Theorising Cultures of Equality

This book sets out a theoretical framework for thinking about equality as a cultural artefact and process, drawing on work from the GRACE (Gender and Cultures of Equality in Europe) project.

In revisiting and reframing conventional questions about in/equality, it considers the processes through which in/equalities have come to be regarded as issues of public concern, the various ways that equalities have been historically defined, and how those ideas and imaginings of equalities are produced, embodied, objectified, recognized and contested in and through a variety of *cultural* practices and sites.

Bringing together an international and interdisciplinary group of contributors, the book will be of interest to scholars from across the humanities and social sciences, including anthropology, sociology, and women's and gender studies.

Suzanne Clisby is a Senior Research Fellow in the Department of Anthropology at Goldsmiths, University of London, Co-Director of the RCUK GCRF Global Gender and Cultures of Equality (GlobalGRACE) Project and Director of the Horizon 2020 Marie S. Curie Gender and Cultures of Equality in Europe (GRACE) Project.

Mark Johnson is Professor of Anthropology at Goldsmiths, University of London and is co-director, with Suzanne Clisby, of the UKRI GCRF GlobalGRACE (Global Gender and Cultures of Equality, 2017–2021) project.

Jimmy Turner is an anthropologist of gender with a focus on Brazil. He is currently a Senior Research Associate and Project Manager for the RCUK GCRF GlobalGRACE Project, based in the Anthropology Department, Goldsmiths, University of London.

GRACE (Global Gender and Cultures of Equality) Project

Theorising Cultures of Equality
Edited by Suzanne Clisby, Mark Johnson and Jimmy Turner

https://www.routledge.com/GRACE-Project/book-series/GRACE

Theorising Cultures of Equality

Edited by
Suzanne Clisby, Mark Johnson and
Jimmy Turner

LONDON AND NEW YORK

First published 2020 by Routledge

2 Park Square, Milton Park, Abingdon, Oxon OX14 4RN

605 Third Avenue, New York, NY 10017

Routledge is an imprint of the Taylor & Francis Group,
an informa business

First issued in paperback 2022

Copyright © 2020 selection and editorial matter, Suzanne Clisby, Mark Johnson and Jimmy Turner; individual chapters, the contributors

The right of Suzanne Clisby, Mark Johnson and Jimmy Turner to be identified as the author[/s] of the editorial material, and of the authors for their individual chapters, has been asserted in accordance with sections 77 and 78 of the Copyright, Designs and Patents Act 1988.

All rights reserved. No part of this book may be reprinted or reproduced or utilised in any form or by any electronic, mechanical, or other means, now known or hereafter invented, including photocopying and recording, or in any information storage or retrieval system, without permission in writing from the publishers.

Notice:
Product or corporate names may be trademarks or registered trademarks, and are used only for identification and explanation without intent to infringe.

Publisher's Note
The publisher has gone to great lengths to ensure the quality of this reprint but points out that some imperfections in the original copies may be apparent.

British Library Cataloguing-in-Publication Data
A catalogue record for this book is available from the British Library

Library of Congress Cataloging-in-Publication Data
A catalog record has been requested for this book

ISBN: 978-1-138-57124-2 (hbk)
ISBN: 978-1-03-233618-3 (pbk)
DOI: 10.4324/9780203702963

Typeset in Times New Roman
by Taylor & Francis Books

Contents

List of figures	vii
List of contributors	viii

1 Theorising Gender and Cultures of Equality   1
SUZANNE CLISBY AND MARK JOHNSON

2 The Promise of the Human: Gender and the Enlightenment's
Culture of Equality   25
LAURA BRACE

3 Equality-Building in Europe: Theorising the Practice of Gender
Training.   38
ATHENA-MARIA ENDERSTEIN

4 Entangled Theorising: Transgender Depathologisation and
Access to 'Disability'   63
LIEKE HETTINGA

5 The (Re)production of (In)equality in Italy: Feminisms and
reproductive labour in the era of populism   76
ELIA A.G. ARFINI AND BEATRICE BUSI

6 Cultures of (In)equality in Poland after 1989   94
ALEKSANDRA M. RÓŻALSKA

7 Why We Need Literature, Art and Fantasy   112
SUSAN STANFORD FRIEDMAN

8 Translating Homosexuality: Urbanism and the masculine *bakla*
in Severino Montano's *The Lion and the Faun*   124
J. NEIL GARCIA

9 The City Animated by the Spirit of Patriarchy   142
JIMMY TURNER

vi *Contents*

10 Power from the Peripheries: Art, culture and masculinities in Rio de Janeiro   158
    TATIANA MOURA, MARTA FERNÁNDEZ AND VICTORIA PAGE

11 Decolonial Joy: Theorising from the art of *Valor y Cambio*   171
    FRANCES NEGRÓN-MUNTANER

Index   195

Figures

9.1	Concrete street furniture on the Rua Felipe Schmidt, central Florianópolis	143
9.2	Men playing dominoes at the north end of the Praça XV de Novembro	145
9.3	Men gather around a card table on Rua Felipe Schmidt in central Florianópolis	150
11.1	Journalist at Latte que Latte, 11 February 2019	174
11.2	Bill 25 with QR code	175
11.3	Participants in line at the Miramar Food Truck location, 16 February 2019	175
11.4	The '21' peso bill portraying Roberto Clemente	177
11.5	The '1' peso bill of the Cordero siblings	178
11.6	The '25' bill featuring three youth leaders to represent the eight communities of El Caño Martín Peña	178
11.7	'Se aceptan pesos' poster at Latte que Latte Cafe, 11 February 2019	179
11.8	Participant holding the Julia de Burgos bill at University High School in Rio Piedras, 13 February 2019	182
11.9	Eduardo Paz showing the '1' bill in Bayamón, 17 February 2019	186

Contributors

Elia A.G. Arfini is Co-Investigator of the MSCA ITN project "GRACE - Gender and Cultures of Equality" for Orlando association in Bologna. They are currently Research Fellow at the Department of Social and Political Sciences of the University of Milan, Adjunct Professor in Gender Studies at the University of Bologna and founding member of the queer transfeminist research centre, CRAAAZI. They have published a book in transgender studies (*Scrivere il sesso*, 2007) and several book-chapters and articles in peer-reviewed journals and curated, with C. Lo Iacono, "Canone inverso. Antologia della teoria queer" (2012). They conduct research in the fields of consumer culture, feminist and queer theory, and disability studies.

Laura Brace is Associate Professor in Political Theory at the University of Leicester. Her research interests are in the politics of property and self-ownership and their relationship to empire, race and gender. Her new book, *The Politics of Slavery*, was published by Edinburgh University Press in 2018, and most recently she has co-edited the volume *Revisiting Slavery and Anti-Slavery: Towards a Critical Analysis* (Palgrave 2018) with Julia O'Connell Davidson. She is currently working on a project to decolonise the feminist theory of Mary Wollstonecraft.

Beatrice Busi is currently involved in fieldwork activities within the IRPPS-CNR project "ViVa – Monitoring, Assessment and Analysis of the Measures to Prevent and Fight Violence against Women" and founding member of the queer transfeminist research centre Centro di Ricerca e Archivio Autonomo transfemminista queer "Alessandro Zijno" CRAAAZI based in Bologna. Since 1999 she has been involved in a number of local and international research projects on contemporary transformations of gender roles, work and social reproduction. Recently, she was Country-expert for Italy within the ERC/Ca' Foscari University of Venice project "DomEQUAL: A Global Approach to Paid Domestic Work and Global Inequalities" (domequal.eu). Among her publications, she has edited a collective volume on the relationships between feminists, women trade unionists and paid domestic workers in Italy in the 1960s and 1970s.

List of contributors ix

Athena-Maria Enderstein was until recently a Research Fellow with the Marie Skłodowska-Curie Innovative Research and Training Network-funded GRACE Project based at Associazione Orlando in Bologna, Italy, and has recently completed a PhD at the University of Hull in the UK. She has a background in psychology and masculinities research and a history of involvement in youth empowerment education and activism in South Africa. Her current work focuses on knowledge circulation and the praxis of gender training as a transformative equality building tool. Athena currently works in Equalities and Diversity for the University of Durham.

Marta Fernández is Director and Adjunct Professor at the Institute of International Relations, Pontifical Catholic University of Rio de Janeiro (IRI-PUC/Rio), which awarded her master's degree and PhD. Previously, she was the co-ordinator of the Graduate Program at IRI/PUC-Rio. She was a research scholar at the University of St Andrews during the first semester of 2010. She is one of the editors of the series *Global Political Sociology* published by Palgrave-Macmillan. She is the academic lead in Brazil of the GlobalGRACE (Global Gender and Cultures of Equality) Project funded by RCUK's Global Challenge Research Fund. She has taught on international relations theory and postcolonial studies. Her current research and publications deal with Brazil's engagement in peacebuilding operations, development, South–South cooperation, theatre, post-colonial and decolonial perspectives, and race and gender relations.

Susan Stanford Friedman is the Virginia Woolf Professor of English and Women's Studies Emerita at the University of Wisconsin-Madison. She publishes widely on feminist theory and women's writing, modernism, narrative theory, migration/diaspora studies and world literature. Recent books include *Planetary Modernisms: Provocations on Modernity Across Time* (2015) and the edited volumes *Contemporary Revolutions: Turning Back to the Future in 21st-Century Literature and Art* (2018) and *Comparison; Theories, Approaches, Uses* (2013). Earlier books include *Mappings: Feminism and the Cultural Geographies of Encounter* (1998). She co-founded the journal *Contemporary Women's Writing,* and her work has been translated into 11 languages.

J. Neil C. Garcia is Professor of Comparative Literature at the University of the Philippines, Diliman, where he serves as Director of the University Press and a Fellow for Poetry in the Institute of Creative Writing. He is the author of numerous poetry collections and works in literary and cultural criticism, including *The Sorrows of Water* (2000), *Kaluluwa* (2001), *Performing the Self: Occasional Prose* (2003), *The Garden of Wordlessness* (2005), *Misterios and Other Poems* (2005) and *Postcolonialism and Filipino Poetics: Essays and Critiques* (2003). In 2009 Hong Kong University Press published its own international edition of his *Philippine Gay Culture* (1996). Between 1994 and 2014, he co-edited the famous Ladlad series of Philippine gay writing. Two other important anthologies he edited are

x *List of contributors*

Aura: the Gay Theme in Philippine Fiction in English, published in 2012, and *Bright Sign, Bright Age: Critical Essays in Philippines Studies*, published in 2017. His poems, essays and books have received much recognition and several prizes, including the Carlos Palanca Memorial Awards, the Philippines Free Press Literary Prize and the National Book Award. He regularly contributes film and theatre reviews to GMA News Online. His most recent books include *The Postcolonial Perverse: Critiques of Contemporary Philippine Culture, Homeless in Unhomeliness: Postcolonial Critiques of Philippine Literature*, and *Myth and Writing: Occasional Prose*. He is currently at work on *Likha*, his seventh poetry book.

Lieke Hettinga was an Early Stage Researcher for the Horizon 2020 Marie S. Curie *Gender and Cultures of Equalities* (GRACE) project and is completing their doctoral research conducted through the GRACE project at Utrecht University. Lieke's research focuses on theorising the gendered body as a site of contest of cultures of equality. Lieke has recently been awarded a Fulbright scholarship from the Fulbright Center in the Netherlands through which will they spend a period of time as a visiting researcher at New York University.

Tatiana Moura is a Senior Researcher at the Centre for Social Studies/University of Coimbra (Portugal), the Coordinator of Promundo Portugal (part of the Global Promundo Consortium, working on masculinities and gender justice) and Associate Director of Instituto Maria and João Aleixo (a Global Think Tank in Maré, Rio de Janeiro, Brazil). She holds a PhD in Peace, Conflicts and Democracy from the University Jaume I (Spain), and her research interests include feminist international relations, masculinities and gender justice, new wars and urban violence. In recent years she has co-ordinated several projects on youth, violence and non-violent trajectories in urban peripheries, particularly in Latin America.

Frances Negrón-Muntaner is a filmmaker, writer, scholar and professor at Columbia University, New York, where she is also the founding curator of the *Latino Arts and Activism Archive*. Among her books and publications are: *Boricua Pop: Puerto Ricans and the Latinization of American Culture* (CHOICE Award, 2004), *The Latino Media Gap* (2014), and *Sovereign Acts: Contesting Colonialism in Native Nations and Latinx America* (2017). Her most recent films include *Small City, Big Change* (2013), *War for Guam* (2015) and *Life Outside* (2016). Negrón-Muntaner has received Ford, Truman, Rockefeller, and Pew fellowships. In 2008 the United Nations' Rapid Response Media Mechanism recognised her as a global expert in the areas of mass media and Latin/o American studies. She is also a recipient of the Lenfest Award—one of Columbia University's most prestigious prizes for excellence in teaching and scholarship (2012), an inaugural OZY Educator Award (2017) and the Latin American Studies Association's Frank Bonilla Public Intellectual Award (2019). In 2019 she launched *Valor y Cambio*, an art, digital storytelling and equitable economy project in Puerto Rico (valorymcambio.org).

List of contributors xi

Victoria Marie Page is a researcher, artist and activist. She holds an MSc in Gender, Development and Globalisation from the London School of Economics and a BA Hons in Development Studies and History from the School of Oriental and African Studies. Victoria has over ten years' experience in non-governmental organisations as well as in the creative arts, specifically in dance and photography, and her particular interests are in visual and performative arts, the collaborative creative process within social movements and feminist visual cultures. Victoria currently leads the communications department of a domestic abuse charity.

Aleksandra M. Różalska is Assistant Professor at the Department of American Studies and Mass Media and Head of the Women Studies Centre, University of Łódź, Poland. She is Co-Investigator for the GEMMA (Erasmus Mundus) and GRACE (Horizon 2020) projects. In 2005–06 she was a Fulbright fellow at the American University, Washington, DC. Her research interests include: intersections of gender, race and religion in media and politics, narratives of 9/11 and the war on terror, as well as media representations of refugees and migrants. She has published works on images of minorities and women in television, as well as on cultural representations of 9/11 and its aftermath. She has co-edited four volumes devoted to feminisms in various cultural contexts (Cambridge Scholars Publishing, Lodz University Press). She is currently working on a book on post-9/11 television discourses from postcolonial and feminist perspectives and on journal articles about media representations of violence against women.

1 Theorising Gender and Cultures of Equality

Suzanne Clisby and Mark Johnson

Introduction

'Everything starts as a story we tell ourselves about ourselves.'
(Jeanette Winterson, 2016)

In an opinion piece written for *The Guardian* newspaper in June 2016, responding to the results of the British EU referendum, the novelist Jeannette Winterson suggested that what is needed is both a renewed story about and an internationalist movement for equality to challenge the post-Brexit narrative and the forces of right-wing conservatism that it threatened to, and indeed subsequently did, unleash. We share Winterson's anxieties and her conviction that we need to tell a different story, and the aim of this volume, *Theorising Cultures of Equality* is to set out the theoretical framework for thinking about equality, and particularly gender equalities, as a cultural artefact and process – something that has been made and must be continuously reshaped and refashioned through stories and actions, both big and small.

The book itself grows out of the GRACE (Gender and Cultures of Equality in Europe) project, an EU-funded, Horizon 2020 Marie Skłodowska-Curie Innovative Research and Training Network that ran from September 2015 until September 2019. The GRACE (Gender and Cultures of Equality in Europe) project, which was directed by Suzanne Clisby, employed 15 Early Stage Researchers (ESR) – from Austria, Italy, Mexico, Poland, Puerto Rico, Romania, Spain, South Africa, Sweden, Syria, Turkey and the United Kingdom – who were based across eight partners in six European countries supported by an International Expert Advisory Panel of academics, artists, curators, film makers and poets[1]. The 15 researchers, many of whom have now completed or are soon to complete their doctoral programmes, conducted research across five sites where cultures of gender equalities are re/produced, transformed and contested by differently situated social agents focused on *mediated* cultures of gender equality, *urban* cultures of gender equality, *intellectual and activist* cultures of gender equality, *textual and artistic* cultures of gender equality and *employing* cultures of gender equality. This is the first of a series of volumes arising from the GRACE project and draws on the work of two of the GRACE ESRs, scholars from within the consortium and

2 Theorising Cultures of Equality

advisory panel, together with invited guests, whose work and ideas have been pivotal in shaping both our project and our thinking about cultures of equality. Although the editors of the volume are based in anthropology, it is important to note at the outset that the volume is firmly located within a tradition of interdisciplinary feminist, gender and queer studies.

Whereas much previous scholarly work focuses on European gender equality policies, their social consequences and political underpinnings (Ahrens, 2018; Arribas and Carrasco, 2003; Pascall and Lewis, 2004; Lombardo and Meier, 2008) the aim of this book, as with the GRACE project out of which it emerges, is to investigate and theorise an under-examined aspect of those processes, namely the production of cultures of equality that underpin, enable and constrain those changing policy and legislative frameworks. We adopt a critical perspective that seeks to provincialise the assumptions of equalities discourses, which are often taken for granted, and through which claims to Europeanness are frequently framed. It is precisely for that reason that we juxtapose and place into conversation here work on and about equalities in European contexts with reflections on and challenges to presumed universal cosmopolitan ideals from within and beyond that. In so doing we develop an approach that understands culture as neither normative frameworks nor ways of representing the world, but more fundamentally as the process through which people create and contest the social worlds that they inhabit.

Questions about equality are frequently posed in terms of asking about how inequalities and social divisions – of age, class, disability, gender, race, religion or sexuality – are produced, recognised, measured and redressed and the processes through which greater equality is achieved, including the transformations required to change people's perceptions about and attitudes towards, for example, racism and sexism. The recognition-versus-rights debate may be seen as one example of that; that is, of whether inequalities are best regarded as a consequence of misrecognition or of the withholding of legal status and political and economic resources.

The questions that we ask are more fundamentally about the processes through which in/equalities have come to be regarded as issues of public concern in the first place, the various ways that equalities have been historically defined and how those ideas and imaginings of equalities are produced, embodied, objectified, recognised and contested in and through a variety of *cultural* practices and sites. The former set of questions tends to identify culture as that which variously legitimates or engenders inequality and, at the same time, treats 'equality' as largely exogenous to 'culture'; that is, we can measure different levels of inequality and explain those differences in terms of more or less essentialised views of gender difference that underpin and naturalise socially produced divisions between women and men. The latter approach views culture as processes through which people create and contest the life worlds that they inhabit and the world views that they articulate, including and perhaps especially ideas about in/equality (Carrithers, 2005; Kapferer, 2013; Wagner, 1981).

Before we continue, we must make a brief note here to clarify how the concept of gender is understood throughout this volume. The idea and use of the term 'gender' continues to be essentialised, politicised, mistrusted, and, in certain contexts, conflated with 'woman' (see for example Aleksandra Różalska's— 2020—chapter in this volume exploring the anti-'gender' backlash in Poland), and so it is important that we define what we mean when we talk about 'gender'. By 'gender' we mean ideologies and embodied practices through which femininities, masculinities, transgender and queer subjectivities are produced, and the relations between people who occupy differently gendered subject positions: subjectivities and subject positions that are shaped in complex ways by intersections of and entanglements with other social divisions and identities, including sexuality, religion, race, ethnicity, nationality, class, disability and age.

Drawing on this understanding of what we mean by gender, as in *'gender equality'*, we build on and critically extend previous work that can be broadly separated into two strands: firstly, comparative sociological, political and policy studies of gender equality regimes; and secondly, comparative studies of national normative cultural frameworks which promote or constrain the emergence of gender equality. The former has seen a shift from comparative studies examining the development and impact of different state welfare regimes on gender relations to more nuanced intersectional considerations of equalities 'architecture' (Walby et al., 2012). Significant advances have been made in creating conceptual and methodological toolkits for helping us to think about the interplay between multiple forms of inequality and changing political landscapes, legal frameworks and institutional practices, as well as dismantling in conditions of austerity and neoliberalism (Tomlinson, 2011; Squires, 2008; Verloo and Walby, 2012; Jacquot 2015). The latter includes micro-studies that examine in more detail the impact of changing policy regimes in producing and sustaining gender (in)equalities in particular places and relations (Harding et al., 2013; Van den Brink et al., 2010; Benschop and Verloo, 2011; Van den Brink and Benschop, 2012; Lyness and Brumit Kropf, 2005).

What is largely absent from the work on different equality regimes is a sustained consideration of 'culture'. That may be explained by the fact that the investigation of cultures of gender equality are less advanced empirically or conceptually, although Athena Enderstein's (2020) detailed analysis of gender equality training and the cultures of equality imbued by equality trainers in Europe, in this volume, goes some way to advancing this knowledge gap. Enderstein's (2020) study aside, many of those studies that do focus on culture may be best characterised as involving two competing approaches. The first approach views culture as a set of shared normative understandings that are deemed to impinge on perceptions of and attitudes towards inequality, the shaping of equalities frameworks and on the preparedness of people to respond positively to processes designed to enhance gender equality. The stronger variant, best exemplified by Inglehart and Norris (2003), takes for granted the view that different countries are characterised by different national cultures and that some are more receptive to change and to equality than others. A more nuanced

4 Theorising Cultures of Equality

sociological variant, in that more consideration is given to the dynamics within putatively national cultures and their interplay with policy and economy, is exemplified by the work of produced and associated with Pfau-Effinger (Stephenson, 2009; Effinger, 2004; Fitzgerald et al., 2014; Röder, 2014; Duncan and Pfau-Effinger, 2012; Pfau-Effinger, 2005). The comparative scope of the latter is European rather than global, although studies increasingly look specifically at whether and how the 'cultures' of non-European migrants shape and affect their receptivity to gender equality when settling in Europe.

Set against that work are what might be deemed the cultural critics, who, despite different vantage points, share a skepticism about the putatively shared normative values of national cultures and a critique of the way that equalities discourse in Europe and North America negatively stereotypes non-European people and cultures as outmoded and resistant to gender equality. These critiques are concerned broadly with cultural essentialism, 'culturalism' in Appadurai's terms and its corollary, the politics of recognition (Benhabib, 2002; Gilroy, 2013; Towns, 2002; Narayan, 2013; Balibar, 2007; Appadurai, 1996). We share the critical concerns of the latter, but think that the perceived risk of culturalism has inadvertently impoverished the study of cultures of equality. In fact, Benhabib's critique of culturalism is also a call for a different way of understanding culture and thinking about the politics of recognition; as she says, '[It] is not a visual but an auditory metaphor that guides my understanding of a complex cultural dialogue. We should view human cultures as constant creations, recreations, and negotiations of imaginary boundaries between 'we' and the 'other(s)' (Benhabib 2002: 12). There are also evident affinities between Benhabib's approach and that recently put forward by Siep Stuurman (2017) in *The Invention of Humanity: Equality and Cultural Difference in World History*, which foregrounds what he refers to as 'bridging frontiers' as sites for the production of cultures of equality.

In this volume, we seek not only to 'provincialise' European claims about equality, but also to treat equality as a culturally contingent, historical artefact. That is, we do not view culture as a thing that belongs to or describes the norms and values of discreet groups of people in ways that inexorably shapes, constrains or enables greater or lesser degrees of gender (in)equality. Rather we view culture not only as a process of communication and a contested arena of meaning making practices, but also as a process of invention and innovation. In that sense, we agree with those scholars who assert that culture matters even if our starting point for thinking about what that means and investigating the way that it matters is different. In sum, if the study of gender equalities regimes is now characterised as an investigation of equalities architectures, the approach put forward here for studying the production of cultures of equality can be best described as the critical investigation and creative co-production of equalities events and artefacts.

To assert that equality is a cultural artefact is to insist that it can be made and done 'otherwise' (Escobar, 2007; Povinelli, 2012; Henare et al., 2007; Sewell, 2005; Sahlins, 2013). To recall Winterson, to recognise that equality is a story that people have created is not to diminish its importance. Rather it is about affirming the necessity of continuously renewing and reinventing that story, recognizing that there are different stories about equality that might be told and exploring the various ways that those stories are and have been narrated, as well as describing their social consequences and political effects. Ours is thus a call for the recognition of the political necessity of the poetics and practices of equality.

What is equality?

This question is inevitably not as simple as it may first appear. On the one hand, equality is, or at least has become, in some institutional and political economic contexts, a kind of pre-theoretical and performative commitment to presumed universalist and neoliberal ideals (Richardson and Munro 2012: 23). On the other hand, as *The Stanford Encyclopaedia of Philosophy* suggests, equality is 'at present probably the most controversial of the great social ideals' (Gosepath, 2011). The author of the latter suggests that there is contention and debate around the definition and concept of equality, questions about organising principles, for example between equality and justice, and the relations with and between whom equality is deemed to matter, as well as questions about what and how to measure equality. People who have been and are involved in struggles against various forms of intersecting oppression are likely to ask about precisely for whom equality has and could ever be taken for granted as a pre-theoretical commitment and invite reflection on the temporality of these present controversies by reminding us that historically claims for (and against) greater equality have always been precisely about struggles over and about the definition and concept of equality. Indeed, as Alison Jagger noted in her introduction to the classic volume, *Living with Contradictions*, on which we draw here, equality has not only been deemed by some to be central to feminist politics but has also been a 'focus of feminist controversy' (1994: 13).

Accepting from the outset that equality is and must remain a contested concept, we want to make the following propositions as a starting point for theorizing equality. First, we want to suggest, following Rae (1981: 132 f., cited in Gosepath, 2011, n.p.), that equality is and must always remain an 'incomplete predicate'; that is, it necessarily generates and provokes questions, among them; equality of what, equality for whom and according to what measures and by whose criteria? These and other related philosophical and political questions and provocations invite critical reflection and demand response rather than providing ready-made answers. That is evident in, among others, traditions of feminist theorizing, from materialist feminists who question the extent to which equality could ever be achieved within a capitalist system (Hennessy and Ingraham, 1997) to critiques of sexual difference theorists who regard equality with suspicion on the grounds that it was about sameness. The latter critique does not arise from ignoring the philosophical logic that the 'judgment of equality presumes a difference between the things being compared' according to which, 'the notion of 'complete' or 'absolute' equality is

6 *Theorising Cultures of Equality*

self-contradictory' Gosepath's (2011, n.p.). Rather, it is about asking whether equality is simply more of the same system of oppression, wrapped up as gift bestowed by men. As Jagger (1994: 24) puts it, it is about recognizing that equality frameworks like other 'familiar western modes of conceptualizing reality in fact are distinctly masculine' and '[r]ather than appearing as the extension to women of the full human status enjoyed by men, sexual equality starts to look like an attempt to masculinise women and negate their special capacities' (Jagger, 1994: 5). Indeed, as Arfini and Busi contend in their chapter in this volume (2020) on feminism and (in)equality in Italy, that ongoing 'radical critique of the concept of equality serve[s] to articulate a revolutionary struggle against the patriarchy'.

The second point that we wish to make is that equality is relational in several senses. Equality is related to, but not simply the inverse of, inequality. That is, how we think about equality – and the questions that equality provokes and enables – is in part a product of and contingent on how we think about inequality and more specifically the relationship between systems of privilege, such as patriarchy, and forms of inequality, for example gender inequality. As the chapters in this book remind us, despite their differences, feminists from Mary Wollstonecraft and Mary Heys in the late 18th century to gender trainers in 21st-century Europe have all foregrounded questions of power, even if there have been significant differences in how the relationship between privilege and inequality is theorised, as well as the means of redress and its relationship (or not) to other systems of privilege. Consider the following quotes from Wollstonecraft and Catherine MacKinnon, respectively, on the way that the denial of political privileges is linked to women being taught to please –men, for example – and on the necessity of feminist jurisprudence in order to disclose fully the extent and operations of male power. In Wollstonecraft's words:

> 'Females, in fact, denied all political privileges, and not allowed, as married women [...] a civil existence, have their attention naturally drawn from the interest of the whole community to that of the minute parts [...] The mighty business of female life is to please, and restrained from entering into more important concerns by political and civil oppression, sentiments become events, and reflection deepens what it should, and would have effaced, if the understanding had been allowed to take a wider range' (Wollstonecraft, 2015 [1792]: 87)

For Mackinnon:

> '[I]nequality is a matter not of sameness and difference, but of dominance and subordination. Inequality is about power, its definition, and its maldistribution [...] Only feminist jurisprudence sees that male power does exist and sex equality does not, because only feminism grasps the extent to which antifeminism is misogyny and both are as normative as they are empirical. Masculinity then appears as a specific position, not just the

Theorising Gender and Cultures of Equality   7

way things are, its judgements and partialities revealed in process and procedure, adjudication and legislation'. (1994: 38).

Our own view, and one that builds on various strands of feminist thought, including the work of the feminist political philosophers Iris Marion Young (2011) and Elizabeth Anderson (1999) on relational equality (see also Fourie et. al., 2015), is that equality is best thought about in relation to inequality, where the latter is conceived as a product and function of privilege; that is, inequality, as Alsheh notes:

> 'is not (solely) a matter of depriving someone from what rightly belongs to them, namely of group B taking away what properly belongs to group A, but has to do with the fact that the greater (often also increasing) well-being of B depends on the lesser (often decreasing) well-being of A.' (Alsheh et al. 2012: 12).

In that way, equality is neither simply about reducing inequality nor providing redress, redistribution or reparation but more fundamentally at some level must be about dismantling the systems of privilege that makes the wellbeing of some contingent on the lesser wellbeing of others. In other words, questions about equality are not, we contend, separable from but inextricably related to questions about social justice, even if, and precisely because, as the work of black feminist and decolonial scholars have especially pointed out, historically the political practices and imaginings of equality have often deferred, displaced and been dependent on, and hence, failed to dismantle and redress, complex and intersecting systems of privilege and oppression. Kimberlé Crenshaw's (1989, 1991) formulation of intersectionality, for example, is evidently a response to the questions posed by a feminist jurisprudence that ignored the ways that the racial privilege of some is contingent on the devaluation and lesser wellbeing of racialised others.

Crenshaw (1994) in particular uses the example of responses to the crime of rape to highlight the ways that theories and statutes centering on equality and discrimination fail to account for Black women's lives and histories. As she states, '[r]ape statutes generally do not reflect *male* control over *female* sexuality, but *white* male regulation of *white* female sexuality'. Locating her analysis in the context of recent American history, she goes on to point out that a:

> 'focus on rape as a manifestation of male power over female sexuality tends to eclipse the use of rape as a weapon of racial terror. When Black women were raped by white males, they were being raped not as women generally, but as Black women specifically: Their femaleness made them sexually vulnerable to racist domination, while their Blackness effectively denied them any protection. This white male power was reinforced by a judicial system in which the successful conviction of a white man for raping a Black woman was virtually unthinkable' (1994: 47).

8 *Theorising Cultures of Equality*

Although the concept of intersectionality in its various forms – structural, political and representational – has been critically extended and refined (see, for example, Lennon and Alsop, 2020: 122 f. for an incisive overview), Crenshaw's analysis remains particularly significant not just for having laid bare the inherent whiteness and ethnocentricity of dominant concepts at work in sociolegal systems, but also for highlighting the importance of attending to complexities of relations of oppression and diverse positionalities and identities in theoretical approaches to in/equality more broadly. In so doing, Crenshaw's work builds on strong foundations of Black feminist theory developed over a long period of time, including of course the work of bell hooks, whose scholarship continues to provide an influential critique of 'white' liberal feminist concerns for equality. In *Feminist Theory: from Margin to Centre* (1984), for example, she presents a powerful challenge to American feminisms and the 'women's liberation' movement at the time and questions what we are really thinking when we talk about equality. We can gain quite a clear sense of her analysis from the following extract, in which she poses the question of whether women share a common vision of what equality means:

> 'Most people in the United States think of feminism or the more commonly used term "women's lib" as a movement that aims to make women the social equals of men. This broad definition, popularized by the media and mainstream segments of the movement, raises problematic questions. Since men are not equals in white supremacist, capitalist, patriarchal class structure, which men do women want to be equal to? Do women share a common vision of what equality means? Implicit in this simplistic definition of women's liberation is a dismissal of race and class as factors that, in conjunction with sexism, determine the extent to which an individual will be discriminated against.' (hooks, 1984: 18).

Here hooks draws on the analysis of Brazilian scholar, Heleith Saffioti, who similarly challenged what she termed 'petty-bourgeois feminism' for representing only segments of society, namely the ruling classes; as she states:

> 'while pretty-bourgeois feminism may always have aimed at establishing social equality between the sexes, the consciousness it represented has remained utopian in its desire for and struggle to bring about partial transformation of society; that it believes could be done without disturbing the foundations on which it rested [...] In this sense, petty-bourgeois feminism is not feminism at all; indeed it has helped to consolidate class society by giving camouflage to its internal contradictions' (Saffioti, 1967, cited in hooks, 1984: 20).

This critique can and has been further extended to show that histories of equality are part and parcel of the emergence of the modern system of gender and racialised privilege, in which the putative equality of some people was socially and culturally dependent on the violent exclusions, expulsions and

Theorising Gender and Cultures of Equality 9

enslavement of other people. Although there is a very partial recognition of that in some earlier European feminist writing, including Mary Wollenstonecraft (on the paradoxes of Wollenstonecraft's vision of equality see Laura Brace—2020—this volume) and other even earlier radical enlightenment thinkers such as François Poulain de la Barre (Stuurman 2004), it is post-colonial, anticolonial and decolonial scholars who have most systematically interrogated the system of racialised oppression that belies even the most radical European enlightenment view of equality. That includes tracing shifts within colonial ideologies from a putatively more universal view of people distinguished on the basis of spiritual perfection (that could theoretically be achieved by all), to that premised on distinctions of race and rationality. This latter position proffered equality to those people accorded the status of humans and legitimated even more extreme forms of dispossession and violence, such as the transatlantic slave trade, against those whom colonisers deemed lesser beings and on whose inhuman degradation the wealth, affluence and wellbeing of colonisers depended (Quijano 2000, 2007; Lugones 2010; Wynter 2003). As Françoise Vergès, writing about post-slavery in French Creole post-slavery societies shows, even after the abolition of slavery in 1848, a paradoxical form of citizenship emerged which was:

'a colonized citizenship, in which equality was qualified. The brother in the colony was equal, but not quite [...] The political demand: 'On what basis aren't we your equals?' was translated into a demand for love and recognition: what do we lack that explains your exclusionary practices?' As equality was offered and postponed, the Creole-colonised citizen (male) became alienated to the desire of the French colonizer, which could not, of course, be satisfied' (Vergès 2001: 11–12).

What these scholars and critics insist on, and as is evident too in many of our contributors' essays here, is the persistence and continuities of coloniality and the racialised basis on which equality, including gender equality, is qualified. As Sarah Wynter (2003: 260) compellingly puts it, 'the struggle of our new millennium will be one between the ongoing imperative of securing the well-being of our present ethnoclass (i.e., Western bourgeois) conception of the human, Man, which over-represents itself as if it were the human itself, and that of securing the well-being, and therefore the full cognitive and behavioral autonomy of the human species itself/ourselves'. Indeed, the final point that we want to make here is that equality is, to borrow from Wynter, an ongoing process; it is not an end point or destination that can or will ever be achieved, but it is an imperative, if, as Wynter suggests, we are to secure the wellbeing not just of one group, at the expense and on the back of another, but the wellbeing of all.

Making equalities: within and beyond the field of cultural production

Cowan, et al.'s (2001) *Culture and Rights: Anthropological Perspectives* sets out a useful critical framework for conceptualising the different ways that

10 *Theorising Cultures of Equality*

Culture and Rights had and could be thought and investigated together and which here serves as a model to begin to think about cultures of equality. As summarised by Cowan (2006: 9) the co-editors identified in particular four ways of thinking about that, as follows: '(1) rights versus culture, (2) the right to culture, (3) rights as culture, and (4) culture as 'analytic' to rights.

The first two frames of thinking are related in so far as the distinction between a view of rights based on enlightenment universalism and ideas of distinctive cultures emerging out of romantic particularism underpins both forms of ethnic nationalism and claims by first peoples about universal rights to and over their culture. There is also a relationship between rights as culture and culture as 'analytic' to rights, even if there are subtle and important differences between them. The former approach treats rights discourse as a historically contingent phenomenon but one that has developed a distinctive set of discourses and procedures that are effectively institutionalised and normatively enforced. The latter, which Cowan et al. (2006) identify most closely with a contemporary critical anthropological approach, recognises the validity of viewing rights as culture but, as with the broader view of culture that they set out, does not regard the culture of rights as a bounded self-sustaining and reproducing system. Rather, this 'culture as 'analytic' to rights' approach thus seeks to tease out the variety of ways that rights discourses and practices are variously produced, taken up, circulated and entangled with and contested by variously positioned people in a variety of situations. Culture can be understood, in that view, as Cowan clarifies, 'not as an object in itself but as an abstraction whose exploration offers a window for seeing and understanding other relations and domains to which it is connected' (2006: 10).

The approach to thinking through cultures of equality that we put forward here is located within, between and, we contend, beyond the space of Equality/ Rights as culture and culture as an analytic of equality. Speaking of cultures of equality (rather than equality as culture in the singular) should be understood as adopting a critical approach both to rights [equalities] (conceived as framed within larger relations of power and knowledge) and a critical approach to culture (understood as contested or contestable), which also acknowledges agency and indeterminacy. Through this theorisation, and drawing on Cowen (2006), we draw attention to the ways that (1) rights [equalities] are both enabling and constraining; (2) rights [equalities] are productive (of subjectivities, of social relations, and even of the very identities and cultures – e.g. genders and sexualities – that they claim merely to recognise); and (3) their pursuit and achievement entails unintended consequences.

There are nonetheless a number of things that are distinctive about the approach that we set out here and that leads us to foreground further the 'cultural' component of cultures of equality. The first is that we are concerned with highlighting the creativity and inventiveness of culture and the corollary that equalities are not just something that have been made but that are in need of continuous remaking. Secondly, while being advocates, Cowan contends that the role of the anthropologist is first and foremost descriptive. Our

Theorising Gender and Cultures of Equality   11

approach is one that understands description and analysis as always already political and cultural. We mean this not merely in the sense that anthropological 'description' is shaped by existing conditions of possibility that enable certain ways of thinking and construing things or of the social relations that make that possible, but also that anthropology is and should embrace its possibilities as a site for inventive and transformative cultural practices. This process also includes, following Linda Smith (1999), the transformation of its own research practices that, as Smith contends, have historically been premised on, and extended, the coloniality of knowledge.

We also want to call attention to the possibilities, as well as evident limitations and contradictions of culture understood specifically in terms of cultural production through art, literature, etc. We recognise that to foreground the inventiveness of culture requires a robust conceptual account that does not put forth a naïve view of people simply making up and creating things out of nothing. Likewise, as Bourdieu (1984, 1993), among others, reminds us, culture, in the sense of cultural production, has in fact become central to and a way through which inequalities and distinctions – distilled in the form of embodied, objectified and institutional cultural capital – are made and reproduced.

Hence, we confront a central paradox, and one that Bourdieu himself was keenly aware of - namely that culture is not merely a signifier of but also foundational to the reproduction of inequalities. However, because of its relative autonomy from the fields of political and economic production, the field of cultural production still remains one of the most important social spaces and set of practices with which to both challenge and reimagine 'equality' and to recreate the *illusio* – that is precisely, as Susan Friedman (2020, this volume) argues, the fantasies and ludic possibilities of alternative readings and novel texts and performances that create the cultural conditions of possibility for more equitable ways of living together.

A final source of inspiration for thinking through the possibilities of cultures of equality comes from Harri Englund's call for a study of 'equality in the vernacular' (2015: 81) for which his ethnography (Englund 2011) of the daily radio programme *Nkhani Zam'maboma* (News from the Districts) in Malawi serves as an exemplar. The challenge, as he described it, was to 'understand what constitutes equality in the absence of an egalitarian ideology' (2011: 14); that is, in a situation where equality is not counterpoised to hierarchy, but is 'intrinsic' to and a condition of the claims that people make on those who are their 'masters, benefactors, and leaders.' The vernacular forms and articulations of equality discerned in the radio programme can be contrasted with what Englund contends are some of the key features of liberal ideologies of egalitarianism, including equality as 'parity' and sameness (2011: 224), 'an attribute of mutually independent individuals' (2011: 14), and as a goal, that is temporally orientated to a utopian future. By contrast, Englund suggests, the vernacular equality evident in *Nkhani Zam'maboma* treats equality as a pre-condition for relations of interdependence, while leaving 'intact' difference and hierarchy, which is an accepted or at least largely

12 Theorising Cultures of Equality

unchallenged corollary of interdependence, and is focused not on an anticipated future but on the present. In summary, Englund describes the vernacular ethos at least as worked out and articulated in and through *Nkhani Zam'maboma* as 'motivated less by the idea of rights than by the idea of obligations' in which obligation, 'presupposes neither acts of charity by the well-off nor overt rebellion by the poor' (2011: 224).

It is evident that Englund's analysis is shaped not just by his encounters and analysis of *Nkhani Zam'maboma* but also by his reading of other theorists including most notably Rancière (2004a; 2004b). In particular, there is resonance between what Englund perceives as the tacit understanding of equality as the precondition for claims of interdependency and obligation in *Nkhani Zam'maboma* and Rancière's (more universalising) contention that equality is a 'point of departure and supposition to be maintained in all circumstances' (Rancière, cited in Hallward, 2006: 109). However, there are some points of difference between Rancière's and Englund's analyses. For Rancière, equality is a precondition for and must continuously be remade through staging acts of insurrection and dissolution of any recurrent and regular – that is to say, institutional, relations which are inevitably seen as weighing down on, policing and constraining equality. In that sense, while equality is a precondition for social action, for Rancière it is only and can only ever be momentarily, fleetingly, established. What Englund suggests is that equality sits within and alongside, and makes possible, ethical claims about reciprocal if asymmetrical obligations within existing hierarchical relations. Englund – drawing on his example of a radio programme – is interested in asking, what are the varieties of ways that people understand equality and how are those ways of understanding equality deployed in and shaped by and through their articulation in a range of public cultural forms in specific social situations? The key takeaway point for us from Englund's ethnography, as from Rancière's theory, is that both put forward an active, creative and inventive, rather than an inherently passive, view of equality.

What has been designated the 'passive view' of equality is attributed to those philosophers and political thinkers who view the task of governance as that of promoting, ensuring and guaranteeing equality through various forms of distributive justice, however that is defined and whatever the criteria used to measure its relative attainment. An active view of equality is one that sees equality not as something to be given or received, but as something to be taken and assumed (May 2008). In terms of political theory and philosophy, our view is that both are necessary and neither is sufficient; that is, that systemic change is unlikely to happen without people making and taking acts of equality, but for that to be effective and enduring beyond the moment of its articulation, it needs to be institutionalised, for example within a particular form of equalities architecture, even if those architectures or platforms must be regarded as provisional, iterative and continuously subject to critique. In terms of cultural theory, we can likewise draw a distinction between those who see the importance of creating cultural change in terms of challenging, shaping and instituting different norms and ideologies and that view of culture as fundamentally

Theorising Gender and Cultures of Equality 13

creative, inventive and imaginative and where there is no necessary, immediate or identifiable linear path between and to the normative.

In summary, what we have been suggesting thus far is that equality is best regarded not as a set of stable ideals or set of procedures but as a provocation; that is, as posing questions about and naming systems of privilege that enable claims about rights, justice and obligations in and against those systems. We understand cultures of equality as the practices and process of asking those questions and making claims which, even if they are not directly talked about in terms of equality, may have what, following Stuurman (2017), can be called equality effects. The latter includes actively creating the space for the imagination (see Friedman, 2020 in this volume; Scott, 1999, cited in Stuurman 2004: 296) that discloses novel ways of apprehending and disclosing those systems of privilege and oppression as well as actively creating new experiments in living together more equitably, among them what Davina Cooper (2014) calls 'everyday utopias'.

Chapter summaries and Overview

The chapters in this book investigate –and may themselves be regarded as – making cultures of equality in that they variously offer novel ways of understanding inequality and systems of privilege, including those that lay at the heart of discourses about equality, extend calls for, and the defence of, fantasy and the imagination and finally that offer reflections on ongoing experiments in living, including and especially those that our contributors themselves are and have been involved with initiating.

Laura Brace's chapter, 'The Promise of the Human: Gender and the Enlightenment's Culture of Equality', is concerned, as she puts it with, 'some of the stories of equality that people have created out of reason, nature and difference' (2020, this volume). In particular, her focus is on the way that the feminist thought of Wollstonecraft and Hays drew on, disrupted and extended 'the politics of the human' at work in late 18th-century European Enlightenment thought. On the one hand, Wollstonecraft and Hays challenged the discourse of rights and freedom, taken to be hallmark of civilisation, because they masked the systems of privilege that makes some men's freedom contingent on the denial of rights and freedoms of other men, as well as women and slaves. Moreover, the perceived weakness in mind and body, naturalised as feminine and attributed by men to women, where they existed, were deemed to be a corollary of a degenerate civilisation premised on and a product of the deprivation of those rights and freedoms. Crucially, in ways that prefigure what are now deemed to be active theories of equality, Wollstonecraft and Hay did not regard equality as something that could be granted to women by men. Rather, the restoration of women to a natural state of humanity required women themselves to make and claim equality with men, whereby the claims of equality simultaneously divest men of their power and through that political action remedy the passivity whereby they were enslaved. On the other hand, Wollstonecraft and Hays variously reinscribe and

14 *Theorising Cultures of Equality*

extend the orientalising discourse that positioned the 'East' – and Muslims in particular – as exemplifying the most extreme form of patriarchy and its corallorary: unnatural femininities. The latter is evidently a form of racism, which operates through the exclusion and abjection of Muslim men while offering conditional and provisional inclusion of Muslim women, which has been enlivened in the 21st century by what Sara Farris (2017) refers to as femonationalism (Farris 2017): that is, a specific coalition or conjunction of anti-immigrant and populist neoliberal politics, as well as some strands of feminism and right-wing women's parties.

We juxtapose Brace's historical chapter on feminist political philosophy in the late 18th century with Enderstein's chapter, 'Equality building in Europe: Theorising the Practice of Gender Training' to show the continuities and changes in the equality stories being developed and deployed at the beginning of the 21st century. Although commonly framed as a story of progress, 'behind this narrative there are both agendas of civilizational supremacy' and 'a seven decades long *transnational* history of women's movement and feminist activism, scholarship, and politics' (Enderstein, 2020, this volume). On the one hand, it is evident among gender trainers whom Enderstein encountered that, as with an earlier generation of feminists, they understood the first step towards greater equality to be based on the necessary 'recognition of power and relations of power' (Enderstein, 2020, this volume). However, the earlier emphasis on reason, stifled by but nonetheless exemplified in the capacity to discern the patriarchal structures of power that suppress and warp people's reasoning, has been replaced by, or perhaps better, reformulated, as the insistence on reflexivity, 'evident not only in the topics and content of trainings but also in the application of feminist pedagogies' (Enderstein, 2020, this volume). On the other hand, the possibilities that are accorded by reflexive knowledge production and its potential to effect political change are constrained, paradoxically, both by the evident currency of particular forms of gender awareness training and the limitations that its marketability imposes, as well as the way that masks and extends other forms of epistemic power and knowledge production. However, rather than simply counterpoise a narrative of feminist failure and complicity against that of putative equalities progress, Enderstein suggests that the struggle for equality requires more complex and robust analytical stories about how precisely gender knowledge circulates and is negotiated in theory and in practice.

While Enderstein's chapter explores both the limitations and possibilities of the sorts of stories that gender experts tell, Leike Hettinga further demonstrates the complicated terrain of equality practices by setting out the political issues at stake in thinking about the depathologisation of transgender in relation to gender and disability theory. Hettinga's chapter, entitled 'Entangled Theorising: Transgender Pathologisation and Access to "Disability"' begins by recounting the ways that publicly announced introduction of gender-neutral toilets at their university, although affirmative in one respect, is troubling in another in that it does not move substantially beyond the performative nature of instutionalised cultures of inclusion and diversity. More specifically, in visibly seeking to distance trans from

Theorising Gender and Cultures of Equality   15

disability, it too easily elides the forms of ableism that are often left intact and uninterrogated. Hettinga contends that engaging critically with the entanglements and disentanglements of transness and disability in theory and practice is not just about sharpening our analytical lens but about opening, rather than foreclosing, the possibility for coalitional politics between transgender and disabled people to address and challenge both ableist and hetero/cisgender forms of privilege.

The subsequent two chapters that conclude the first part of the book explore issues around cultures of equality from the vantage point of two country-specific situations: Italy and Poland, respectively. These chapters foreground the diversity of feminist approaches to thinking about equality across Europe and highlight the different historical and political circumstances within which people are making and pressing claims for gender justice and equality, while recognising that, as Enderstein contends, these movements are always already part of transnational circulations of ideas related to gender (in)equality.

Elia A.G. Arfini and Beatrice Busi's chapter, 'The (re)production of (in) equality in Italy: feminisms and reproductive labour in the era of populism', provides an insightful overview of some of the recurrent themes and tensions in Italian feminism, which centres in particular on the contested domain of reproductive labour as a – and perhaps *the* – key site for the making of cultures of equality. Indeed, more than any of our other contributors, Arfini's and Busi's chapter reminds us of that important strand of feminist thought and praxes that aims not so much for equality, but for a just society premised on the realisation and affirmation of sexual difference. As they forcefully contend, 'Italian feminist critiques of equality understood as parity, inclusion, representation, protection of a minority, or efficiency in the late capitalist project of economic growth, represent the distinguishing features of a feminist political culture that is currently under the pressure of populism and economic crisis but also ambitious in its intersectional and radical scope' (Arfini and Busi, 2020, this volume).

Aleksandra M. Różalska's chapter 'Cultures of (In)equality in Poland after 1989' homes in on the rise of populism and the gendered dynamics of a resurgent nationalism that belies the assumed correlation between neoliberal political economic transformations and the emergence of socially progressive cultures of equality. What Różalska shows is that the reinvention of traditional gender regimes is increasingly marked and made in public culture by their specific opposition to feminism and an openly stated anti-gender stance. These are a set of reactionary transnational discourses that have come to characterise various nationalist populist movements across Europe and elsewhere. Despite those visible public denunciations of gender ideology and, more precisely, because of the threats to women's reproductive rights that they enabled, the alliance between right-wing and conservative religious groups and leaders produced a counter-movement and mass public action arising in the form of the Black Protest and All Women's Strike organised in Poland in the autumn of 2016 that successfully saw off the introduction of legislation to radically restrict access to abortion. For Różalska, the lasting significance of the protest was both in installing an idea of solidarity among women who, 'refuse to be sacrificed for the greater good—be it

16   *Theorising Cultures of Equality*

God, the Nation or just higher fertility rates' (Korolczuk 2016a: 105), and enabling the effective – because affective – mainstreaming of key feminist principles through collaborative and non-hierarchical forms of organising around women's assertion of control over their bodies.

The chapters in the second section of the book take up and extend in further detail attention to various fields of cultural production as sites of and for the making and remaking of equalities.

Susan Friedman's chapter, "Why We Need Literature, Art, and Fantasy', foregrounds in particular the necessity of the arts in creatively illuminating intersecting forms of privilege and inequality and in imagining alternative futures. More than simply a trenchant critique of the withdrawal of public funding and support for arts and humanities, which she contends is a corollary of the assault on gender ideology, it is also a call to renew and further enliven and expand feminist traditions of story-telling. In particular, Friedman, who is engaged in ongoing conversation and dialogue with the multi-media artist Kabe Wilson, draws on the latter's recycling of Virginia Woolf's *A Room of One's Own*, in which each word from Woolf's novel was reassembled and reordered and in the process reimagined from the perspective of a queer and black subjectivity, to 'consider ways in which contemporary feminists might re-mix (or, more precisely, according to Kabe Wilson, might *recycle*) previous feminisms into ones suited for the intersectional feminism of the 21st century that envisions broadly conceived cultures of equality' (Friedman, 2020, this volume). Indeed, the metaphor and practice of recycling at the heart of Wilson's work offers a different and complementary way of understanding and extending both feminist reflexivity and contested circulations of gender knowledge proposed by Enderstein – one in which revolution is a continuous process of 'turning back to turn forward' (Friedman 2020, this volume).

Neil Garcia's chapter, 'Translating Homosexuality: Urbanism and the Masculine Bakla' in Severino Montano's *The Lion and the Faun*, is likewise about the possibility of 'turning back, to turn forward' (ibid.) that is attentive to the slippages and failures, as well as possibilities and opportunities of those returns to the future. In particular, Garcia returns to the work of one of the most celebrated Filipino writers and dramatists of the early part of the 20th century, Montano. For Garcia, Montano's unpublished novel, *The Lion and the Faun*, describes the cultural conditions of possibility both for the emergence and translation of lesbian, gay, bisexual and transgender (LGBT) subjectivities in urban centres in the Philippines and for the political movements that continue and which have been closely intertwined with the emergence of a Filipino LGBT literary tradition. If, as Garcia suggests, *The Lion and the Faun* is best read as Montano's fictionalised autobiography, then we might also suggest that the postcolonial reading and act of translation necessary to understand and decipher it is a story about the continuing ways that writers and readers within and beyond that Filipino LGBT tradition struggle within, against and between the cosmopolitan promise of neocolonial claims to equality and the forms of inequality that it produces, as well as the pluralities of embodied subjectivities and relational dynamics alongside of which it emerges in particular situations.

Theorising Gender and Cultures of Equality 17

The following chapters, nine and ten, are, we suggest, best read as a pair that offer distinctive if complementary perspectives on cultures of in/equality thought about and understood from the vantage point of two urban contexts in Brazil. Jimmy Turner's 'The City Animated by the Spirit of Patriarchy' draws on ethnographic encounters in the southern Brazilian city of Florianópolis to extend ways of thinking about people's experiences of gender inequality in urban situations. In particular, Turner's essay invites us to consider the ways that cultures of inequality are not simply produced in practice and objectified in objects, bodies and institutions but rather are a product of, and animated by, ongoing sets of human and non-human relations that are discernible both in their everyday and persistent social consequences and effects and in their material and embodied affects. While Turner's essay gestures to the way that overcoming the spirit of patriarchy and producing cultures of equality necessitates attending simultaneously to social relations and their material effects and affects, Tatiana Moura, Marta Fernández and Victoria Page's chapter, 'Power from the peripheries: Art, Culture and Masculinities in Rio de Janeiro' provides a concrete example of the way that some men and women are attempting that precisely. Drawing on a decolonial approach, they foreground the way that the space of the city is both animated by gender inequalities and divided clearly by class and racialised forms of privilege and marginality – divisions that replay and coincide with those of the 'modernity/coloniality binomial'. Against the violent policing not just of the boundaries and the movement of black people, men especially, into white spaces, as well as the denigration and criminalisation of the former, Moura, Fernández and Page disclose some of the creative and artistic practices, in particular *passinho* and slam, that not only disrupt and transgress those racialised and territorialised divides but more importantly, to recall Wilson, return to reclaim the urban periphery both as vantage point to observe and return the white gaze and as a site for the institution of an alternative set of effective and affective relations, including new models of gender relations and of masculinity in particular.

The final chapter of the volume, 'Decolonial Joy: Theorising from the Art of Valor y Cambio' by Frances Negrón-Muntaner extends ways of thinking about cultures of equality as sites and practices through which people can imagine and, in her terms, ' "feel" the possibility of a different future, one where neither colonialism nor coloniality rules over their lives'. The *Valor y Cambio* (Value and Change) project, conceived and co-launched by Negrón-Muntaner working with the visual artist Sarabel Santos Negrón, alongside a team of designers and engineers, produced and distributed a newly minted currency, 'Personas de Peso Puerto Rico (people of weight Puerto Rico), or pesos for short' (Negrón-Muntaner, 2020, this volume). The bank notes, ranging from 1 to 25 Pesos, feature historical figures, women and men alike, and an iconic community and that in different ways represented values of gender equality and social justice. Bank notes were dispensed from a recycled ATM (named VyC) where people were invited to share stories about the things that they valued in exchange for receipt of a banknote. The project successfully achieved its ambition to kick-start public conversations about value, as well as instituting a community currency and

18　*Theorising Cultures of Equality*

initiate a practice of non-capitalist exchange in the midst of multiple economic and environmental crises and catastrophes conditioned by colonialism. However, the focus of Negrón-Muntaner's chapter is of being, to borrow from C.S. Lewis (1995), 'surprised by joy'; that is the joy expressed by participants especially on receiving and holding the Peso in their hand. For Negrón-Muntaner this is not about, following Sara Ahmed (2010), the joy of being a feminist, or in this case, anti-colonial killjoy. Rather, drawing together decolonial and black feminist writing with that of theologians and philosophers, Negrón-Muntaner posits decolonial joy as the collective, shared and tangible experience of touching and sensing – and hence enlivening their claims to – alternative futures, amid pain and dispossession of coloniality in the present, as well as in the past.

Conclusion: 'Footnotes on' and Footsteps towards Equality

In a recent issue of the journal *Debate Feminista*, Anne Phillips asks, 'Why don't gender theorists talk more about gender equality?' She poses the question against a backdrop of the proliferation and mainstreaming of equality policies and frameworks the world over, from the UN to the Council of Europe, to the Gender Equality Observatory set up by the Economic Commission for Latin America and the Caribbean, and a backlash against notions of gender equality and indeed against the very idea of 'gender' itself in places and situations across the world. Indeed, it is precisely within and against those seemingly opposed processes, that Philipps, like Lennon and Alsop (2020), affirm the necessity for and renewal of gender theory in troubled times and more specifically for putting, 'thinking about gender equality back at the heart of gender theory'. (Phillips, 2019: 29).

This book, as with the GRACE project generally, may be regarded as one response to that call in so far as we place equality and, more specifically, cultures of equality at the heart of our gender theory and praxes. We have done so, however, not by offering an answer to the question about, 'what it is to be free and equal' (Phillips, 2019: 24–5), but rather by proposing that equality is and must a remain a provocation. In order to understand equality, we must begin not with a fixed set of ideas about what counts or qualifies as equality, but rather by listening to various competing and contested claims about equality, learning from struggles to dismantle systems of privilege and oppression and creating, and participating in, experiments in more equitable ways of living and working or dwelling together.

We want to end here by drawing our readers' attention in particular to the researchers on the GRACE project whose work, both individually and collectively, and in particular the exhibition Footnotes on Equality (footnotesonequality.eu) offers important insights on and suggestions for future footsteps towards equality (see, for example, Benitez-Silva 2018; Calderón 2017; Drage 2017, 2018; Enderstein 2017, 2018; Grabher 2020; Levy 2018; Rosado Pérez 2018; Trilló 2017, 2018, 2020; Verderi 2020). Working with Negrón-Muntaner, Rosemarie Buikema and Vassos Belia, as well as designer Anja Groten and web-designer

Theorising Gender and Cultures of Equality   19

Joana Chicau, the GRACE researchers created a physical and virtual exhibition that launched on International Women's Day, 8 March 2019 at CASCO Art Institute in Utrecht and which then went on a European tour to cities of the participating GRACE partners. The exhibition centres on the collection of art and everyday objects, together with film, that had been found, made and produced by the 15 GRACE researchers over the course of their doctoral projects. The objects and installations that comprise the exhibition, as the accompanying exhibition narrative explains, 'tell stories around instances when (in)equality is experienced, but also around moments of resistance to a discourse on equality that has come to reinforce European geopolitical boundaries, creating spaces of 'achieved equality' and global horizons of the 'not there yet.' [It provides] an artifactual analysis as a way to both engage and disseminate, as well as produce "new" sites and events of and about cultures of equality'(Footnotes on Equality Exhibition Catalogue, 2019).

What we wish to draw out in particular is the curators' notion of 'embodied discomfort' that informed both the stories that they told and the way that they sought to organise the exhibition in each of its forms. It was, as the group described it, a way of exploring the role of the body in its encounter with various texts and objects and an invitation to 'understand better, but also to witness present glimpses of equality's potentiality' (Footnotes Exhibition Catalogue, 2019), as well as to be discomfited, literally and metaphorically, by excessively easy assumptions about equality and equitability. We might also add, as the authors, together with Jimmy Turner, of the project bid that created the opportunity to, indeed demanded, the development and curation of an exhibition, that the discomfort that the researchers allude to is also no doubt a reflection of the considerable demands placed on them as researchers to engage in a different mode of creative inquiry and practice, in addition to and alongside their doctoral research.[2] The critical engagement with the cultural productions of equalities enabled by the GRACE project has clearly demonstrated the importance of creative praxis in theorising gender and cultures of in/equalities. For us, the beauty of GRACE has been the fruitful and indeed joyful coming together of theory and creative arts to engage with and enable diverse sections of the public to think through, challenge, contest and embrace, as well as discomfit, what equality can mean, feel, hear and look like to them.

Notes

1 GRACE is a consortium of gender studies scholars based at Associazione Orlando (Italy), Central European University (Hungary), University of Bologna (Italy), University of Granada (Spain), University of Hull (UK), University of Lodz (Poland), University of Oviedo (Spain), University of Utrecht (Netherlands) together with partners Kingston upon Hull City Council Equalities Unit (UK) & ATRIA (Institute on Gender Equality & Women's History, Netherlands)
2 In addition to Footnotes on Equality, the GRACE researchers successfully designed, created and launched Quotidian – http://graceproject.eu/quotidian/ – a feminist smartphone app, which also launched in March 2019 and is freely available to download through the usual app stores. Researchers also produced a series of films that showcased

20   *Theorising Cultures of Equality*

their research, some of which are incorporated in the Footnotes on Equality exhibition. Finally, as part of the GRACE project, Associazone Orlando built the GRACE digital HUB as an experiment in bespoke feminist digital architecture. It runs on its own platform and is not reliant on any pre-existing digital framework. Project co-ordinators and researchers used this platform very effectively for daily communication, knowledge-sharing, uploading data and images, etc. in the development of the Museum, smart phone, films, etc.

Bibliography

Ahrens, P. (2018). 'Indirect opposition: diffuse barriers to gender equality in the European Union.' In M. Verloo (ed.) *Varieties of Opposition to Gender Equality in Europe.* London: Routledge, 77–97.

Alsheh, Y., Filc, D., Frumer, N. and Snir, I. (2012). 'Equality', *Political Concepts.* www.politicalconcepts.org/equality-collaboration. Accessed 8 July 2019.

Ahmed, S. (2010). 'Killing joy: Feminism and the history of happiness', *Signs: Journal of Women in Culture and Society,* 35(3), 571–594.

Anderson, E.S. (1999). 'What is the Point of Equality?' *Ethics,* 109(2), 287–337.

Appadurai, A. (1996). *Modernity at Large: Cultural Dimensions of Globalization.* Minneapolis, MN: University of Minnesota Press.

Arribas, G. andCarrasco, L. (2003). 'Gender Equality and the EU. An Assessment of Current Issues', *Eipascope,* 1, 22–31.

Balibar, E. (2007). 'Is there a 'neo-racism'?'. In: das Gupta, T. (ed.), *Race and Racialization: Essential Readings.* Toronto: Canadian Scholars Press: 85–88.

Benitez-Silva, A. (2018). 'Sport: A Site of Exclusion or Space for Equality?' *Studies on Home and Community Science,* 11(2): 97–107.

Benhabib, S. (2002). *The Claims of Culture: Equality and Diversity in the Global Era.* Princeton, NJ: Princeton University Press.

Benschop, Y. andVerloo, M. (2011). 'Gender change, organizational change, and gender equality strategies'. In *Handbook of Gender, Work, and Organization.* Hoboken, NJ: John Wiley & Sons Ltd: 277–290.

Bourdieu, P. (1984). *Distinction: A Social Critique of the Judgement of Taste.* Translated by Richard Nice. Cambridge, MA: Harvard University Press.

Bourdieu, P. (1993). *The field of cultural production: Essays on art and literature.* New York: Columbia University Press.

Calderón, O. (2017). 'Feminist documentary cinema as a diffraction apparatus for the visualisation of care labour: the Spanish collective film Cuidado, resbala (2013)', *Feminist Media Studies,* 17(2).

Carrithers, M. (2005). 'Why anthropologists should study rhetoric', *Journal of the Royal Anthropological Institute,* 11(13): 577–583.

Cooper, D. (2014). *Everyday Utopias: The Conceptual Life of Promising Spaces.* Durham, NC: Duke University Press.

Cowan, J.K., Dembour, M.B. and Wilson, R.A. (Eds.). (2001). *Culture and Rights: Anthropological Perspectives.* Cambridge: Cambridge University Press.

Cowan, J. (2006). 'Culture and Rights after Culture and Rights ', *American Anthropologist,* 108(1): 9–24.

Crenshaw, K. (1989). 'Demarginalizing the intersection of race and sex: a black feminist critique of antidiscrimination doctrine, feminist theory and antiracist politics', *University of Chicago Legal Forum,* 140: 139–167.

Theorising Gender and Cultures of Equality 21

Crenshaw, K. (1991). 'Mapping the margins: intersectionality, identity politics, and violence against women of color', *Stanford Law Review*, 43(6): 1241–1299.

Crenshaw, K. (1994). 'Demarginalizing the Intersection of Race and Sex: A Black Feminist Critique of Antidiscrimination Doctrine, Feminist Theory, and Antiracist Politics'. In Jagger, A. (ed.), *Living with Contradictions: Controversies in Feminist Ethics*. Oxford: Westview Press: 38–52.

Drage, E. (2017). 'In the Hard Times, (and the Good): Solidarities Beyond Race and Gender in Critical Utopian and Dystopian Women's Science Fiction', *deGenere: Small Islands? Transnational Solidarity in Contemporary Literature and Arts*, no. 3.

Drage, E. (2018). 'Science, Myth, and Spirits: Re-inventions of Science Fiction by Women of Colour Writers, Between Africa, Europe and the Caribbean', *Studies on Home and Community Science*, vol. 11, no. 2.

Duncan, S.Pfau-Effinger, B.. (2012). *Gender, Economy and Culture in the European Union*. London: Routledge.

Effiinger, B.P. (2004). *Development of Culture, Welfare States and Women's Employment*. Aldershot: Ashgate.

Enderstein, A.M. (2017). 'European Identity and Gender Equality Policies: Shaping the Practice of Gender Expertise', *Journal of Research in Gender Studies* 7(2): 109–135.

Enderstein, A.M. (2018). '"First of all, Gender is Power": Intersectionality as Praxis in Gender Training', *Studies on Home and Community Science* 11(2): 44–56.

Englund, H. (2011). *Human Rights and African Airwaves: mediating equality on the Chichewa radio*. Bloomington, IN: Indiana University Press.

Englund, H. (2015). 'Equality in the Vernacular – Response by Harri Englund. Forum Section: Anthropologists Debate (In)Equality', *Suomen Antropologi: Journal of the Finnish Anthropological Society*, 2015(1): 79–81.

Escobar, A. (2007). 'Worlds and knowledges otherwise 1: The Latin American modernity/coloniality research program', *Cultural studies*, 21(2–3): 179–210.

Farris, S.R. (2017). *In the Name of Women s Rights: The Rise of Femonationalism*. Durham, NC: Duke University Press.

Fitzgerald, R. et al. (2014) 'Searching For Evidence of Acculturation: Attitudes Toward Homosexuality Among Migrants Moving From Eastern to Western Europe', *International Journal of Public Opinion Research* 26(3): 323–341.

Fourie, C., Schuppert, F., and Wallimann-Helmer, I. (Eds). (2015). *Social Equality: On What it Means to be Equals*. Oxford: Oxford University Press.

Gilroy, P. (2013). *Between Camps: Nations, Cultures and the Allure of Race*. London: Routledge.

Gosepath, S. (2011). 'Equality', *The Stanford Encyclopedia of Philosophy* (Spring2011 Edition), Edward N. Zalta (ed.). Accessed 8 July 2019. Retrieved from https://plato.stanford.edu/archives/spr2011/entries/equality.

Grabher, B. (forthcoming, 2020). 'The Privilege of Subversion. Reading Experiences of LGBT-themed Events during Hull UK City of Culture 2017 through Liminality'. In I. Lamond and J. Moss (eds.), *Liminality and Liminoid Spaces*. London:Routledge.

Hallward, P. (2006). 'Staging Equality: On Rancière's Theatrocacy', *New Left Review*37, Jan–Feb. 2006.

Harding, N. et al. (2013). 'Is the 'F'-word still dirty? A past, present and future of/for feminist and gender studies in Organization', *Organization*, 20(1): 51–65.

Henare, A. et al. (eds.) (2007). *Thinking Through things: Theorising Artefacts Ethnographically*. London: Routledge.

22 Theorising Cultures of Equality

Hennessy, R., and Ingraham, C. (1997). 'Introduction: reclaiming anticapitalist feminism'. In R. R. and C. Ingraham, (eds), *Materialist Feminism: A Reader in Class, Difference and Women's Lives*. London: Routledge: 1–16.

Hooks, b. (1984). *Feminist Theory: from Margin to Centre*. Boston, MA: South End Press.

Inglehart, R. and Norris, P. (2003). *Rising Tide: Gender Equality and Cultural Change around the World*. Cambridge: Cambridge University Press.

Jacquot, S. (2015). *Transformations in EU Gender Equality: From Emergence to Dismantling*. Basingstoke: Palgrave Macmillan.

Jagger, A. (ed.) (1994). *Living with Contradictions: Controversies in Feminist Ethics*. Oxford: Westview Press.

Kapferer, B. (2013). 'How anthropologists think: configurations of the exotic', *Journal of the Royal Anthropological Institute*, 19(4): 813–836.

Khader, S.J. (2018). *Decolonizing Universalism: A Transnational Feminist Ethic*. Oxford:Oxford University Press.

Korolczuk, E. (2016a). 'Explaining mass protests against abortion ban in Poland: the power of connective action', *Zoon Politikon*, 7: 91–113.

Lennon, K. and Alsop, R. (2020). *Gender Theory in Troubled Times*. Cambridge: Polity.

Lewis, C.S. (1995). *Surprised by Joy: The Shape of My Early Life*. Boston, MA: Houghton Mifflin Harcourt.

Levy, J. (2018). 'Of Mobiles and Menses: Researching Period Tracking Apps and Issues of Response-Ability', *Studies on Home and Community Science*, 11(2): 108–115.

Lombardo, E. and Meier, P. (2008). 'Framing gender equality in the European Union political discourse', *Social Politics: International Studies in Gender, State and Society*, 15(1): 101–129. doi:10.1093/sp/jxn001.

Lugones, M. (2010). 'Toward a decolonial feminism', *Hypatia*, 25(4): 742–759.

Lyness, K. and Brumit Kropf, M. (2005). 'The relationships of national gender equality and organizational support with work-family balance: A study of European managers', *Human Relations*, 58(1): 33–60.

Mackinnon, C. (1994). 'Towards Feminist Jurisprudence'. In Jagger, A. (ed.) (1994) *Living with Contradictions: Controversies in Feminist Ethics*. Oxford: Westview Press: 28–33.

Narayan, U. (2013). *Dislocating Cultures: Identities, Traditions, and Third World Feminism*. London: Routledge.

Pascall, G. andLewis, J. (2004). 'Emerging gender regimes and policies for gender equality in a wider Europe', *Social Policy*, 33(3): 373–394.

Pfau-Effinger, B. (2005). 'Culture and welfare state policies: Reflections on a complex interrelation', *Journal of Social Policy*, 34(1): 3–20.

Phillips, A. (2019). 'Why Don't Gender Theorists Talk More About Gender Equality?', *Debate Feminista*, Año 29, Vol. 57, April–September.

Povinelli, E.A. (2012). 'The Will to Be Otherwise/The Effort of Endurance', *South Atlantic Quarterly*, 111(3): 453–475.

Quijano, A. (2000). 'Coloniality of power and Eurocentrism in Latin America', *International Sociology*, 15(2): 215–232.

Quijano, A. (2007). 'Coloniality and modernity/rationality', *Cultural Studies, 21* (2–3):168–178.

Rae, Douglas, et al. (1981). *Equalities*, Cambridge, MA: Harvard University Press.

Rancière, J. (2004a). *The Philosopher and his Poor*. Durham, NC: Duke University Press.

Rancière, J. (2004b). *The Politics of Aesthetics: the Distribution of the Sensible*, translated by G. Rockhill. London: Continuum.

Richardson, D. and Munro, S. (2012). *Sexuality, Equality & Diversity*. Basingstoke: Palgrave Macmillan.

Röder, A. (2014). 'Explaining religious differences in immigrants' gender role attitudes', *Ethnic and Racial Studies* 37(14): 2615–2635.

Rosado Pérez, W. (2018). 'Literary Activism for "Mental Equality" in Mary Robinson's Proto-Feminist Pamphlet A Letter to the Women of England on the Injustice of Mental Subordination with Anecdotes (1799)', *Studies on Home and Community Sciences*, 11(2): 66–76.

Sahlins, M. (2013). *Islands of History*. Chicago, IL: University of Chicago Press.

Sewell Jr, W.H. (2005). *Logics of History: Social Theory and Social Transformation*. Chicago, IL: University of Chicago Press.

Squires, J. (2008). 'Intersecting inequalities: reflecting on the subjects and objects of equality', *The Political Quarterly*, 79(1): 53–61.

Smith, L.T. (1999). *Decolonizing Methodologies: Research and Indigenous Peoples*. London: Zed Books.

Stephenson, C.M. (2009). 'Gender equality and a culture of peace'. In *Handbook on Building Cultures of Peace*. New York: Springer: 123–138.

Stuurman, S. (2004) *François Poulain de la Barre and the Invention of Modern Equality*. Cambridge, MA: Harvard University Press.

Stuurman, S. (2017). *The Invention of Humanity: Equality and Cultural Difference in World History*. Cambridge, MA: Harvard University Press.

Tomlinson, J. (2011). 'Gender equality and the state: a review of objectives, policies & progress in the European Union', *The International Journal of Human Resource Management*, 22(18): 3755–3774.

Towns, A. (2002). 'Paradoxes of (In)Equality: Something is Rotten in the Gender Equal State of Sweden', *Cooperation and Conflict*, 37(2): 157–179.

Trilló, T. (forthcoming, 2020). 'Troubling coalitions: Some remarks on the (hardly audible) voice of pro-equality men's groups in gender equality advocacy', *Acta Universitatis Lodziensis. Folia Sociologica*, 69/2020.

Trilló, T. (2018). 'Performing Feminist Resistance on Twitter: The case of #Parliamone-Sabato in the Italian Twittersphere', *Władza sądzenia/Power of Judgment*, 14(1): 75–92.

Trilló, T. (2017). 'Communicating anti–violence policy on Twitter: The European Commission and #SayNoStopVAW', *Styles of Communication*, 9(1): 9–24.

Wagner, R. (1981). *The Invention of Culture*. Chicago, IL: University of Chicago Press.

Walby, S. et al. (2012). 'Intersectionality and the Quality of the Gender Equality Architecture', *Social Politics*, 19(4): 446–481.

Verderi, S. (forthcoming, 2020). 'Visualizing violence: political imaginations from the Syrian diaspora in the Netherlands'. In L. Passerini, M. Trakilovick and G. Proglio (eds.), *The Mobilities of Memory across European Borders and Beyond*. Oxford: Berghahn Books.

Vergès, F. (2001). 'The Age of Love', *Transformations*, 47: 1–17.

Winterson, J. (2016). 'We need to build a new left. Labour means nothing today', *The Guardian*, 24 June. Accessed 10 September 2019. Retrieved from www.theguardian.com/politics/2016/jun/24/we-need-to-build-a-new-left-labour-means-nothing-jeanette-winterson

Van den Brink, M. et al. (2010). 'Transparency in academic recruitment: a problematic tool for gender equality?', *Organization Studies* 31(11): 1459–1483.

Van den Brink, M. andBenschop, Y. (2012). 'Slaying the Seven-Headed Dragon: The Quest for Gender Change in Academia', *Gender, Work & Organization*, 19 (1): 71–92.

24   *Theorising Cultures of Equality*

Verloo, M. and Walby, S. (2012). 'Introduction: The implications for theory and practice of comparing the treatment of intersectionality in the equality architecture in Europe', *Social Politics: International Studies in Gender, State & Society* 19(4): 433–445.

Wollstonecraft, M. (2015 [1792]). *A Vindication of the Rights of Woman*. London: Vintage Books.

Wynter, S. (2003). 'Unsettling the Coloniality of Being/Power/Truth/Freedom: Towards the Human, After Man, Its Overrepresentation—An Argument', *The New Centennial Review*, 3(3): 257–337.

Young, I.M. (2011). *Justice and the Politics of Difference*. Princeton, NJ: Princeton University Press.

2 The Promise of the Human

Gender and the Enlightenment's Culture of Equality

Laura Brace

Introduction

This chapter explores Enlightenment conceptions of equality and the place of gender in wider deliberations about rationality, autonomy and self-legislation. In the 18-century debates about reason, human rationality was understood to be self-created and self-creating through an endless historical process, and humanity, civilisation and history were chained to colonial values and the imperial project and therefore to underlying structures of gender, race, class and nation. As Rachel Sturman argues, the 'plural and proliferating politics of the human have mobilised gender in a variety of ways', and gender has come to signal the 'exclusions inherent in the universal category of humanity' (2011: 230). In the writings of Mary Wollstonecraft and Mary Hays in the late 18th century, we can trace the simultaneous creation of the universal and the particular in the development of the politics of the human as they made the claim for women's humanity and equality in the contexts of history and of nature. Their arguments show us the 'complex interrelatedness of the condition of women with the history of forms of property and of legal and political rights' (O' Brien, 2009: 104) and the limitations of the promise of the human for guaranteeing equal rights for women.

Natural history

Much of the work of humanisation in the 18th century centred around competing discourses of natural history – an area of enquiry that was emerging, as Niekerk argues, as a privileged field and a popular science, and as a leading arena for debate. It focused on a whole new set of questions from which nature emerged as 'flexible and full of connections, transitions, and metamorphoses' (Niekerk, 2004: 479). In the late 18th century, scientists were finding more similarities than differences between human, animal and plant life, and coming to the conclusion that 'man was not to be regarded as a separate species, set apart from and central to a divinely ordained hierarchy' (Ruston, 2008: 57). Late 18th-century natural history was about the search for the link between humanity and non-human animals, and the key player in this story was the orang-utan. Enlightenment controversies about human nature and culture centred around the character of

26 *Theorising Cultures of Equality*

the relation between mankind and the great apes, which were regarded as 'most immediately adjacent to us in the natural world' (Wokler, 2012: 4). Rousseau drew a flexible boundary around the human and argued for the powerful effects of diverse climates, air, food, ways of living and habits that might make it possible that those characterised as beasts were in effect primitive men who had not been able to develop their faculties or reach any degree of perfection.

Most 18th-century natural historians agreed on the orang-utan's striking resemblance to humans. The exercise of reason and the command of language were usually taken to be the leading distinctions between animals and men, but these were the subject of debate in the speculative philosophies at the end of the 18th century. Thinkers were exploring and complicating the connections between nature, reason and revelation, and the acquisition of language was at an uncomfortable boundary between the natural and the cultural. Rousseau argued that being able to speak and communicate using language was something that had to be acquired and mastered, and as such, this was not a natural characteristic of humans. Orang-utans, he speculated, might not use language because they lacked the opportunities to develop their vocal organs, or even because they chose to pretend not to speak in order to avoid being put to work (Wokler, 2012: 9). Robert Wokler sees the 18th-century thinkers as 'attempting to establish the zoological frontiers of humanity', directing their attention to the conceptual boundaries of humanity by addressing themselves to language rather than anatomy. 'Enlightenment anthropologists', he argues, 'perceived their subject plainly in terms of the relation between the biological and social characteristics of man, without supposing that human nature was either an assemblage of instincts or a product of culture' (Wokler, 2012: 5).

Much of this discussion about how to balance out the natural and the cultural and to determine the boundaries of the human centred on the idea of the great chain of being, the 'chain of subordination' (Spencer, 2012: 429) that was used as a framework to try and make sense of the variety of living species and of the flimsiness of the borders between them. The principle of continuity, Jane Spencer argues, meant that the distinctions between species and kinds were understood to be finely graduated, and 'in theory, wherever two distinct beings are found next to each other on the chain it should be possible to find a third being in between the two with characteristics of both – the 'link' between them' (Spencer, 2012: 430). This approach meant understanding the natural world through a series of gradations and elegant variations. The flying squirrel united the bird to the quadruped, while the ape linked the quadruped to the man (Spencer, 2012: 430).

It was possible to focus on almost imperceptible nuances of difference between the species in the chain and on the closeness of the resemblances between them, but Wokler concludes that 'it was in the Enlightenment taken for granted that the chain as a whole was essentially fixed and static, that its main links were points of cleavage rather than conjunction, and that man and ape were separated by a qualitative gulf which, as Buffon put it, even Nature could not bridge' (Wokler, 2012: 7). It is important for us to understand the ways in which the chain was tied to time and history in the 18th century, so that it became 'a theory

The Promise of the Human   27

that gave expression to [Nature's] still uncompleted programme' (Wokler, 2012: 10). Orang-utans could in the 1790s be perceived by the naturalist William Smellie and other biologists as primitive members of our species, rather than as degenerate men. As Wokler argues, this is an exact reverse in temporal perspective and a significant milestone in understanding our origins. Niekerk sees two competing models of natural history at work in the 18th century: one based on the older paradigm of a static, eternal order of nature, and a newer model based on 'the dynamic and therefore developmental aspect of natural history' that introduced the element of time (Niekerk, 2004: 478). Accounts of 'natural' peoples entailed what Sankar Muthu has identified as a 'temporal claim' within which the New World represented the earliest stage of human history, an 'infant world' in contrast to the decrepitude and moral bankruptcy of a European civilisation that was now in decline (Muthu, 2003: 23). The study of natural history brought with it elements of time and space, but there was no unified discourse of the relationship of man to ape. As Niekerk argues, much remained unsaid or contradictory, and the different agendas of the Enlightenment were not always in agreement. Wokler is describing a progressive moment that underpins both much later and more modern accounts of evolution, as well as an understanding of humans as 'constitutively cultural agents' (Muhtu, 2003: 67) living within complex webs of inherited institutions, practices and beliefs that they consciously formed and maintained. The progressive moment described by Wokler did not last, however, and by the early 19th century the great apes had been reaffirmed as sub-human (Wokler, 2012: 11). If man and ape were related, then some humans had to be closer to apes than others, and their claim to humanity was called into question. There were, as Roxann Wheeler points out, 'multifaceted ways to adjudicate the boundaries of human similarity, and these changed over time' (Wheeler, 2000: 240–1).

Smellie argued that man in his lowest condition was close to the orang-utan, so that the stupid Huron and the Hottentot could be identified as the kinds of human who were furthest away from the high condition of the 'profound philosopher' (Spencer, 2012: 432). This was complicated by Rousseau's account, which argued that savages must have had stronger powers of sight, hearing and smell than their civilised counterparts, and that whole peoples, such as Hottentots, 'were able to see as far with the naked eye as Europeans with a telescope' (Wokler, 2012: 7). For Rousseau, this was part of a story of decline, of human animals moving away from their natural state in ways that were detrimental and damaging, making us dull and frail, until we 'are hardly any longer even animals of a certain degenerate kind, but only pets, or prey, broken in by ourselves – weak, docile, fattened and fleeced' (Wokler, 2012: 8). In other words, as Wokler puts it, civilisation emerges from Rousseau's account as 'a self-imposed form of domestication' (Wokler, 2012: 8). There is a clear link from here to Wollstonecraft's arguments about hyper-femininity and partial civilisation and the uneven domestication of men and women. In her review of Smellie's work, Wollstonecraft argued that the docility of animals was of the most ignoble kind, produced by fear. Caged animals, she argued, soon forget their tricks when they are well

28 *Theorising Cultures of Equality*

fed, and they are not reminded of the cruel treatment that they endured while they were learning them. Women's limbs and faculties 'are cramped with worse than Chinese bands, and the sedentary life which they are condemned to live, while boys frolic in the open air, weakens the muscles and relaxes the nerves' (Ruston, 2008: 68). Women of fashion were weak, but proud of their weakness, their exquisite sensibility, which raised them up the social scale while 'simultaneously sinking her lower down the chain of being' (Ruston, 2008: 69). In Wollstonecraft's account, the chain of being was a chain of subordination, but it was not fixed and static, but a dynamic element in women's subordination and in men's power. Women in Wollstonecraft's narrative 'appear to be suspended by destiny' between heaven and earth – not quite reduced to livestock, but not enlightened by reason or given the opportunity to struggle against the world, unfold their faculties or acquire the dignity of conscious virtue. Without a clear set of morals and principles, women became passive and indolent and bore the marks of inferiority and degeneration (Wollstonecraft, [1792] 1995: 105). Wollstonecraft's argument was that men were 'actively and purposefully trying to push women further down the chain of being' (Ruston, 2008: 66).

Spencer's work has shown how the relationship between animals and humanity was an important influence on the development of enlightenment feminism, which was based on 'a belief in the essential rational equality of human beings regardless of sex, and a commitment to the possibility of social progress' (Spencer, 2012: 428). They were interested in the general similarity yet endless variety of the human race from physical and moral causes alike. They used natural history to argue that variety was natural and beneficial. Their core argument was that women's natural state was unknowable, because the relations between the sexes had been so distorted and corrupted by the unnaturalness of contemporary society. 'It cannot be demonstrated', Wollstonecraft argued, 'that woman is essentially inferior to man because she has always been subjugated' (1995: 108). She set out to show that women were capable of reason and thus to prove that they were part of mankind 'in its most universal sense, and therefore entitled to the rights of man' (Ruston, 2008: 64). Sturman argues that the limitations imposed by the idea of the 'Rights of Man' 'defined the terrain of women's struggle' and structured women's claim to humanity (2011: 229). Their struggle made clear that exclusions were inherent in the category human because the claim to inclusion and equality 'necessarily reproduced the differentiation of women from the universal category of 'Man' they sought to overcome' (Sturman, 2011: 229).

Equality, reason and the human

Enlightenment feminism began with the claim to equality. Virtue and good morals were inherent in the soul of man because they had been placed there by God. Women had been formed by God to resemble men in their desire for happiness, in having their own wills, in pursuing the attainment of their own ends, and in being able to form opinions for themselves. There were no distinctions in the moral perfection or the religious duties of men and women.

The Promise of the Human   29

Women, in Hays' view, did not differ materially from men, and it was fair and natural for them to wish to be guided by God and their own consciences in the same way as men. Hays argued that women bore the unequivocal marks of dignity that came from having been created by God, and this put them on a footing of equality. Women had been included in the original promise of the human, and their exclusion was a result of men's active intervention. Men had fostered women's inferiority 'till women are almost sunk below the standard of rational creatures' (Wollstonecraft [1792] 1995: 105) and unable to attain 'conscious dignity by feeling themselves only dependent on God' (1995: 106). Humanity was a status that came from an original grant from the Creator, but it was also an achievement and not just a species-specific characteristic (Scott, 2004: 91). It was being consciously and unreasonably withheld from women when men imposed dependence on them. Hays addressed men directly, 'Ye unjust, ye unreasonable, ye tyrannical beings! Are ye not all formed by the same hand? made of the same flesh and blood? And subject alike to common frailties?' (Hays, 1798: 22). Reason, she argued, went hand in hand with religion 'in opposing the claims of the one sex, to a right of subjecting the other' (Hays, 1798: 25). Men, in her view, had clothed themselves with authority of their own assumptions and privilege and maintained their empire by force alone. Women, as a result, were 'an oppressed, -a degraded, - and an excluded portion of the human race' (Hays, 1798: 41). The claim for inclusion in the rights of man came out of a claim of exclusion from the human.

In this account, the conditions of modern social life were understood to deform and dehumanise individuals. Men were attempting to affix 'universal weakness' to women for their own convenience and to perpetuate an unfortunate 'system of politics in morals' that rested on partitioning and drawing internal distinctions within the category of human beings (Hays, 1798: 57). Men's arrogance and vanity made them presume to interpret women's road to happiness and perfection 'as lying only through the medium of submission and obedience' to them as men (Hays, 1798: 149). The whole system, Hays argued, was raised and supported by men and relied on degrading the understandings and corrupting the hearts of women. Women, as Wollstonecraft argued, had lost their dignity, almost removing them from the human species, losing their grip on the rank assigned to them by reason ([1792] 1995: 117). Neither nature, reason nor revelation could justify such 'an arbitrary exclusion, such a mortifying distinction; as that which the men have established between the sexes, by governing women without control, without representation, and without limitation; and by leaving them in almost every circumstance of life, exposed to every species of injury, without a possibility of redress' (Hays, 1798: 153).

For both Wollstonecraft and Hays, the intellectual and moral inferiority of women was the corrupt effect of civilisation. It was women, rather than all humans, who were treated as pets and prey and educated for docility and dependence. Women bore the marks of inferiority, stripped of the virtues that should clothe humanity (Wollstonecraft, [1792] 1995: 107). Mary Hays argued that it was an infallible truth that any class of rational beings held in a state of

30　*Theorising Cultures of Equality*

subjection and dependence from generation to generation would degenerate both in body and mind (Hays, 1798: 69). For her, the state of women in general was to be degraded and humiliated in society, held in a constant state of dependence until they had lost any clear idea of what they might have been, or what they still might be. They were bound by such heavy and complicated chains 'that they more they are considered, the less hope remains of being able to unloose them by perseverance, or break through them by force' (Hays, 1798: 70). Their status as rational moral agents was constantly being called into doubt, and the possibility that they could be transformed into moral beings was complicated by these questions of debasement and inferiority. The threshold for autonomy and conscious dignity, for full inclusion in the category of the human, was undecided and uncertain. It was possible for women to move up and down the chain of being, to be excluded from the human and to make themselves unworthy of being counted as members of the human species. The boundary of the universal category of 'Man' always carried the potential for disruption, rupture and contradiction.

Animals to men to monsters

Enlightenment feminism drew attention to the fact that the whole discourse of rights was 'premised on preserving societal forms of inequality intact' (Sturman, 2011: 229) and on the simultaneous creation of the universal and the particular. The liberal focus was on rights grounded in theories of property and autonomy, and that meant that rights that were designated as natural had to be understood as specific social relations. As Wollstonecraft made clear in her opposition to property (Brace, 2016; Halldenius, 2014) freedom had come to be understood as 'class privilege, applicable only in full to a group entitled to it by property, reason and virtue' (Rozbicki, 2001: 39). Liberty was a cultural artefact that reflected inequalities, which in turn were regarded as just and justifiable, and so as natural (Rozbicki, 2001: 40). Rousseau shared this critique of rights, arguing that inegalitarian property relations underpinned divisions between rich and poor, ruler and ruled, master and slave: 'In civilized societies we have come to be imprisoned by our symbols, ensnared by the images of our freedom as we run headlong into our chains, altogether captivated by our accomplishments which are in fact no more than the trappings of culture' (Wokler, 2012: 18). As Rozbicki points out, this distorted notion of freedom rested on a combination of inequality and elite contempt that amplified class distinctions and reinforced hierarchical social relations (Rozbicki, 2001: 44). It had the same amplifying effect on gender.

In this process of being imprisoned by symbols and running headlong into our chains, Wokler points to what he sees in Rousseau as 'the double metamorphosis from animals to men to monsters of our own making' (Wokler, 2012: 22). This monstering was highly gendered. Women were implicated in particular ways in the process of being captivated by accomplishments and the trappings of culture, and they were blamed for making themselves into monsters, despots and tyrants. Women of fashion, as Wollstonecraft argued,

The Promise of the Human   31

were weak and neglected all the duties of life, preferring to recline on their sofas. They were depraved and 'dissolved in luxury', with the truth hidden from them and their characters wholly artificial, built on the trappings of culture rather than the authenticity of nature (Wollstonecraft, [1792] 1995: 116). Women were forced to avail themselves of the only weapons that they were permitted to yield. They were, Hays argued, compelled to subterfuge, whining and flattery by the injustice of men's actions, employing low cunning, as the weak have no other weapons against the strong (Hays, 1798: 91). These weapons of the weak were handed to women under the disguise of prudence. They were 'the miserable shifts that women were reduced to' (Hays, 1798: 212) – pitiful arts that were supposed to succeed with men, all of them focused on the 'art of insnaring and entrapping' to attain and manage a husband (Hays, 1798: 219). Hays and Wollstonecraft shared Rousseau's belief that all people had come to be imprisoned and duped by the inequalities of property and rank. Even those who consider the human species from a liberal and extensive point of view, Hays argued, had come to accept the idea that the necessity of subordination on one side was unavoidable (Hays, 1798: 91). The complicated social interrelations of power meant that men everywhere submitted to oppression and at the same time endeavoured to enslave women and to transmit their servitude through the generations, debasing individual women in the process (Wollstonecraft, [1792] 1995: 155, 161). Hays' language made clear that women's subordination was inseparable from a deeply hierarchical understanding of society and from ideas about property, liberty and virtue. Men considered the authority that had been assumed by their sex 'not only as an inheritance against which no claim can avail; but as a birthright given them from above, which it is their duty as much as their inclination to maintain' (Hays, 1798: 102). They were fully convinced that they were fitter to govern than women and that women were unable to govern themselves, and this mesh of assumptions and imagined authority formed a mysterious veil of law, prejudice and precedent that needed to be ripped apart. Behind the veil, men's patriarchal authority was revealed to be a cultural artefact and built on deeply unstable foundations. Matrimony is a civil contract that is, as Hays pointed out, influenced by love, which in turn can be deceived, or can degenerate under the influence of ambition and avarice. Power is 'an engine of too dangerous, and of too ready execution, in domestic life, to be trusted in the hands of man', who is subject to error, passion and caprice (Hays, 1798: 264).

Women living behind the veil and subject to this kind of arbitrary patriarchal control had been kept ignorant of their own rights, such that they did not have it in their power to claim them. In the Enlightenment account, reason depended on ideas, and ideas depended on an environment of reflection and on the possibility of using the mind and expanding its horizons (Carey, 2006). Without these expanded horizons, reason no longer operated as a clear marker of humanity. Women kept in a state of dependence were bound to find that there was a disjuncture between their natural potential and what they could actually do with their reason (Hirschmann, 2008). Rationality, as Roland Marden argues, defines human beings as human, but not all human beings are able to exercise this

32   *Theorising Cultures of Equality*

capacity properly (2006: 87). Wollstonecraft asked the readers of the *Vindication of the Rights of Man*, 'In what respect are we superior to the brute creation, if intellect is not allowed to be the guide of passion? Brutes hope and fear, love and hate; but, without a capacity to improve, a power of turning these passions to good or evil, they neither acquire virtue nor wisdom' (Wollstonecraft, [1792] 1995: 31). The creator had given reason to all human beings, but women were treated as though they were incapable of acquiring virtue or wisdom, or of acting on fixed principles. The 'fair ladies' who inflicted tortures on captive slaves were monsters who imagined themselves to be sensitive to the feelings of others, civilised and cultivated. Some of them, 'after the sight if a flagellation, compose their ruffled spirits and exercise their tender feelings by perusal of the last imported novel' (Wollstonecraft, [1792] 1995: 46). This was a particularly gendered transformation from animal to human to monster, driven by the instability and untrustworthiness of the female imagination. The question was not only how far a woman could control it, but also how far it could be corrupted, warped and distorted by the restriction of her horizons. Wollstonecraft's description of the fair ladies' tender feelings drew on a long tradition of figuring women's weak minds as particularly susceptible to superstition and of understanding the imagination as a threat to a stable and coherent self (Buckley, 2017). In the case of the 'fair ladies' in Wollstonecraft's account, the minds of women had been enfeebled by false refinement and the enforcement of blind obedience to men.

Tyrants of all denominations, as Wollstonecraft pointed out, were eager to crush reason and so 'to force all women, by denying them civil and political rights, to remain immured in their families groping in the dark' (Wollstonecraft, [1792] 1995: 69). Women were kept in the dark by men who wanted only slaves and playthings. The key to change was education, so that women would be 'awakened to a sense of their injuries, they would behold with astonishment and indignation, the arts which had been employed, to keep them in a state of PERPETUAL BABYISM' (Hays, 1798: 97). For Hays, the problem was that from the first dawnings of reason, women find that their part in life has been already prescribed for them: 'They find themselves enclosed in a kind of magic circle, out of which they cannot move, but to contempt or destruction. And however confined and mortifying to their feelings this prison of the soul may be, they can never hope for emancipation, but from superior power' (Hays, 1798: 111). They see that they are injured, but they cannot see any means of redress, and so they turn to vanities and follies, captivated by the trappings of culture. Women are entirely dependent on their senses, rather than their reason, for employment and amusement, so that there is nothing to curb their emotions and 'no noble pursuit sets them above the little vanities of the day' (Wollstonecraft, [1792] 1995: 98). For Hays, women were wasting their lives, their passions forced into wrong channels: 'Thus many a good head is stuffed with ribbons, gauze, fringes, flounces, and furbelows, that might have received and communicated, far other and more noble impressions' (Hays, 1798: 79). Patience and industry had been dissipated, and intense thought and ceaseless anxiety had been spent on the pursuit of vanity, rendering women passive and

The Promise of the Human   33

indolent, with just a few superficial accomplishments, and their thoughts constantly directed to the most insignificant part of themselves.

Claiming humanity and equality

The solution was a reformation in female manners. It was time to restore women's lost dignity 'and make them, as a part of the human species, labour by reforming themselves to reform the world' (Wollstonecraft, [1792] 1995: 117). They needed to exert themselves, to unfold their own faculties and so acquire the dignity of conscious virtue. Every being could become virtuous by exercising its own reason (Wollstonecraft, [1792] 1995: 89), and once women could maintain the habits of virtue, they could make themselves independent. It was up to women to de-monster themselves, to refuse to be broken in, to enlarge their minds and to give up their sinister tricks for governing their husbands. Sharon Ruston argues that this proposed revolution in female manners was about women taking on the responsibility of being 'part of the human species' (2008: 69), asserting both their humanity and their equality, bringing them both into existence at the moment that they claimed them (Phillips, 2015: 69–70), and making the human a political matter (Phillips, 2015: 78). The feminist writers of the 18th century were creating a claim-based account of humanity that focused attention on those still battling to achieve a status as fully human, to be 'accepted as full equals' (Phillips, 2015: 74). They were demanding equality when it was not being granted, and when they had been made vulnerable, insecure and unequal from exposure to differential power.

This claim to humanity was being made at a particular moment in the development of commercial society that involved what Karen O'Brien identifies as 'a simultaneous naturalisation and historicisation of the female sex' (2009: 101). The question of what it meant to be part of the human species, and what responsibilities that brought with it, was part of a wider ambivalence about commercial society in the 18th century, when the pursuit of wealth was a source of moral unease, seen as bringing with it ostentation, emasculation, vanity, luxury and selfish effeminacy, loaded with risk and danger, a vortex that sucked in and destroyed virtue and discipline. These dangers were embodied by the slave trade, an 'abominable mischief' and 'stigma on our nature' that had been allowed to continue from motives of self-interest and expediency in the face of its manifest injustice and inhumanity (Wollstonecraft, [1792] 1995: 53). At the same time, the new commercial society was regarded as a source of value, of improvement, prosperity, taste, elegance and refinement (Taylor, 2012: 81). Women as a category were central to this ambivalence. They were regarded as particularly susceptible to the seductions of consumption and to gaming and dissipation (Brace, 2010, 2013), but they were also central to the 'social optimism' identified by Taylor in the recognition that human beings are naturally disposed to care for one another. Women as the 'guardians of sociality' helped to foster and guarantee sensibility and generous civility. The proper exercise of domestic duties, 'the sweet circle of domestic life' could lay the

34 *Theorising Cultures of Equality*

foundations of virtue and charity (Hays, 1798: 81). Women may have had different duties from men to fulfil, as Wollstonecraft argued, but they were human duties, and if they were allowed to carry them out in rational fellowship with men, rather than in slavish obedience, they would become more generous, social and affectionate daughters, sisters, wives and mothers – 'in a word, better citizens' (Wollstonecraft, [1792] 1995: 240).

Citizenship and humanity were bound up with masculinity, and the concept of the free citizen was both equal and gendered. Demanding civic recognition for women drew Wollstonecraft away from a discourse of humanity and towards identification with 'masculine' values. Hays made clear that the idea of a masculine woman was considered a term of reproach, even where she emulated virtues and accomplishments 'which as common to human nature, are common to both sexes' (Hays, 1798: 173). There was nothing wrong, she argued, with a woman being rational and acquiring knowledge, although she needed to avoid 'aukward imitations' of the masculine (1798: 179). Like Wollstonecraft, Hays emphasised the physical differences between the sexes, arguing that nature had denied women the bodily strength, abilities and inclination for being soldiers, masons, carpenters, blacksmiths or farriers. A woman should not pursue knowledge or accomplishments in a way that could interfere with her duty 'in any of the leading characters of the sex, as daughter, sister, wife, or mother; a woman of sense and virtue will not for a moment balance between these' (Hays, 1798: 202). The comfort, happiness and security of men depended on the fidelity and chastity of the women, and this strand of Enlightenment feminism told a story about equality that rested on the conscious dignity of women being fostered and maintained by her domestic roles and duties. Humanity, in this sense, was 'a relational encounter' (Pin-Fat, 2018) between men and women that rested on doing gender in particular ways.

These idealisations of the domestic were, Taylor argues, not just about femininity and the family, but about the 'fate of "social affections" in a competitive market economy' (Taylor, 2012: 83). In order to understand the promise of the human as it was held out in the 18th century, we need to see the importance of the feminine influence, the influence of gender at the heart of modernising process. Women, as Taylor argues, were constructed as the leading agents of social progress, civilising men, transforming them into proper persons as good citizens and polite gentlemen. The corruption of women's morals was presented as a consequence of European refinement, and there was a clear 'sense of a tension between men and women's innate humanity and their socially ascribed identities' (O'Brien, 2009: 182). Wollstonecraft thought about gender in evolutionary terms, presenting modern women as a relic of feudal history and associating their oppression with the customs of the 'East'. She and Hays positioned women's subordination both in the past, as part of the temporalising of natural history, and in the historic present of the colonial gaze where 'all opinions degrading to women, are grounded on the rude ideas of savage nations, where strength of body is the only distinguishing feature, and supposed to carry every other degree of

The Promise of the Human 35

superiority along with it' (Hays, 1798: 131). Wollstonecraft uncritically associated the East with despotism and tyranny, imagining 'gendered despotism' as a defining feature of Eastern life and as a corruption of Western values (Zonana, 1993: 600). Women in the East, she said, 'languish like exotics' ([1792] 1995: 107), lived in harems where they were indolent, confined, under-educated and over-sexualised. Women in the West were subjected to books of instruction that were written by men in which 'in the true style of Mahometanism, they are treated as a kind of subordinate beings, and not as a part of the human species' (Wollstonecraft, [1792] 1995: 74). They were educated 'in worse than Egyptian bondage' (1995: 202). Women's slavish dependence was amplified in her imagined version of the East, which was populated by tyrants and sensualists and blasted by a despotism that killed virtue and genius in the bud ([1792] 1995: 116). Women's humanity was most at risk in this Eastern context –a place where they could not make a claim to be accepted as full equals. The Enlightenment feminism of Wollstonecraft, Hays and Catharine Macaulay constructed women who lived in the regions of the East as in a state of slavery (Macaulay, 1790: 31), and the 'East' itself as a site of 'imperial irresponsibility' where Islam imposed an inferior status on women who were thought to have no souls (Howard, 2004: 69). They used anti-Muslim stereotypes to highlight the barbarism of patriarchal marriage in primitive and Orientalist terms and to underscore the themes of confinement, imprisonment and sexual control in men's domination of women (Botting and Kronewitter, 2012). In making their claim for inclusion in the universal category of Man, they used the otherness of Eastern subordination to provide 'a reassuring substrate to their own oppression, assuring them of their relative privilege as English women in a civilized society' (Paugh, 2014: 640).

The tension between humanity and socially ascribed identities was also expressed through class. Inequalities of property and distinctions of rank were presented as 'uniquely unfavourable to the humanity of women' (O'Brien, 2009: 182), driving them away from their maternal duties by encouraging them to employ wet nurses. Women were rendered weak and luxurious by wealth (Wollstonecraft, [1792] 1995: 235). For Hays, the problem was that social affections and domestic duties were not valued by aristocratic women, so that they fell into the disuse among them, and then their corrupted social practices were emulated by the middle classes, and 'spoiled by prosperity and goaded on by temptation and the allurements of pleasure, they give a loose rein to their passions, and plunge headlong into folly and dissipation' (Hays, 1798: 82). Women had the potential to be the companions and equals of men, and they were entitled to esteem regardless of their class status. They were originally intended, Hays insisted, to be the helpmates of men, and 'not their drudges in the common ranks, and the tools of their passions and prejudices in the higher' (Hays, 1798: 128).

Conclusion

Women's claim to humanity, in the end, had to rest on nature. Enlightenment feminism found itself caught between a conjectural model of gender as

36   *Theorising Cultures of Equality*

progress and the category of 'natural' woman, which was used as 'a yardstick with which to measure some abuses of civilisation' (O'Brien, 2009: 100). The fair ladies and the baby-women had moved too far away from the sweet circle of domestic life, and they needed to find a path back through duty and independence. Nature had placed great trust in their virtue and formed their modesty from the beginning, so that 'modesty is innate in a greater degree in women than in men', demonstrated in the history of all nations 'of the human race, wild and tame, social and savage' (Hays, 1798: 231–2). They all agreed on the truth that a great degree of modesty and purity in behaviour and conduct was expected and required in the female character. Hays was arguing for the gradual emancipation of women and its salutary effects in this enlightened age. Like Wollstonecraft's, it was an argument against dependence and for the redistribution of wealth and the enlargement of women's opportunities for employment. Married women felt the shallowness of their participation in the community of fortune and the humiliation of being completely dependent on their husbands until 'a wife is neither more, nor less, than – a great baby in leading-strings' (Hays, 1798: 281–2). She was arguing for a reformation to restore women to their natural rights, so that they could find themselves at ease in their proper places. Her vision was of men and women living together 'like people in short of the same species, who feel that they are of equal consequence to each other's happiness and comfort'. Differences between the sexes could produce variety without degrading half of the human race (Hays, 1798: 292). This claim to humanity would mean that 'both sexes are upon a footing of equality, when they are permitted to exert in their different spheres of action, the talents their Creator has been pleased to bestow on them' (Hays, 1798: 62).

The politics of the human at work in late 18th-century natural histories and in the development of feminist thought show us some of the stories of equality that people have created out of reason, nature and difference. They are stories that demonstrate the tensions between the static, eternal order of nature and a newer dynamic model of the human and of equality as forged in history, and in relation and encounter with the other. This more dynamic approach revealed the uncertainty and porosity of the boundary around the human, as well as the politics behind the claim and commitment to equality. The promise of the human in the 18th century should remind us that in trying to achieve equality, we need to do more than claim our own humanity and remember that we have a responsibility not to be complicit in reproducing, sustaining and policing inequitable hierarchies of humanity (Pin-Fat, 2018).

Bibliography

Botting, E. and Kronewitter, S. (2012). 'Westernization and Women's Rights: Non-Western European Responses to Mill's Subjection of Women, 1869–1908', *Political Theory*, 40:4, 466–496.

Brace, L. (2010). 'Improving the Inside: Gender, Property and the Eighteenth-Century Self', *British Journal of Politics and International Relations*, 12:1, 111–126.

The Promise of the Human 37

Brace, L. (2016). 'Mary Wollstonecraft and the Properties of (Anti)Slavery', in S. Berges and A. Coffee (eds), *The Social and Political Philosophy of Mary Wollstonecraft*. Oxford: Oxford University Press.

Buckley, J. (2017). *Gender, Pregnancy and Power in Eighteenth-Century Literature: The Maternal Imagination*. London: Palgrave Macmillan.

Halldenius, L. (2014). 'Mary Wollstonecraft's Feminist Critique of Property: On Becoming a Thief from Principle', *Hypatia*, 29:4, 942–957.

Hays, M. (1798). *An Appeal to the Men of Great Britain in Behalf of Women*. London: Johnson and Bell.

Hirschmann, N. (2008). *Gender, Class and Freedom in Modern Political Theory*. Princeton, NJ and Oxford: Princeton University Press.

Macaulay, C. (1790). *Letters on Education with Observations on Religious and Metaphysical Subjects*. Dublin: Chamberlaine and Rice.

Marden, R. (2006). '"That all men are created equal": "Rights talk" and exclusion in North America', in G. Bhambra and R. Shilliam (eds), *Silencing Human Rights*. London: Palgrave Macmillan.

Muhtu, S. (2003). *Enlightenment Against Empire*. Princeton, NJ: Princeton University Press.

Niekerk, C. (2004). 'Man and Orangutan in Eighteenth-Century Thinking: Retracing the Early History of Dutch and German Anthropology', *Monatshefte*, 96:4, 477–502.

O'Brien, K. (2009). *Women and Enlightenment in Eighteenth-Century Britain*. Cambridge: Cambridge University Press.

Paugh, K. (2014). 'The Curious Case of Mary Hylas: Wives, Slaves and the Limits of British Abolitionism', *Slavery and Abolition*, 35:4, 629–651.

Pin-Fat, V. (2018). 'On Claiming and Acknowledging Humanity: Grammatical Remarks on The Politics of the Human and Black Lives Matter', *Contemporary Political Theory*, Vol. 17, no. 2.

Phillips, A. (2015). *The Politics of the Human*. Oxford: Oxford University Press.

Rozbicki, M. (2001). '"To Save Them from Themselves": Proposals to Enslave the British Poor, 1698–1755', *Slavery and Abolition*, 22, 29–50.

Ruston, R. (2008). 'Natural Rights and Natural History in Anna Barbauld and Mary Wollstonecraft', *Essays and Studies*, 61, 53–71.

Scott, D. (2004). *Conscripts of Modernity*. Durham, NC and London: Duke University Press.

Spencer, J. (2012). '"The Link which Unites Man with Brutes": Enlightenment Feminism, Women and Animals', Intellectual History Review 22:3, 427–444.

Sturman, R. (2011) 'Gender and the Human: An Introduction', *Gender and History*, 23:2, 229–234.

Taylor, B. (2012). 'Enlightenment and the Uses of Woman', *History Workshop Journal*, 6:3, 435–450.

Wheeler, R. (2000). *The Complexion of Race: Categories of Difference in Eighteenth-Century British Culture*. Philadelphia, PA: University of Pennsylvania Press.

Wokler, R. and Garsten, B. (2012). *Rousseau, the Age of Enlightenment, and their Legacies*. Oxford: Oxford University Press.

Wollstonecraft, M. (1995). *A Vindication of the Rights of Men and a Vindication of the Rights of Woman*. Ed. S. Tomaselli). Cambridge: Cambridge University Press.

Zonana, J. (1993). 'The Sultan and the Slave: Feminist Orientalism and the Structure of "Jane Eyre"', *Signs*, 18:3, 592–617.

3 Equality-Building in Europe
Theorising the Practice of Gender Training

Athena-Maria Enderstein

Introduction

This book begins with the assertion of the importance of the stories that we tell. European equality stories are typically progress narratives (Hemmings, 2011), which exalt gender equality as a fundamental European value (Abels and Mushaben, 2012). However, behind this narrative there are both agendas of civilisational supremacy and imperialism (Shore, 2000; MacRae, 2010; Enderstein, 2017) and a seven-decades-long transnational history of women's movement and feminist activism, scholarship, and politics. To adequately theorise equality in Europe, it is necessary to render visible the interconnections, incongruences and reformulations of this ongoing story and the ways in which equality concepts and strategies are circulated. In this chapter I do this by focusing on gender training as a tool through which equality is disseminated in Europe. I propose a theoretical architecture for analysing gender training and gender expertise which can act as an instrument of critical analysis to study how cultures of equality are constituted and contested.

To begin, I briefly map a genealogy and political economy of gender expertise in this region to illuminate significant themes and dynamics. I posit that these factors demonstrate what might be required to adequately theorise gender training praxis as an activity in European equality-building. Namely, the multi-level nature of gender training; the interconnection of equality actions and actors and the interrelation thereof with other social systems; and the effects of the movement of knowledge through these systems. I suggest that collectively this scholarship establishes an imperative to render gender knowledge and the concept of equality itself the subject of analysis and to critically engage with the power dynamics which adhere to the circulation of knowledge and the transformative intent of equality work. I then mobilise a conceptual lexicon based on social complexity theory and gender knowledge as an analytical device to propose an original model of knowledge circulation through gender training. I argue for a theorisation of gender and feminist knowledges, which leaves these open to revision and reformulation. The theoretical architecture that I propose consists of three tessellating parts. I argue for the understanding of gender knowledge as an analytical device; the incorporation of circulatory understanding of the movement of knowledge; and the application of key concepts from social complexity theory. In conclusion, I supply theoretical tools that allow the analysis of how equality concepts are circulated through gender training and the associated dynamics of change and resistance. Consequently, I expose how gender and feminist knowledges are in formation through exchange and circulation and advocate for revision of equality stories in transnational perspective.

Gender expertise and gender training in Europe: mapping the field

The practice of gender expertise has evolved in reciprocity with gender equality strategies and policy developments, both internationally and in the European context (Mazey, 1995, 1998; Rossili, 2000; McBride and Mazur, 2010). This is evident from legislative cases for equal pay in the 1960s (Ostner, 2000; Abels and Mushaben, 2012); to positive action in the 1980s (Vallance and Davies, 1986; Mazey, 1995; Hoskyns, 1996; Richardson and Mazey, 2015); to gender mainstreaming in the 1990s (Jacquot, 2010; Abels and Mushaben, 2012); and finally to current diversity mainstreaming efforts (Squires, 2008; Woodward, 2008; Lombardo and Verloo, 2009; Kantola and Nousiainen, 2009; Krizsàn et al., 2012). This has established gender inequality as a policy problem (Bacchi, 1999), and concretised "an international network of gender experts and a distinctive body of expertise on gender relations" (Thompson and Prügl, 2015). Specific research on gender experts is scarce (see Hoard, 2015; Thompson and Prügl, 2015; Kunz et al., 2019), but an inventory of the kinds of professional activities that they carry out can be found in the dense body of evaluative research on gender mainstreaming (Rees, 1998; Beveridge et al., 2000; Booth and Bennett, 2002; Moser and Moser, 2005; Stratigaki, 2005; Walby, 2005; Squires, 2005; Lombardo and Meier, 2006; Hafner-Burton and Pollack, 2007; Prügl, 2011; Milward et al., 2015; Clisby and Enderstein, 2017)[1]. These activities and roles make up the field of equality-building work in Europe and constitute a diverse network of positionalities and approaches. In the wide range of tasks that gender experts carry out they employ and enact specific and specialised knowledge, experience and skills (Berg, 1994; Standing, 2004; Kunz et al., 2019), which are not available to the general public (Schudson, 2006; Collins and Evans, 2007). This knowledge comes from 'specialised training as well as a sophisticated understanding of gender relations' (Beveridge et al., 2000: 390) and forms part of a 'field of technical expertise' (Macdonald, 1994: 16). Different kinds of 'gender knowledge' are developed and practiced through the different locations in which experts are active. There is the procedural knowledge of femocrats and feminist politicians who are inside institutions and therefore adept in norms, regulations and procedures relating to policymaking and legislation. There is the technical or technocratic knowledge of academics and researchers who generate research and theoretical and empirical analysis of gendered inequalities. Lastly, there is the experiential knowledge of actors embedded in women's movements and non-governmental organisations resulting from their contact with local communities and their involvement in European transnational networks (Mazey, 1995; Locher, 2003; Hoard, 2015).

40   *Theorising Cultures of Equality*

There are strong interconnections between these specific fields of knowledge, differently located experts and the institutions and organisations that are involved in European equality initiatives. Writing on the development of gender equality policies references these interrelationships that have been built through a genealogy of women's and feminist activism, the evolution of feminist and gender theorising and institutionalised scholarship and the development of equality architecture in Europe (Mazey, 1995; Halsaa, 1998; Vargas and Wieringa, 1998; Woodward, 2003; Holli, 2008; McBride and Mazur, 2010). For example, Halsaa (1998) states that 'strategic partnerships' describe the co-operation between women politicians, women bureaucrats and women in the autonomous women's movement. For Vargas and Wieringa (1998: 3) the term 'triangles of empowerment' is more appropriate to the dynamism of 'the interplay between three sets of actors—the women's movement, feminist politicians and feminist civil servants (femocrats)'. Woodward (2003) later uses the term 'velvet triangle', but categorises the three parts as 'organisations of the state, of civil society and universities and consultancies' (Woodward, 2003: 84). Holli (2008) suggests 'women's co-operative constellations' to describe the actions of these constellations and the interrelationships between 'actors, allies and arenas involved in the co-operation' (Holli, 2008: 180). Although the terms and configurations may differ, this literature emphasises the formative power of these interconnections. Indeed, comparative policy research evidences that these relationships and networks of co-operation between women's movements activists, femocrats, and women politicians are indispensable to the success of equality policies and strategies (Mazur, 2002; McBride and Mazur, 2010; Hoard, 2015).

Gender experts are located in a range of sites throughout the public, private and civil society sectors, and interrelate through co-operation and collaboration. Within this map, gender training is a key tool for facilitating the development and exchange of feminist and gender knowledges as these are translated into utilisable formats for policymakers and practitioners across sectors. The United Nations Women Training Centre (UNWTC) (2016b: 3) defines gender training as a 'transformative process that aims to provide knowledge, techniques and tools to develop skills and changes in attitudes and behaviours'. Referencing this definition, the European Institute for Gender Equality (EIGE) describes gender equality training as part of a long-term process aiming to equip training participants with the relevant knowledge, skills and values that allow them to contribute to the effective implementation of the gender mainstreaming strategy in their contexts (EIGE, 2012: 2). Over the past 30 years, a substantial body of resources has emerged in the form of tools, checklists and training manuals, which focuses on methods and techniques in gender training (Rao et al., 1991; Wong et al., 2016). This is paralleled by scholarship on gender training work in the field of gender and development, which details tools for analysis, practitioner experiences, techniques and activities, and contextually specific examples (Mackenzie, 1993; Moser, 1993; Wiliams, 1994; Bhasin, 1996; Sweetman, 1998; Smyth and March, 1998; Porter and Smyth, 1998).

Equality-Building in Europe 41

More recent research on gender training in Europe builds on this transnational work and illustrates how the complexities and tensions of equality work are amplified in gender training (Wong et al., 2016; Bustelo et al., 2016b; Ferguson, 2018, 2019). This practice is a site at which macro-level discursive constructions of equality meet meso-level infrastructures and micro-level interpersonal exchange. In this sense, gender training is a multi-level phenomenon. Wong et al. (2016) emphasise the significance of reflexivity, intersectionality and resistances in gender training. Training is a political and a social process, and both discursive and organisational elements shape the contexts in which training takes place (Wong et al., 2016: 10). Trainers have to strategically operate within the constraints of these contexts while integrating theory and pedagogy to catalyse transformative change (Ferguson, 2018). Given that the aim of gender training is 'a transformation in gendered power relations for more equal societies, workplaces, polices, and communities' (Bustelo et al., 2016: 3) it is often referred to as an act of 'feminist knowledge transfer' (see Ferguson and Forest, 2011; Wong et al., 2016; Bustelo et al., 2016b). This use of the term feminist points to an ongoing debate regarding the practice of gender expertise in which there are complex relationships and tensions between power, knowledge and ideals of social transformation (Prügl, 2016). In the following section I outline some of the key questions, tensions and challenges that affect the practice of gender expertise and gender training, thus evidencing dynamics that need to be addressed in the theorisation of equality.

Tensions and challenges in equality work

Gender training and gender expertise is driven by transformatory intent and politically charged through its relationship to feminism. A feminist practice of gender training involves an understanding of gendered inequalities as 'structural' and 'systemic' and of knowledge as situated and collectively produced (Rose, 1997; Prügl, 2010, 2013; Wong et al., 2016; Bustelo et al., 2016b). The recognition of power and relations of power within the production of feminist and gender knowledges is indispensable (Prügl, 2010; Lilja and Vinthagen, 2014; Davids and van Eederwijk, 2016; Mukhopadhyay, 2017). In this, reflexivity – a critical awareness and analysis of individual positionality and social location – is recognised as fundamentally important (Adkins, 2004; Mukhopadhyay and Wong, 2007; Wong et al., 2016; Mukhopadhyay, 2017; Ferguson, 2018). In gender training this is evident not only in the topics and content of trainings but also in the application of feminist pedagogies (Bustelo et al., 2016a; Ferguson, 2018, 2019). Both Thompson and Prügl (2015) and Hoard (2015) report that the majority of gender experts in their studies applied feminist principles and have feminist goals, but that these are often diluted or muted in application.

Although adherence to feminist principles in gender expertise and gender training is much discussed (Bustelo et al., 2016b; Ferguson, 2018, 2019), as feminist knowledge is packaged and processed into the format of gender expertise complex power relations and dynamics of epistemic authority occur

42 Theorising Cultures of Equality

(Prügl, 2010). The dense body of literature on the analysis and evaluation of national and transnational equality policies in Europe highlights key issues in the current practice of gender expertise. Hostile policy contexts, opposition and the co-optation of feminism and gender expertise are dominant unifying themes across this literature. Gender experts are caught in a paradox. They have to advocate transformative gender equality awareness, but are often forced to adopt strategic framing and engage in depoliticisation in order to be hired (Mazey, 1998; Ghodsee, 2004; Pascall and Lewis, 2004; Squires, 2008; Kantola and Squires, 2012; Ferguson, 2015). The institutionalisation of gender expertise entails legitimisation of the related skills and competencies, an attached market value, as well as an epistemic authority. However, many authors have argued that this has also brought about depoliticisation in practice and application (Pollack and Hafner-Burton, 2000; Perron, 2005; Lombardo and Meier, 2008; Gerhards et al., 2009; Jacquot, 2010; Kantola and Squires, 2012). Wong et al. (2016: 5) observe that, in the case of gender training, this manifests in the typical format of a one-off workshop-based event, with limited scope, focused on memorisation and information transfer. Gender training has typically been 'constructed, manualised and packaged' (Lazreg, 2002: 132), particularly in relation to gender mainstreaming, as 'a set of skills, which can be straightforwardly delivered and reproduced' (Mukhopadhyay, 2014: 362). The result is trainings that can be conceptually stripped down and politically hollow. In Ahmed's (2012) assessment, the commissioning of training in these cases comes to stand in tokenistically for actual organisational restructuring, resulting in dynamics of co-optation. Consequently, there is an ongoing debate in gender training around issues of universal standards, the privatisation of funding and the marketisation of inequalities (Prügl, 2016; Bustelo et al., 2016a; Ferguson, 2018, 2019).

The debate around the 'co-optation of feminisms' (see Clisby and Enderstein, 2017; de Jong and Kimm, 2017), is strongly linked to the marketisation of gender expertise. Writing on the transformation of feminism with, and through, capitalism is well established (Fraser, 2009; Eisenstein, 2009; Roberts, 2012; Kantola and Squires, 2012; Prügl, 2015; Farris, 2017). It is visible, for example, in the neoliberalisation of feminism in women's empowerment projects run by transnational companies. These approaches privilege competition, markets, customers and outcomes by interweaving feminism with neoliberal economic principles and ideologies (Prügl, 2015: 617). Gender experts are expected to deploy these discourses of economic efficiency, and in the process they become accountable to funders and employers rather than communities who are discriminated against (Mazey, 1995; Rossili, 2000; Pascall and Lewis, 2004; Ghodsee, 2004; Squires, 2008; Kantola and Squires, 2012). Ferguson (2015) argues that this business case for equality poses a particular dilemma for gender experts as they have to negotiate complicity and legitimacy against remuneration for their work, concluding that working 'as a gender expert with transformative feminist goals is indeed a messy business' (Ferguson, 2015: 393).

The 'utilitarian market model' (Squires, 2008: 59) of equality work is supported by the intensification of an evidence-based policy-making format,

Equality-Building in Europe 43

which further inculcates competition and rationales of efficiency, becoming symptomatic of the managerialist dynamics of neoliberal governance. Kantola and Nousiainen (2010: 48) state that these new modes of public governance have increased the discursive presence of equality through the work of gender experts, while delivering comparatively little on a material level. These modes of governance privilege a heavy cognitive dimension of systematic knowledge dissemination, which is carried out in part through gender training. Marketisation has profound effects, it 'not only tends to shape what gender training looks like; it also makes the tools and methodological approaches developed by trainers a competitive matter, as trainers need to sell their competences on a developing market' (Ferguson and Forest, 2011: 55). Trainers are required to make gender concepts intelligible for participants in their trainings, resulting in a reductive approach that shifts from changing attitudes towards exclusively transmitting measurable skills, whereby participants are 'professionals' who simply need to apply gender knowledge according to discrete checkboxes (Mukhopadhyay and Wong, 2007).

The field of gender expertise and gender training is driven by an emancipatory ethos, but as institutionalisation and professionalisation has progressed tensions and debates have arisen regarding the inevitable exercise of power that accompanies the notion of 'expert knowledge' (Walby, 2005; Lilja and Vinthagen, 2014). Within the field of specialised equality knowledge, some kinds of knowledge and knowers are hegemonic (Connell et al., 2017; Collyer et al., 2017), creating epistemic hierarchies that are problematic both practically and politically (Ferguson, 2015: 386). They can result in the devaluing of plural feminist and other critical epistemologies (see Mukhopadhyay and Wong, 2007) and replicate Eurocentric hegemonies in knowledge production (Shore, 2000; Raj, 2006; Enderstein, 2017; Connell et al., 2017).

In addition to the challenges of marketisation, equality advocates routinely face high resistance and unreceptive 'policy hinterlands'. These are 'national political and cultural traditions, hegemonic values and the characteristics of the politico administrative systems' (Mazey, 1998: 145) which heavily impact their work. Gender experts continue to face institutional resistance to transformation and competition for scarce resources (Pollack and Hafner-Burton, 2000, 2007). While institutions discursively commit to gender mainstreaming, gender experts consistently face resistance at many levels (Mazey, 1995; Perron, 2005; Chiva, 2009; Lombardo and Mergaert, 2013). Gender experts face the challenge of making gender equality palatable and uncontroversial, to develop messages on gender that successfully circumnavigate this resistance and appeal to institutions while promoting change within them (Lombardo and Meier, 2006; Ferguson, 2015). Furthermore, on the interpersonal level, gender training is a point of intersection between different kinds of gender knowledge and different paradigms, which gives rise to resistance.

Resistances can take multiple implicit and explicit forms (Agocs, 1997; Lombardo and Mergaert, 2013; Mukhopadhyay, 2017; Enderstein, 2018; Verloo, 2018a), and these reflect an 'expression of resistance and opposition

44 *Theorising Cultures of Equality*

to gender+ equality' (Ahrens, 2018: 79) and response to a perceived disciplinary power (Lilja and Vinthagen, 2014: 123). I argue that current resistances and opposition should be seen within the context of the transnational history of equality projects. For example, the recent growth of anti-gender movements in Europe further entrenches and legitimises implicit and explicit resistance against equality initiatives (Grzebalska, 2016; Graff and Korolczuk, 2017; Kuhar and Paternotte, 2017; Verloo, 2018a). Anti-gender movements consist of networks of 'individuals, already existing organizations and newly formed groups' which typically engage in media campaigns and political actions against what they term 'gender ideology', or 'gender theory' (Lavizzari and Prearo, 2019: 424). These movements, although diverse between them (Kuhar and Paternotte, 2017, 2018), respond to supranational and national gender mainstreaming policies. As Weislander and Nordvall (2019: 2) assert, in this moment, 'when feminist truth claims are broadly challenged, it is important to analyse the dynamics of back-lashes and resistance against feminist discourses'. A conceptual lexicon which facilitates the analysis of this reciprocity and the multi-level and interrelated nature of gender training is required to theorise gender training and the culture of equality that it seeks to actualise.

Theorising gender training: knowledge concepts, circulation, and complex systems

The themes that I have detailed here provide the co-ordinates for building a theoretical architecture to investigate gender training and thus shed light on how concepts of equality travel and are shaped in Europe. Gender expertise is prac-ticed over multiple locations and a diversity of activities and roles, and central to this field are the interconnections between these structures and actors. In this field gender training is an instrument of knowledge circulation through which these links and interactions are facilitated. Ideas of equality, and the valorisation or delegitimisation thereof, move and are shaped through these interactions. As evidenced, gender training is strongly linked to the feminist project through its transformatory intent and a transnational history of activism, scholarship and politics. Complex dynamics of knowledge and power have evolved, whereby gender training is imbricated both in technologies of governance and projects for emancipation. This takes place in an environment constituted by political, eco-nomic and social factors that reciprocally shape one another. Thus, multiple factors impact how equality is translated and communicated through gender training in an ongoing dynamic of reformulation.

Analysis of these mechanics and dynamics necessitates a theoretical frame-work, which addresses the movement of knowledge through gender training and acknowledges different forms of gender knowledges or epistemological positions regarding gender. This should include flexibility for plurality, because gender training does not fill a deficit, but is rather an encounter between actors of the feminist project and 'others whose truth commitments are structured around different premises' (Bustelo et al., 2016b: xi). A conceptualisation is required that tracks the sequences of the movement of feminist and gender knowledges, including obstacles and redirections and the relation thereof to epistemic hierarchies and hegemonies. This framework should render legible not only the interrelation of different systems and the multilevel nature of gender training, but the change effects that equality actions can bring about, whether transformative or regressive. In synthesis, this theoretical architecture needs to address both the constraints and opportunities of current equality-building work, with a close attention to "what is lost in the process and what is perhaps gained" (Prügl, 2015: 614) in order to deepen the understanding of what 'equality' means in Europe and the theorisation thereof. In the following section I outline such an architecture based on social complexity theory and gender knowledge as an analytical device to propose an original model of knowledge circulation through gender training.

Gender knowledge

A key question in gender training is that of knowledge – how it is acquired, how it is used and the epistemological and practical implications of different kinds of knowledge (Mukhopadhyay and Wong, 2007; Young and Scherrer, 2010; Bustelo et al., 2016b). Commissioners, trainers and participants each bring their own maps of the world – and their understandings of gender – to a gender training workshop. Gender training is not about simply transferring knowledge about gender to address a deficit. It is about facilitating a paradigmatic shift to a critical understanding of gender among workshop participants in such a way that they are inspired to work against gendered inequalities. Indeed, as psychological studies on behaviour change illustrate, information provision alone is simply inadequate to catalyse change (see Glanz et al., 2015), least of all change that requires individuals to challenge intimate and enduring beliefs such as those surrounding gender and relations of power. Thus, to study how equality is translated in gender training, and in relation to processes of social change, a concept of plurality in gender knowledges and epistemologies is required. I propose the concept of gender knowledge as an analytical device (Andresen and Dölling, 2005; Young and Scherrer, 2010; Cavaghan, 2010, 2017).

The 'gender knowledge as a concept' (Cavaghan, 2010: 19) approach departs from the assumption that 'every form of knowledge – be it everyday knowledge, expert knowledge and popularised knowledge – is based upon a specific, often tacit and unconscious, form of gender knowledge' (Young and Scherrer, 2010: 9). In this understanding, rather than gender knowledge as a specific empirical and theoretical body of work upon which only gender experts draw, gender knowledge is ubiquitous. As such, gender knowledge refers to the 'explicit and implicit representations concerning the differences between the sexes and the relations between them, the origins and normative significance of these, the rationale and evidence underpinning them and their material form' (Cavaghan, 2017: 48). This renders it possible to track how different knowledge forms are articulated and how these relate to truth claims by different social actors.

46 *Theorising Cultures of Equality*

Gender knowledge can be differently classified according to relation and provenance. Andresen and Dölling (2005: 50) distinguish between collectively held 'objective' macro-level gender knowledge and 'subjective' micro-level gender knowledge. Collectively held gender knowledge is common ideas about gender and gender relations, and subjectively held gender knowledge refers to an individual's knowledge of their gender and position in society (Çağlar, 2008; Cavaghan, 2010). These kinds of knowledge can further be organised into three forms: practical everyday knowledge, institutionally produced knowledge and popular knowledge. Schwenken (2008: 773, citing Dolling, 2005: 52) describes these three levels as follows:

> tacit and unreflected everyday knowledge and knowledge of experience; knowledge and meanings generated by institutions such as religion, academia, or law; and popularised knowledge that is dispersed through media, guidebooks, and social movements, among other forces, and that often links everyday and expert knowledge.

Within this framework, each of these forms may incorporate different understandings and positions about gender, these epistemologies are interpretative frameworks according to which gender knowledge is understood and analysed. For example, schematically speaking, a feminist interpretive framework may see gender as socially and relationally constructed, focusing on the dynamics of interaction between systems of power and oppression that sustain inequalities. In contrast, a religious perspective may state that gender and sex are God-given.

Gender knowledge understood in this way sheds light on the dynamics of competing epistemologies as interpretative frameworks. Crucially it acknowledges gender as 'always already there' as part of collective and subjective knowledge, and that gender experts are also gendered beings. This approach holds together macro-level discursive constructions of gender and equality and the micro-level political struggles in different organisational and bureaucratic contexts. Through this understanding it is possible to track the movement of gender and feminist knowledges in gender training practice, thus illuminating how these interpretive frameworks are negotiated in relation to one another. By treating gender knowledge as a concept, dynamics of the negotiation of epistemic status are revealed and the plurality within feminist and gender theorising is acknowledged (Harding, 1987; Reinharz, 1992; Beasley, 1999). This illuminates the co-existence and interaction of different understandings of gender and feminism. The dynamic between the feminist project and opposition changes from one of forceful, almost static juxtaposition to one of interaction and the possibilities for counterstrategies are rendered more transparent (see Verloo, 2018b).

Circulation

The gender knowledge concept presupposes movement as forms of knowledge are communicated and pass between actors and social systems. The term

Equality-Building in Europe 47

most frequently used to describe this movement of knowledge in the case of gender training is 'transfer' (Thompson and Prügl, 2015; Bustelo et al., 2016b). Following my theorisation of gender trainings as moments of intersection and interaction, I argue for a more dynamic and fluid understanding. Bustelo et al. (2016b: 4) refer to gender training as a process of *feminist knowledge transfer*, where *feminist* is used to designate the political, power imbued, and contested features of gender training praxis. However, as these authors themselves acknowledge, *transfer* holds 'one-dimensional connotations and the danger of creating and sanctioning hierarchies of feminist knowledges' (Bustelo et al., 2016b: 4). In my appraisal, the term transfer states a unidirectionality and does not allow space for opposition or reformulation. Transfer conveys a notion of a fixed temporality, a single instance of knowledge delivered and presupposes an empty, dislocated space through which knowledge moves directly from an expert to a passive and neutral target. Rather, as Kunz (2016: 43) asserts, 'feminist knowledges circulate in many different ways and directions, defying the simplistic, linear top-down version of the transfer scenario'. Thus, I propose a redefinition of the movement of knowledge through gender training as one of circulation.

Circulation acknowledges the transnational history of knowledge production and political economy in which the trainers are embedded. The term has a long history across disciplines as the descriptor for delivery systems of processes that move 'discrete objects, images, and people between defined points in space and time' (Aronczyk and Craig, 2012: 93). More recently, it has come to prominence in the field of the sociology of science and knowledge, particularly as terminology relating to the movement of concepts and ideas within international social sciences through South-North and South-South interactions (Keim et al., 2014; Collyer et al., 2017). I use the term 'circulation' (Keim, 2014: 84) from this field because it is especially relevant to the practice of gender expertise and gender training. Women's, Gender and Feminist Studies (WGFS) as an academic discipline actively participates in the circulation of knowledge and concepts in the broader field of international social sciences (Wöhrer, 2016), but it is also strongly linked to actors and activities outside of this field, as highlighted in the first section of this chapter. The establishment of WGFS in the European region, albeit with significant local and national diversity (see do Mar Pereira, 2017), was catalysed by feminist and women's movement activism and continues to share strong links with these projects and gender equality policies in Europe and internationally (Holli, 2008; Lang, 2009; Young and Scherrer, 2010; Baksh et al., 2015).

Co-operative constellations between actors located in different sites across private, public and civil society sectors continue to constitute links and joins across which concepts and practice travel. By focusing on circulation, I centre this movement and 'the historical contingency and mutation of existing notions and practices' (Raj, 2006: 20) that this brings. Furthermore, these links and interactions hold a particular transnational quality in the case of feminist and gender knowledges, where they reach past individual local contexts in a 'coalescence of organisations, networks, coalitions, campaigns, analysis, advocacy and actions that politicise women's rights and gender equality issues beyond

48   *Theorising Cultures of Equality*

the nation-state' (Baksh and Harcourt, 2015: 5). The relations of this transnationalism are shot through with colonialities of power, and WGFS is not wholly the counter-hegemonic multi-centre discipline that we would wish (Wöhrer, 2016: 340). My use of the circulation concept applies a recognition and analysis of these relations, a task for which 'transfer' is inadequate.

I do not subscribe to a rhetoric of circulation which pivots on 'overcoming of boundaries and restrictions, through which all this excitement appears positive for everyone involved' (Tsing, 2000: 332). Neither do I think of circulation as a unidirectional diffusion of knowledge from the metropole to the rest of the world. Rather, I draw on Keim's (2014) proposed three variants of circulation. In reception a theory or concept is taken from somewhere else and applied by a scholar to their own work; exchange involves the 'multidirectional prolongation' of reception in which the field or concept is co-developed through controversy and co-construction (Keim, 2014: 97). The third type of circulation is that of *negotiating theory and practice*, which involves exchange between academics and practitioners. Gender training is an example of this last configuration.

My conceptualisation of circulation is made up of several conjoined and interacting elements which respond to the key issues in gender training. Circulation of knowledge is a communicative act, one which is firmly located in, and mediated by, the environments where it takes place (Raj, 2006). Circulation involves a process of collective exchange and ongoing development (Kunz, 2016); knowledge is contested, rejected and developed in power-laden social, economic and cultural spaces (Keim, 2014). Circulation is carried out by agents located in these spaces and the individual labour which produces the social product of knowledge 'is also part of a collective process in which knowledge formations come into existence, are sustained, applied and transformed' (Collyer et al., 2017: 24). Over time, knowledge is subject to revision and reformulation through circulation (Collyer et al., 2017; Connell et al., 2017), both by dominant and subversive forces, although in asymmetric ways (Meyer et al., 2001; Keim, 2014). In a learning encounter such as gender training, both the educator and the learner participate in constructing and developing circulated knowledge (UNWTC, 2016a). Marx Ferree (2015: 82) explains, 'learners are not "empty mugs" awaiting new and better knowledge from the "jug" of formal gender expertise; instead, training works best when it acknowledges its role in encouraging and supporting contestation'. Crucially, the concept of circulation is part of a framework of thinking about equality that as 'something that has been made and must be continuously reshaped and refashioned through stories and actions' (Clisby and Johnson, 2019; this volume). In the next section, I outline concepts of complex systems and change to complete this theoretical architecture, incorporating the movement inherent to circulation and addressing the multi-level nature of gender training.

Social complexity theory concepts

Here I build on the theoretical pillars introduced above to describe and analyse concurrent interactions and relationships between multiple elements of

Equality-Building in Europe 49

complex systems. It is certainly not the only framework that could have been used, nor is it without critique (Houchin and MacLean, 2005; Byrne and Callaghan, 2013; Verloo, 2018c), but it provides useful theoretical footholds for the issues which are central to the theorisation of gender training and equality in Europe. This takes into account the simultaneous coexistence of multiple levels derived from Walby's (2002, 2005, 2009, 2012) work and the extension of her theorising presented by Verloo (2018c). In essence, gender training is about addressing inequalities to facilitate social transformation. Walby's (2002, 2005, 2009, 2012) implementation of social complexity theory foregrounds these same concerns – the centrality of inequalities in the configuration of societies and the focal points of multiple interacting elements and interrelating systems in the mechanics of social change. This includes the unexpected – and multiple – directions that this change may take.

Walby's (2004, 2009) interpretation of social complexity theory follows from her analysis that traditional sociological thought has neglected the significance and centrality of social inequalities in the making of society. As this scholar explains, in order to understand intersecting inequalities it is necessary to theorise the 'ontological depth of each set of social relations' while also theorising 'more fully the relationship between systems of social relations and how they affect each other together with the dynamics of social change' (Walby, 2007: 454). I distil the basic assertions of this theory as follows. There are two kinds of systems, domains and regimes. Domains refer to the set of institutions in an area, termed institutional domain, these are the polity (states, nations, organised religions, hegemons and emerging global institutions), economy (marketised activities, domestic labour and state welfare), violence (power exercised by interconnected individuals, groups, states and armed forces, as well as the criminal justice system and interpersonal violence) and civil society (civic engagement, culture, sexuality and education). Regimes refer to sets of social relations; examples of regimes of inequality are gender, class and race, and these are multiple and co-existing within and across domains.

The distinction between regimes of inequality and domains renders visible how complex relationships between social relations occur across different sets of institutions. Each system has as its environment all the other systems, meaning that they are co-existing and contemporaneous in their relations each to the other (Walby, 2009: 65). Systems are overlapping, but they are not necessarily nested, they are not reducible to one another, and they do not saturate the territory in which they are located. These systems mutually adapt and co-evolve, but they may have different spatial and temporal reach. In the interrelation of domains and regimes, there is competition, contestation and co-operation (Walby, 2009: 43). Drawing on biologist Kauffman's (1993, 1995) writings on co-evolution, Walby (2009: 59) explains that the co-evolution refers to the relationships between social systems, resulting from mutual interactions and mutual effects in which they hold 'unequal power to alter the rules of their global environment'. This understanding of social systems is particularly appropriate to theorising gender training because of the idea of emergence,

50　*Theorising Cultures of Equality*

which links individual, structure and system in co-existence. Emergence refers to how individual elements on a lower level collectively come to constitute a higher level. In other words, it is the 'way in which social systems emerge from the multiple actions of individuals, but are not reducible to them', the concept of emergence links 'a focus on human reflexivity to social systems' (Walby, 2009: 74). It is across these links that knowledge circulates.

Within this theoretical architecture gender training is located at the intersection of different domains. The domain of civil society includes several social spheres (civic engagement, culture, sexuality and education). There are multiple forms of knowledge created and circulated by powerful sets of institutions. These are institutions across which complex regimes of inequality play out. This knowledge gives shape to and interacts with concepts of gender and gender relations in all domains, and it is an integral part of gender inequality regimes across the micro, meso, and macro dimensions of social life. In affective terms, this is the stuff with which individuals build meanings and lives. Thus, I am in agreement with Verloo's (2018c) proposed revision and extension of Walby's (2004, 2009) domains. This locates civic engagement – linking citizenship and democracy – in the polity and adds two domains to the model: cathexis and episteme. Cathexis is the domain where biopolitics are most visible; it is the system through which bodies and relationships are shaped in terms of reproduction, sexuality and kinship (Verloo, 2018c: 40). The episteme is the 'system that produces and organises knowledge and truth, located strongly in social fields such as religion, education, media and research' (Verloo, 2018a: 22). It is in the episteme that truth and knowledge are claimed and different forms of gender knowledge are generated by powerful sets of institutions such as those of religion, sciences, education and media. These institutions are involved in the consolidation of feminist politics through the legitimation of feminist theory and research, but they also provide channels to propose and disseminate 'oppositional gender "truths"' (Verloo, 2018a: 22). The conceptualisation of episteme as a separate domain facilitates a more detailed view of the circulation of gender knowledge as it moves through and within domains and relates to regimes of inequality.

Gender training takes place in the borders, overlaps and interrelations between the episteme and other domains; it is a point where material and discursive features of domains interact in mutual adaption. Consider, for example, training on gender mainstreaming and gender equality architecture within the polity, or workforce participation and diversity management initiatives in the economy, or awareness-raising on reproductive rights and families in the domain of cathexis, or training on peace and security in the institutions of the domain of violence. In each of these contexts, training is a mechanism for the circulation of knowledge and truth claims that represents, in part, the theoretical content of academic gender studies within the episteme, but also the discursive and material features of the feminist project, as well as the actions of more dispersed communities, such as transnational networks of women's organisations.

Within these systems, a project is 'a set of processes and practices in civil society that creates new meanings and social goals, on a range of rhetorical

Equality-Building in Europe 51

and material resources' (Walby, 2011: 6). Regimes of inequality have projects linked to them that are working to reduce this inequality (Verloo, 2018c: 42). A project can occur in any time or space; it is characterised by fluidity and dynamism, and it is driven forward by certain groups or individuals attempting social change. In these terms, feminism is a project working for gender equality, and there is a great deal of diversity and plurality within this (Walby, 2007). Projects are typically located in the domain of civil society, but they have 'counterparts' in policy, government and legislature (such as equal opportunities measures or equality architecture). Gender training is an activity of the feminist project and its counterparts. Resistance against the change proposed by projects can take the form of oppositional projects themselves (Verloo, 2018c): for instance, the anti-gender movements in Europe.

I value this view because systematic interrelatedness is a constant, but the nature of the interconnections and interactions is not presupposed. This eliminates a fixed hierarchy of systems and allows space for mutual impact and reciprocity between systems (Walby, 2007, 2009). Processes of change in these interrelating systems take place through interaction, as opposed to one-way impact, because each system constitutes the environment in which the other systems reside. Tipping points, feedback loops and path dependency are important mechanisms of change relative to mutual adaption (Walby, 2007; Walby, 2009; Verloo, 2018c). The speed of change may be gradual and incremental or may occur in the form of saltations – fast and unexpected jumps. *Tipping points* refer to moments where gradual and incremental change in a phenomenon build up to a clear and substantial shift in the nature of the phenomenon, a moment of irreversibility. *Feedback loops*, whether positive or negative, describe how changes in one factor in turn affect other factors. In a negative feedback loop, change in one factor is met with a counterbalance in another, which stagnates or reduces change in the system. A positive feedback loop is one where one change in a system is reinforced by another, making the probability of a subsequent change higher or stronger (Walby, 2009: 85–86). As Verloo (2018c) articulates it, the value of this concept is that it allows us to see the relationships between projects, their oppositions and social change. In this understanding, change is a concatenation of interrelated events in interconnected systems occurring at varying rates. However, some changes have enduring consequences, a dynamic encapsulated in the concept of *path dependency*. Path dependency, which is a concept widely used in social sciences, refers to the fact that 'the order in which things happen affect how they happen; the trajectory of change up to a certain point constrains the trajectory after that point' (Kay, 2005: 535). This is useful in order to talk about how history can narrow the possible future trajectories of a system such that it is later difficult to deviate from this path. Each of these concepts is useful for the analysis of how equality is built, contested and opposed; and for the understanding of the temporality and potential multi-directionality of this process.

To illustrate the theoretical architecture and conceptual vocabulary outlined above, I propose the following schematic example. In Italy, the Catholic Church pre-dates the state, and it is not nested within the Italian state, either in terms of its influence or in its spatial reach. The regime of gender inequality

52 *Theorising Cultures of Equality*

across these two domains interacts with other regimes of inequality such as class, ethnicity and age, but is not reducible to any one of these. For instance, neither the Catholic Church nor the Italian state polity saturates the territory in terms of reproductive rights; rather, they co-operate and conflict with one another – abortion is legal in Italy but healthcare professionals can register as 'conscientious objectors', which is the refusal to comply with this law on religious, ethical or ideological grounds (see Vázquez, 2018). Here both the polities of the state and organised religion are exercising authority, overlapping and co-existing, in regimes of gender relations and intimacy. Co-evolution of these polities can be seen in the interactions of the polities of the supranational European Union (EU), the Italian state and the organised religion of the Catholic Church as they mutually adapt to one another.

Building on equal treatment and positive action policies, the UN Women's Conferences of the 1990s legitimised the use of the term 'gender' and gave rise to policies such as gender-mainstreaming, resulting from the actions and activism of the transnational feminist project (Nagar and Swarr, 2010; Baksh and Harcourt, 2015). This led to the adoption of gender mainstreaming in the EU (Jacquot, 2010; Bego, 2015), which represents a tipping point in gender equality policy, whereby the state adoption rates of the international norm led to its broad acceptance (see Finnemore and Sikkink, 1998). In Italy, gender equality legislation and norms such as gender-mainstreaming were adopted following pressure to comply with European directives (see Guadagnini and Donà, 2007). However, the Catholic Church's response to the Beijing Platform for Action was the initiation of anti-gender campaigns to renaturalise the concept of gender (Garbagnoli, 2016; Paternotte and Kuhar, 2018). Given the strong presence of the Vatican in Italian politics, Italy was one of the first countries in which a powerful movement against 'gender ideology', fronted by the *Sentinelle in Piedi* (Standing Sentinels) and supported by a wide range of Catholic groups and conservative political actors, established political prominence.

The demonstrations and actions of these groups have subsequently succeeded in blocking legal and social reforms on reproductive health and lesbian, gay, bisexual, transgender, queer and other (LGBTQ+) rights. Right-wing populist politicians mobilise the anti-gender discourse to rail against 'ideological colonisation' by a secular, capitalist, pro-equality EU identity as the Catholic Church collaborates to maintain its institutional authority 'concerning the sexual order and a powerful supplier of services to Italian families' (Garbagnoli, 2016: 190). In the domain of education, the current *crociata 'anti-gender'* (anti-gender crusade) (Biemmi and Satta, 2017: v) has resulted in vitriolic public reprisal of teachers and calls to oppose corruptive 'gender ideology' in schools (Ottaviano and Mentasti, 2017). In turn, this strongly negatively affects the work of gender trainers who work in educational contexts, such as those delivering gender and sex education programmes in schools (see Lavizzari and Prearo, 2019). This example elucidates dynamics of interrelation, mutual adaptivity and co-evolution between social systems, and how the meaning of equality and the impact of equality work such as gender training is shaped in this environment, following processes of change that can play out in multiple directions.

Conclusion

In this chapter I have proposed a theoretical architecture for the theorisation of gender training as an instrument through which understandings and meanings of equality are shaped. In the first section of the chapter I mapped the factors that are relevant to the critical analysis of gender training in Europe. In the second section I developed the conceptual lexicon to theorize the mechanics and dynamics of this work and how the meaning of equality is shaped through this practice.

I began with a genealogy of several decades of equality policies and actions carried out by activist, political and academic actors in different sectors and institutions. There are strong connections and interrelations between these actors and the networks of institutions, organisations and gender equality architecture at national and supranational level. Gender training circulates feminist and gender knowledges, as well as concepts of equality, through these networks and co-operative constellations. In gender training, the issues and concerns that affect the practice of gender expertise are amplified, as discursive constructions of equality and organisational politics play out in interpersonal dynamics of exchange and contestation. The environment in which this takes place is shaped by transnational histories, supranational and national sociopolitical contexts, funding and governance trends and opposition against equality-building. I introduced the relationship between feminism and gender expertise and elucidated the debate around the co-optation and marketisation of gender expertise and gender training and the association between institutionalisation and depoliticisation. In these terms, equality is both a transformative ideal and a rationalised objective outcome that is subject to tokenism and devalorisation. I identified the need for a theoretical framework that addresses interrelation, complex systems and environments, actor- and structure-driven dynamics, multidirectional processes of change and dynamics of opposition and reformulation.

In the second section of the chapter I constructed a tripartite theoretical architecture to respond to these needs. First, within this framework the theorisation of gender knowledge as an analytical device reveals the ubiquity of gender knowledge in different forms as these develop across institutional domains and through regimes of social relations that co-evolve over time. Second, I described the movement of feminist and gender knowledges through these systems as one of circulation. My utilisation of circulation incorporates an understanding of gender trainings as moments of intersection and interaction, where the environment in which they take place mediates this dynamic. I pointed to the potential for opposition, plurality and extended temporality that circulation acknowledges. I also emphasised the dynamics of collective exchange, iteration and reformulation that a circulatory view of knowledge renders possible. Lastly, I outlined how gender knowledge and circulation as concepts combine with elements of social complexity theory to offer a way to visualise and understand change within social systems and the diffusion of European equality stories and the opportunities and challenges in the practice of gender training. These three

54 Theorising Cultures of Equality

elements can be used to analyse gender training in such as way as to expose how equality concepts are carried through different systems, how these are shaped through contextual revision and opposition, and what kinds of processes of change, in multiple directions, result. These insights are essential to a critical and reflexive theorisation of equality, but they are also valuable for the development of effective responses in equality work to the current European and global sociopolitical environment.

Note

1 The most frequently mentioned activities are the following: gender training, gender monitoring; gender-based institutional and procedural review; generating gender-disaggregated statistics; developing equality indicators; gender budgeting; conducting gender impact assessments; participating in gender studies scholarship; measurement and monitoring, implementation of policies and processes; creating awareness and engaging relevant stakeholders; gender-proofing; and processes of monitoring and evaluation (Arribas and Carrasco, 2003; Rees, 2005; Beveridge and Velluti, 2008; Jacquot, 2010).

References

Abels, G. and Mushaben, J.M. (eds) (2012) .*Gendering the European Union. New Approaches to Old Democratic Deficits*. Basingstoke: Palgrave Macmillan.

Adkins, L. (2004). 'Reflexivity: Freedom or Habit of Gender'. In *L.* Adkins and *B.* Skeggs (eds) *Feminism after Bourdieu*. Oxford: Blackwell Publishers: 191–211.

Agocs, C. (1997). 'Institutionalized resistance to organizational change: denial, inaction and repression', *Journal of Business Ethics*, 16(9), 917–931. doi:10.1023/A:1017939404578.

Ahmed, S. (2012). *On Being Included. Racism and Diversity in Institutional Life*. Durham, NC: Duke University Press.

Ahrens, P. (2018). 'Indirect opposition: Diffuse barriers to gender equality in the European Union'. In *M.*Verloo (ed.) *Varieties of Opposition to Gender Equality in Europe*. London: Routledge: 77–97.

Andresen, S. and Dölling, I. (2005). 'Umbau des Geschlechter-Wissens von ReformakteurInnen durch Gender Mainstreaming'. In *U.* Behning *and B.* Sauer (eds). *Was Bewirkt Gender Mainstreaming Evaluierung durch Policy-Analysen*. Frankfurt: Ulrike Helmer Verlag: 171–187.

Aronczyk, M. and Craig, A. (2012). 'Introduction: cultures of circulation', *Poetics*, 40 (2), 93–100. doi:10.1016/j.poetic.2012.02.001.

Arribas, G. and Carrasco, L. (2003). 'Gender equality and the EU. An assessment of current issues', *Eipascope*, 1, 22–31.

Bacchi, C. (1999). *Women, Policy and Politics. The Construction of Policy Problems*. London: SAGE Publications.

Baksh, R. and Harcourt, W. (eds) (2015). *Oxford Handbook of Transnational Feminist Movements*. New York: Oxford University Press.

Baksh, R., Harcourt, W. and Moghadam, V.M. (2015). 'Transnational Feminist Activism and Movement *Building'*. In *R.* Baksh and *W.*Harcourt (eds). *Oxford Handbook of Transnational Feminist Movements*. New York: Oxford University Press: 53–81.

Equality-Building in Europe   55

Beasley, C. (1999). *What is Feminism: an Introduction to Feminist Theory*. St Leonards, NSW: Allen & Unwin.

Bego, I. (2015). *Gender equality policy in the European Union. A fast track to policy for the New Member states*. Basingstoke: Palgrave Macmillan.

Berg, G. (1994). 'Structures to promote gender within MS'. In *M*.Macdonald (ed.). *Gender Planning in Development Agencies*. Oxford: Oxfam: 167–172.

Beveridge, F., Nott, S. and Stephen, K. (2000). 'Mainstreaming and the engendering of policy-making: a means to an end?' *Journal of European Public Policy*, 7(3): 385–405. doi: https://doi.org/10.1080/13501760050086099.

Beveridge, F. and Velluti, S. (2008). *Gender and the Open Method of Coordination*. New York: Ashgate Publishing.

Bhasin, K. (1996). 'Gender workshops with men in South Asia: experiences and reflections', *Convergence*, 29(1), 46–60. doi:10.1080/741922356.

Biemmi, I. and Satta, C. (2017). 'Infanzia, educazione e genere. La costruzione delle culture di genere tra contesti scolastici, extrascolastici e familiari', *AG AboutGender International Journal of Gender Studies*, 6(12): 1–21. doi:10.15167/2279-5057/AG2017.6.12.491.

Booth, C. and Bennett, C. (2002). 'Gender mainstreaming in the European Union: towards a new conception and practice of equal opportunities?' *European Journal of Women's Studies*, 9(4): 430–446. doi:10.1177/13505068020090040401.

Bustelo, M., Ferguson, L. and Forest, M. (2016a). 'Conclusions'. In *M*. Bustelo, *L*. Ferguson and *M*.Forest (eds). *The politics of feminist knowledge transfer: gender training and gender expertise*. New York: Palgrave Macmillan: 157–175.

Bustelo, M., Ferguson, L. and Forest, M. (2016b). *The Politics of Feminist Knowledge Transfer. Gender Training and Gender Expertise*. London: Palgrave Macmillan.

Byrne, D. and Callaghan, G. (2013). *Complexity Theory and the Social Sciences: The State of the Art*. London: Routledge.

Çağlar, G. (2008). 'Unravelling the hidden gender knowledge in the field of global economic governance: implications for gender-sensitive international economic policies', Fourth Conference on Interpretative Policy Analysis. Essex, 19–21 June. Essex: University of Essex.

Cavaghan, R. (2010). 'Gender knowledge: a review of theory and practice'. In *C*. Scherrer and *B*. Young (eds). *Gender Knowledge and Knowledge Networks in International Political Economy*. Baden-Baden: Nomos Verlagsgesellschaft: 18–35.

Cavaghan, R. (2017). 'Bridging rhetoric and practice: new perspectives on barriers to gendered change', *Journal of Women, Politics & Policy*, 38(1), 42–63. doi:10.1080/1554477X.2016.1198209.

Chiva, C. (2009). 'The limits of Europeanisation: EU accession and gender equality in Bulgaria and Romania', *Perspectives on European Politics and Society*, 10(2): 195–209. doi:10.1080/15705850902899230.

Clisby, S. and Enderstein, A. (2017). 'Caught between the orientalist–occidentalist polemic: gender mainstreaming as feminist transformation or neocolonial subversion?', *International Feminist Journal of Politics*: 1–16. doi:10.1080/14616742.2016.1258262.

Collins, H. and Evans, R. (2007). *Rethinking Expertise*. London: University of Chicago Press.

Collyer, F., Maia, J. and Morrell, R. (2017). 'Toward a global sociology of knowledge: post-colonial realities and intellectual practices', *International Sociology*, 32(1): 21–37. doi:10.1177/0268580916676913.

56 *Theorising Cultures of Equality*

Connell, R., Pearse, R., Collyer, F., Maia, J. and Morrell, R. (2017). 'Negotiating with the North: how Southern-tier intellectual workers deal with the global economy of knowledge', *The Sociological Review*, 66(1): 41–57. doi:10.1177/0038026117705038.

Davids, T. and van Eederwijk, A. (2016). 'The Smothering of Feminist Knowledge: Gender Maintreaming Articulated through Neoliberal Govermentalities'. In *M. Bustelo, M.*Forest and *L.* Ferguson (eds). *The Politics of Feminist Knowledge Transfer. Gender Training and Gender Expertise.* Palgrave Macmillan: London: 80–90.

de Jong, S. and Kimm, S. (2017). 'The co-optation of feminisms: a research agenda', *International Feminist Journal of Politics*, 19(2): 185–200. doi:10.1080/14616742.2017.1299582.

do Mar Pereira, M. (2017). *Power, Knowledge and Feminist scholarship: An Ethnography of Academia.* London: Routledge.

Eisenstein, H. (2009). *Feminism Seduced: How Global Elites Use Women's Labor and Ideas to Exploit the World.* Boulder, CO: Paradigm Publishers.

Enderstein, A. (2017). 'European identity and gender equality policies: shaping the practice of gender expertise', *Journal of Research in Gender Studies*, 7(2): 109–135.

Enderstein, A. (2018). '(Not) just a girl: reworking femininity through women's leadership in Europe', *European Journal of Women's Studies*, 25(3). doi:10.1177/1350506818765029.

European Institute for Gender Equality. (2012). *Mapping of gender training policies and practices in the European Union: Summary of findings.* Vilnius: European Institute for Gender Equality.

Farris, S.R. (2017). *In the Name of Women's Rights: the Rise of Femonationalism.* Durham, NC: Duke University Press.

Ferguson, L. (2019). 'Exploring privilege through feminist gender training', *European Journal of Politics and Gender*, 2(1): 113–130. doi:10.1332/251510819X15471289106059.

Ferguson, L. (2018). *Gender Training: a Transformative Tool for Gender Equality.* London: Palgrave Pivot.

Ferguson, L. (2015). 'This is our gender person', *International Feminist Journal of Politics*, 17(3): 380–397. doi:10.1080/14616742.2014.918787.

Ferguson, L. and Forest, M. (2011). *OPERA final report. Advancing gender+ training in theory and practice.* Available online: www.quing.eu/files/results/final_opera_report.pdf. [Accessed 24 May 2018].

Finnemore, M. and Sikkink, K. (1998). 'International norm dynamics and political change', *International Organization*, 52(4): 887–917. doi:10.1162/002081898550789.

Fraser, N. (2009). 'Feminism, capitalism and the cunning of history', *New Left Review*, 56: 97–117.

Garbagnoli, S. (2016). 'Against the heresy of immanence: Vatican's 'gender' as a new rhetorical device against the denaturalisation of the sexual order', *Religion and Gender*, 6(2): 187–204. doi:10.18352/rg.10156.

Gerhards, J., Shafer, M.S. and Kampfer, S. (2009). 'Gender equality in the European Union: the EU script and its support by European citizens', *Sociology*, 43(3): 515–534. doi:10.1093/sp/jxh024.

Ghodsee, K. (2004). 'Feminism-by-design: emerging capitalisms, cultural feminism, and women's nongovernmental organizations in postcolonial Eastern Europe', *Signs*, 29(3): 727–753. doi:10.1086/380631.

Glanz, K., Lewis, F.M. and Viswanath, K. (2015). *Health Behaviour: Theory, Research, and Practice.* 5th ed. San Francisco, CA: Jossey-Bass.

Equality-Building in Europe 57

Graff, A. and Korolczuk, E. (2017). 'Towards an illiberal future: anti-genderism and anti-globalization', *Global Dialogue*, 7(1): 1–3.

Grzebalska, W. (2016). 'Why the war on "gender ideology" matters—and not just to feminists. Anti-genderism and the crisis of neoliberal Democracy', *Visegrad Insight*, 7: 1–5.

Guadagnini, M. and Donà, A. (2007). 'Women's policy machinery in Italy between European pressure and domestic constraints'. In *J.* Outshoorn *and J.* Kantola (eds). *Changing State Feminism*. London: Palgrave Macmillan: 164–181.

Hafner-Burton, E. and Pollack, M.A. (2007). 'No revolution: the disappointing implementation of gender mainstreaming in the European Union', Newsletter of the European Politics and Society Section of the American Political Science Association, 6(1): 11–13.

Halsaa, B. (1998). 'A strategic partnership for women's policies in Norway'. In *G.* Lycklama a Nijeholt, *V.* Vargas and *S.* Wieringa (eds). *Women's Movements and Public Policy in Europe, Latin America and the Caribbean*. New York and London: Garland: 167–189.

Harding, S. (1987). *Feminism and Methodology*. Bloomington, IN: Indiana University Press.

Hemmings, C. (2011). *Why Stories Matter: the Political Grammar of Feminist Theory*. Durham, NC: Duke University Press.

Hoard, S. (2015). *Gender Expertise in Public Policy. Towards a Theory of Policy Success*. Basingstoke: Palgrave Macmillan.

Holli, A.M. (2008) Feminist triangles: a conceptual analysis. *Representation*, 44(2), 169–185. doi:10.1080/00344890802080407.

Hoskyns, C. (1996). *Integrating Women, Law and Politics in the European Union*. Oxford: Oxford University Press.

Houchin, K. and MacLean, D. (2005). 'Complexity Theory and Strategic Change: an Empirically Informed Critique*', *British Journal of Management*, 16(2): 149–166. doi:10.1111/j.1467-8551.2005.00427.x.

Jacquot, S. (2010). 'The paradox of gender mainstreaming: unanticipated effects of New Modes of Governance in the gender equality domain,' *West European Politics*, 33(1): 118–135. doi:10.1080/01402380903354163.

Kantola, J. (2010). *Gender and the European Union*. Basingstoke: Palgrave Macmillan.

Kantola, J. and Nousiainen, K. (2009). 'Institutionalizing intersectionality in Europe', *International Feminist Journal of Politics*, 11(4), 459–477. doi:10.1080/146167409 03237426.

Kantola, J. and Squires, J. (2012). 'From state feminism to market feminism', *International Political Sciences Review*, 33(4), 382–400. doi:10.1177/0192512111432513.

Kauffman, S. (1995). *At Home in the Universe: the Search for Laws of Self-Organization and Complexity*. London: Viking.

Kauffman, S. (1993). *The Origins of Order: Self-organisation and Selection in Evolution*. Oxford: Oxford University.

Kay, A. (2005). 'A critique of the use of path dependency in policy studies', *Public Administration*, 83(3): 553–571. doi:10.1111/j.0033-3298.2005.00462.x.

Keim, W. (2014). 'Conceptualizing circulation of knowledge in the social sciences'. In *W.* Keim, *E.*Çelik, *C.* Ersche and *V.*Wöhrer (eds). *Global Knowledge in the Social Sciences. Made in Circulation*. Farnham: Ashgate: 87–113.

Keim, W., Çelic, E., Ersche, C. and Wöhrer, V. (eds). (2014). *Global Knowledge Production in the Social Sciences. Made in Circulation*. Farnham: Ashgate.

Krizsàn, A., Skejei, H. and Squires, J. (2012). *Institutionalizing Intersectionality: the Changing Nature of European Equality Regimes*. London: Palgrave Macmillan.

58 Theorising Cultures of Equality

Kuhar, R. and Paternotte, D. (2017). *Anti-gender Campaigns in Europe: Mobilizing against Equality.* London: Rowman and Littlefield International.

Kunz, R. (2016). 'Windows of opportunity, Trojan horses, and waves of women on the move: de-colonizing the circulation of feminist knowledges through metaphors'. In *M.* Bustelo, *L.* Ferguson and *M.* Forest (eds). *The Politics of Feminist Knowledge Transfer. Gender Training and Gender Expertise.* Palgrave Macmillan: Basingstoke: 98–117.

Kunz, R., Prügl, E. and Thompson, H. (2019). 'Gender expertise in global governance: contesting the boundaries of a field', *European Journal of Politics and Gender,* 2(1): 23–40. doi:10.1332/251510819X15471289106112.

Lang, S. (2009). 'Assessing advocacy: transnational women's networks and gender mainstreaming' *Social Politics: International Studies in Gender, State and Society,* 16(3): 327–357. doi:10.1093/sp/jxp016.

Lavizzari, A. and Prearo, M. (2019). 'The anti-gender movement in Italy: Catholic participation between electoral and protest politics', *European Societies,* 21(3): 422–442. doi:10.1080/14616696.2018.1536801.

Lazreg, M. (2002). 'Development: Feminist Theory's Cul-de-sac'. In *K.* Saunders *(ed.). Feminist Post-development Thought: Rethinking Modernity, Postcolonialism and Representation.* London: Zed Books: 123–145.

Lilja, M. and Vinthagen, S. (2014). 'Sovereign power, disciplinary power and bio-power: resisting what power with what resistance?'. *Journal of Political Power,* 7(1): 107–126. doi:10.1080/2158379X.2014.889403.

Locher, B. (2003). '*International norms and European policy making: trafficking in women in the EU'.* Portland, OR: Annual Meeting of the International Studies Association.

Lombardo, E. and Verloo, M. (2009). 'Institutionalizing intersectionality in the European Union', *International Feminist Journal of Politics,* 11(4): 478–495. doi: https://doi.org/10.1080/14616740903237442.

Lombardo, E. and Meier, P. (2008). 'Framing gender equality in the European Union political discourse', *Social Politics: International Studies in Gender, State and Society,* 15(1): 101–129. doi:10.1093/sp/jxn001.

Lombardo, E. and Meier, P. (2006). 'Gender mainstreaming in the EU. Incorporating a feminist reading?', *European Journal of Women's Studies,* 13(2): 151–166. doi:10.1093/sp/jxn001.

Lombardo, E. and Mergaert, L. (2013). 'Gender mainstreaming and resistance to gender training: a framework for studying implementation', *NORA – Nordic Journal of Feminist and Gender Research,* 21(4): 296–311. doi:1080/08038740.2013.851115.

Macdonald, M. (1994). 'Issues arising from the workshop'. In *M.* Macdonald (ed.). *Gender Planning in Development Agencies.* Oxford: Oxfam: 15–64.

Mackenzie, L. (1993). *On our feet. Taking steps to challenge women's oppression. A handbook on gender and popular education workshops.* Bellville: German Adult Education Association and University of the Western Cape, Centre for Adult and Continuing Education.

MacRae, H. (2010). 'The EU as a gender equal polity: myths and realities', *JCMS: Journal of Common Market Studies,* 48(1): 155–174. doi:10.1111/j.1468-5965.2009.02046.x.

Marx Ferree, M. (2015). *Training for gender equality as a source of organisational change.* Santo Domingo: UN Women Training Centre.

Mazey, S. (1998). 'The European Union and women's rights: from the Europeanization of national agendas to the nationalization of a European agenda?', *Journal of European Public Policy,* 5(1): 131–152. doi:10.1080/13501768880000061.

Equality-Building in Europe 59

Mazey, S. (1995). 'The development of EU equality policies: bureaucratic expansion on behalf of women', *Comparative and International Administration*, 73(4): 591–609. doi:10.1111/j.1467-9299.1995.tb00848.x.

Mazur, A.G. (2002). *Theorizing Feminist Policy*. Oxford: Oxford University Press.

McBride, D. and Mazur, A. (2010). *The Politics of State Feminism: Innovation in Comparative Research*. Philadelphia, PA: Temple University Press.

Meyer, J., Kaplan, D. and Charum, J. (2001). 'Scientific Nomadism and the New Geopolitics of Knowledge', *International Social Science Journal*, 53(168): 309–321. doi:10.1111/1468-2451.00317.

Milward, K., Mukhopadhyay, M. and Wong, F. (2015). 'Gender mainstreaming critiques: signposts or dead ends?', *IDS Bulletin*, 46(4): 75–81. doi:10.1111/1759-5436.12160.

Moser, C. (1993). *Gender Planning and Development: Theory, Practice and Training*. London: Routledge.

Moser, C. and Moser, A. (2005). 'Gender mainstreaming since Beijing: A review of success and limitations in international institutions', *Gender and Development*, 13 (2): 11–22. doi:10.1080/13552070512331332283.

Mukhopadhyay, M. (2017). *Feminist Subversion and Complicity: Governmentalities and Gender Knowledge in South Asia*. New Delhi: Zubaan Publishers.

Mukhopadhyay, M. (2014). 'Mainstreaming gender or reconstituting the mainstream? Gender knowledge in development', *Journal of International Development*, 26(3): 356–367. doi:10.1002/jid.2946.

Mukhopadhyay, M. and Wong, F. (eds). (2007). *Revisiting Gender Training: the Making and Remaking of Gender Knowledge. A Global Sourcebook*. Amsterdam: KIT Publishers.

Nagar, R. and Swarr, A.L. (2010). *Critical Transnational Feminist Praxis*. Albany, NY: State University of New York Press.

Ostner, I. (2000). 'From equal pay to equal employability: four decades of European gender policies'. In *M.* Rossili (ed.). *Gender policies in the European Union*. New York: Peter Lang Publishing: 26–42.

Ottaviano, C. and Mentasti, L. (2017). 'Differenti sguardi cattolici sull'educazione di genere nella scuola italiana: chiusure identitarie o aperture di nuove sfide?', *AG About Gender*, 6(12): 160–189.

Pascall, G. and Lewis, J. (2004). 'Emerging gender regimes and policies for gender equality in a wider Europe', *Social Policy*, 33(3): 373–394.

Paternotte, D. and Kuhar, R. (2018). 'Disentangling and locating the "global right": Anti-gender campaigns in Europe', *Politics and Governance*, 6(3): 6–19. doi:10.176 45/pag.v6i3.1557.

Perron, D. (2005). 'Mainstreaming and gender equality in the New (Market) Economy: an analysis of contradictions', *Social Politics: International Studies in Gender, State and Society*, 12(3): 389–411. doi:10.1093/sp/jxi021.

Pollack, M.A. and Hafner-Burton, E. (2000). 'Mainstreaming gender in the European Union', *Journal of European Public Policy*, 7(3): 432–456. doi:10.1080/135017 60050086116.

Porter, F. and Smyth, I. (1998). 'Gender training for development practitioners: only a partial solution', *Gender and Development*, 6(2): 59–64. doi:10.1080/741922724.

Prügl, E. (2010). Gender expertise and feminist knowledge, *Gender Politics in International Governance*. 6–8 October 2010, Geneva: Graduate Institute of International and Development Studies.

60 Theorising Cultures of Equality

Prügl, E. (2016). 'How to wield feminist power'. In *M.* Bustelo, *L.* Ferguson and *M.* Forest (eds). *The Politics of Feminist Knowledge Transfer. Gender Training and Gender Expertise.* Basingstoke: Palgrave Macmillan: 25–42.

Prügl, E. (2015). 'Neoliberalising feminism,' *New Political Economy*, 20(4): 614–631. doi:10.1080/13563467.2014.951614.

Prügl, E. (2013). 'Gender expertise as feminist strategy'. In *Feminist Strategies in International Governance.* London: Routledge: 79–95.

Prügl, E. (2011). 'Diversity management and gender mainstreaming as technologies of government', *Politics & Gender*, 7(1): 71–89. doi:10.1017/S1743923X10000565.

Raj, K. (2006). *Relocating Modern Science: Circulation and the Construction of Knowledge in South Asia and Europe, 1650–1900.* Delhi: Permanent Black.

Rao, A., H. Feldstein, K. Cloud and K. Staudt. (1991). Gender training and development planning: learning from experience. *Conference Report.* Bergen, May. New York: Population Council.

Rees, T. (2005). 'Reflections on the uneven development of gender mainstreaming in Europe', *International Feminist Journal of Politics*, 7(4): 555–574. doi:10.1080/14616740500284532.

Rees, T. (1998). *Mainstreaming Equality in the European Union. Education, Training and Labor Market Policies.* London: Routledge.

Reinharz, S. (1992). *Feminist Methods in Social Research.* Oxford: Oxford University.

Richarson, J. and Mazey, S. (2015). *European Union: Power and Policy-making.* New York: Routledge.

Roberts, A. (2012). 'Financial crisis, financial firms…and financial feminism? The rise of "transnational business feminism" and the necessity of Marxist-feminist IPE', *Socialist Studies/ETudes Socialistes*, 8(2): 85–108. doi:10.18740/S40W2K.

Rose, G. (1997). 'Situating knowledges: positionality, reflexivities and other tactics', *Progress in Human Geography*, 21(3): 305–320. doi:10.1191/030913297673302122.

Rossili, M. (2000). *Gender Policies in the European Union.* New York: Peter Lang Publishing.

Schudson, M. (2006). 'The trouble with experts–and why democracies need them', *Theory and Society*, 35(5–6): 491–506. doi:10.1007/s11186-006-9012-y.

Schwenken, H. (2008). 'Beautiful victims and sacrificing heroines: exploring the role of gender knowledge in migration policies', *Signs: Journal of Women in Culture and Society*, 33(4): 770–776. doi:10.1086/528744.

Shore, C. (2000). *Building Europe. The Cultural Politics of European Integration.* London: Routledge.

Smyth, A. and March, C. (1998). *A Guide to Gender Analysis Frameworks.* Oxford: Oxfam.

Squires, J. (2008). 'Intersecting inequalities: reflecting on the subjects and objects of equality', *Political Quarterly*, 79, 53–61. doi:10.1111/j.1467-923X.2008.00902.x.

Squires, J. (2005). 'Is mainstreaming transformative? Theorizing mainstreaming in the context of diversity and deliberation', *Social Politics: International Studies in Gender, State and Society*, 12(3): 366–388. doi:10.1093/sp/jxi020.

Standing, H. (2004). 'Gender, myth and fable: the perils of mainstreaming in sector bureaucracies', *IDS Bulletin*, 35: 82–88. doi:10.1111/j.1759-5436.2004.tb00159.x.

Stratigaki, M. (2005). 'Gender mainstreaming vs. positive action an ongoing conflict in EU gender equality policy', *European Journal of Women's Studies*, 12(2): 165–186. doi:10.1177/1350506805051236.

Sweetman, C. (ed.). (1998). *Gender, Education, Training.* Oxford: Oxfam.

Equality-Building in Europe 61

Thompson, H. and Prügl, E. (2015). *Gender Experts and Gender Expertise. Results of a Survey*. Geneva: The Graduate Institute of International and Development Studies.

Tsing, A. (2000). 'The Global Situation', *Cultural Anthropology*, 15(3): 327–360.

United Nations Women Training Centre. (2016a). *Compendium of good practices in training for gender equality*. Santo Domingo.

United Nations Women Training Centre. (2016b). *Education and training for gender equality*. Santo Domingo.

Vallance, E. and Davies, E. (1986). *Women of Europe: Women MEPs and Equality Policy*. Cambridge: Cambridge University Press.

Vargas, V. and Wieringa, S. (1998). 'The triangle of empowerment: Processes and actors in the making of public policy for women'. In G. Lycklama a Nijeholt, V. Vargas and S. Wieringa (eds). *Women's Movements and Public Policy in Europe, Latin America and the Caribbean*. New York and London: Garland: 3–23.

Vazquez, M. (2018). 'Conscientious objection in Swedish and Italian healthcare: paradoxical secularizations and unbalanced pluralisms'. In K. Topidi (ed.). *Normative Pluralism and Human Rights*. London: Routledge: 144–162.

Verloo, M. (2018a). 'Gender knowledge, and opposition to the feminist project: extreme-right populist parties in the Netherlands', *Politics and Governance*, 6(3): 20–30. doi:10.17645/pag.v6i3.1456.

Verloo, M. (2018b). 'Introduction: dynamics of opposition to gender equality in Europe'. In M. Verloo (ed.). *Varieties of Opposition to Gender Equality in Europe*. London: Routledge: 3–18.

Verloo, M. (2018c). 'Understanding the dynamics of opposition to gender-equality change: lessons from and for social complexity theory'. In M. Verloo (ed.). *Varieties of Opposition to Gender Equality in Europe*. London: Routledge: 38–54.

Walby, S. (2011). *The Future of Feminism*. Cambridge: Polity.

Walby, S. (2009). *Globalization and Inequalities: Complexity and Contested Modernities*. London: Sage.

Walby, S. (2007). 'Complexity theory, systems theory, and multiple intersecting social inequalities', *Philosophy of the Social Sciences*, 37(4): 449–470. doi:10.1177/0048 393107307663.

Walby, S. (2005). 'Gender mainstreaming: productive tensions in theory and practice', *Social Politics: International Studies in Gender, State and Society*, 12(3): 321–343. doi:10.1093/sp/jxi018.

Walby, S. (2004). 'The European Union and gender equality: emergent varieties of gender regime', *Social Politics: International Studies in Gender, State and Society*, 11(1): 4–29. doi:10.1093/sp/jxh024.

Walby, S. (2002). 'Feminism in a global era', *Economy and Society*, 31(4): 533–557. doi: https://doi.org/10.1080/0308514022000020670.

Walby, S., Armstrong, J. and Strid, S. (2012). 'Intersectionality: multiple inequalities in social theory', *Sociology*, 46(2): 224–240. doi:10.1177/0038038511416164.

Wieslander, M. and Nordvall, H. (2019). 'When gender training backlashes: participants' resistance and the fragility of commonsensical feminism', *Adult Education Quarterly*, 69(3): 207–224. doi:10.1177/0741713619841128.

Wiliams, S. (1994). *The Oxfam Gender Training Manual*. Oxford: Oxfam.

Wöhrer, V. (2016). 'Gender studies as a multi-centred field? Centres and peripheries in academic gender research', *Feminist Theory*, 17(3): 323–343. doi:10.1177/146470 0116652840.

62 *Theorising Cultures of Equality*

Wong, F., Vaast, C. and Mukhopadhyay, M. (2016.) *Review and Mapping Exercise for Conceptualizing Professional Development of Gender Trainers.* Amsterdam: KIT Gender and UN Women's Training Centre.

Woodward, A. (2008). 'Too late for gender mainstreaming? Taking stock in Brussels', *Journal of European Social Policy*, 18(3): 289–302. doi:10.1177/0958928708091061.

Woodward, A. (2003). 'Building velvet triangles: gender and informal governance'. In *T.*Christiansen and *S.* Piattoni (eds). *Informal Governance in the European Union.* Cheltenham: Edward Elgar Publishing: 76–93.

Young, B. and Scherrer, C. (2010). *Gender Knowledge and Knowledge Networks in International Political Economy.* Baden-Baden: Nomos Verlagsgesellschaft.

4 Entangled Theorising
Transgender Depathologisation and Access to 'Disability'

Lieke Hettinga

Introduction

In a now expected move towards flagging trans* inclusivity across institutional frameworks, Utrecht University in the Netherlands announced that it was opening gender-neutral bathrooms in three of the university's buildings.[1] While gender-neutral bathrooms already existed in most buildings in the form of disability accessible stalls, one of the rationales behind the infrastructural change was to disassociate gender non-conformity from disability, so that the former is no longer linked to 'negative associations', as stated in the university's news outlet (Waterlander, 2018).

As with most moments in which transgender and gender nonconforming emancipation coalesces with institutions publicly showcasing their inclusion and diversity policies, the announcement prompts mixed sensations and thoughts. Feeling affirmed yet troubled, I am curious what this institutional move – both in terms of local architectural rearrangements as well as part of a wider cultural phenomenon of neoliberal inclusivity campaigns – signals about the splitting of trans* and disability politics. What would it mean for trans* people to be able to move away from 'negative associations', and what is the assumed project towards 'positivity' behind such a stated aim for a trajectory of transgender justice? How is becoming transgender a project of becoming an abled subject?

Without devaluing the important change towards gender-neutral bathrooms, I take this vignette to signal two issues that open my inquiry into contemporary cultural and theoretical contestations vis-à-vis politics of the body. Firstly, this anecdote points to how the unprecedented forms of transgender and genderqueer emancipation in contemporary Euro-American culture are entangled with disability, where disability functions as a stigmatised site from which trans* and gender nonconforming people can move away, or, as Eli Clare (2013) and Jasbir Puar (2017) argue, whose capacitation is contingent on a disavowal of relationships to disability. Secondly, the overlapping bathroom accessibility needs of trans* and disabled people demonstrate an opportunity of a coalitional politics geared toward an expansive notion of access – an opportunity that is missed out on when these sites of politics are disentangled.[2]

64 *Theorising Cultures of Equality*

In order to explore these issues in their complexity, I consider the affinities, dissonances and potentials of transgender and disability politics a form of 'entanglement', in the sense that Karen Barad mobilises the term. For Barad (2007: 35), material-discursive factors such as gender or race materialise and come to matter through their intra-action. Entanglement, then, does not show how previously disconnected entities come to be intertwined, but instead captures how they come to be meaningful through their interaction. In other words, rather than mobilising 'transgender' and 'disability' as categories that pre-exist their emergence, I am interested in looking at ways in which they both materialise as forms of embodied experiences contingent on discourses, infrastructures and bodily capacities that sometimes coalesce and other times operate as mutually exclusive. A crucial way in which these material-discursive categories are entangled is through histories of medicalisation and pathologisation, which transgender and disability studies and activist movements have contested and continue to grapple with. As I explore in more detail below, this also entails moving away from treating identity categories as intersectional axes on an equal plane that are interchangeable, but to reckon with the force of their entanglement.

Taking the dis/entanglement of transness and disability as its central concern, this chapter moves beyond the bathroom as an iconic site in which trans* and disability politics meet, and reviews the ways in which this dis/entanglement takes place in the movement towards the depathologisation of transgender identity. First, in light of the shared vexed relationships to medicalisation from trans and crip[3] perspectives, I explore the ways in which theories of the body in disability studies are useful in contributing to critical transfeminist perspectives of medicalised notions of 'Gender Dysphoria'. I do this through a discussion of Alexandre Baril's (2015) proposition to consider transness a form of disability – a claim that I argue is both useful in resisting the splitting of trans and disability politics, but that also exposes some problems that arise with doing intersectional analysis. Second, leaning on Jasbir Puar's (2017) work on debility and capacity, I interrogate the epistemological coherence of categories of 'transgender' and 'disability' as intersectional axis of identity. To conclude my review of these debates, I discuss Dean Spade's (2003) critical trans perspective on the sociopolitical factors which influence people's capacity to access a legal definition of disability. Hence, this chapter deploys a two-fold meaning of 'access', shifting emphasis from the question of accessible bathrooms, infrastructure and social worlds, to the question of the ability to access an identity category such as 'disability'.

From Bathrooms to Diagnoses: Transgender Depathologisation and Compulsory Able-bodiedness

In recent years, bathrooms have become a key site of regulation through which transgender issues have received cultural visibility, from legislative battles over transgender bathroom access in the USA to the introduction of gender-neutral bathrooms. As Alison Kafer (2013: 156) argues in her work on queer, crip and feminist coalitions, there is an unexplored potential for a politics of affinity centred around the bathroom, and she suggests that disability movements might take the lead in undoing gendered conventions of the bathroom. Noting how it is generally accepted that disability bathrooms are used by people of various gender presentations, she points out how the regulation of gender segregation is less strong in this case, because disabled people are already considered outsiders, owing partly to being cast as asexual subjects (Ibid.: 155). Gender neutral bathrooms only become threatening if flagged specifically as such, which demonstrates the underlying assumption that the creation of gender-neutral bathrooms caters for genderqueer able-bodied users. For Kafer, disability movements have the opportunity to go beyond demanding access to pre-existing conventionally gendered bathrooms and instead foreground demands for infrastructural change in which disability access and trans access are not separate issues.

But bathrooms are not coherent microcosms that capture the stakes of transgender and/or disability organising and their possible affinities, not least because this example lends itself easily to a specific form of visibility politics that performatively celebrates emancipation while keeping structural inequalities intact. As Jack Halberstam (2017: 50) points out, in the context of the United States, the celebration of transgender children who have challenged bathroom restrictions in their schools is part of a particular cultural iconography that occludes struggles faced by trans subjects less easily celebrated or habilitated on the terms of racialised and classed norms of state recognition, struggles around issues such as the safety of sex workers, the increasing violence against trans women of colour, transgender youth facing homelessness or the impact of police brutality on transgender people. Similarly, Robert McRuer's (2018: 44) work on the place of disability in processes of globalisation and ongoing austerity measures highlights a comparable dynamic in which certain disabled subjects receive a cultural and representational currency that functions as what activist Stella Young has called 'inspiration porn', while the infrastructure for the livelihood of disabled people is being erased through the impact of extreme cuts in government spending. While the iconicity of the bathroom allows for a clear site around which activist organising takes place, as well as an easy symbol for institutional recognition, the (dis)entanglements of frameworks of trans* and disability organising that I am interested in exploring here go beyond the question of whether or not shared bathroom access needs are met. Taking the announcement of Utrecht University's gender-neutral bathrooms as an entry point into analysing a problematic of how transgender emancipation relies on a disassociation with disability, I am interested in exploring how this dynamic plays out in the movement towards transgender depathologisation.

Transgender depathologisation is a crucial part of transgender activist movements across the world, and the primary aim is to fight the medical as well as cultural notion that being transgender is a pathology. As Amets Suess, Karine Espineira, and Pau Crego Walters (2014: 74) outline, the activist and academic movement towards trans depathologisation includes:

> the questioning of the current diagnostic classification of gender transitions, the demand of a recognition of trans rights, among them legal and

66 *Theorising Cultures of Equality*

health rights, the revision of the trans health care model, and the claim of an acknowledgment of gender/body diversity.

Hence, the removal of gender-related diagnoses in psychiatric manuals, or introducing a non-pathologising reformulation, is a key aim, as the positioning of transgender identity as a mental illness continues to support the process of stigmatisation and discrimination. Writing this on the heels of the announced changes in transgender-related diagnoses in the World Health Organization's International Classification of Diseases (ICD), the results of the labour of transgender activists and advocacy organisations working towards the depathologisation of transgender identity are becoming visible. The new ICD-11, which was introduced in June 2018, is changing how transgender experiences are formulated as conditions to be diagnosed (WHO, 2018). In the previously used ICD-10, gender identity-related diagnoses such as 'Gender Identity Disorder' or 'Transsexualism' were listed under 'Mental Health Disorders'. This has been replaced with 'Gender Incongruence' under the heading 'Conditions related to sexual health' in the ICD-11. Advocacy groups such as Transgender Europe or Global Action for Trans Equality celebrate the change the ICD as a crucial step forward in the depathologisation of transgender identity, while recognising how significant problems continue to exist despite these adjustments, such as the pathologisation of intersex people, as well as the proposed usage of the contested diagnosis of 'Gender Incongruence in Childhood'.

The changes in the ICD mirror the shifts that have taken place in gender-related diagnoses in the *Diagnostic and Statistical Manual of Mental Disorders* (DSM), the globally used diagnostic manual from the American Psychiatric Association. 'Gender Identity Disorder' has been replaced with 'Gender Dysphoria' in the DSM-V, where, according to the central diagnostic criteria, one must show 'a marked incongruence between one's experienced/expressed gender and primary and/or secondary sex characteristics' (American Psychiatric Association, 2013: 452). With both the ICD and the DSM now emphasising the notion of 'incongruence', the updated changes in diagnostic criteria now describe gender dysphoria as being a distress that is a result of stigmatisation, not an inherent experience of being transgender. In this way, we can see how the medical perspective of transgender identity has absorbed aspects of a social understanding of gender identity, where it underscores how gendered social arrangements in the world have the potential impact of dysphoria for transgender people. The cause of distress, then, is not being transgender, but the social response to one's gendered experiences and expressions. However, these diagnostic tools have historically had a crucial function in creating, defining and regulating what we understand as 'transsexuality' and 'transgender' and inform a structure of gatekeepers who regulate access to medical procedures, access which is often denied to those who fail to perform and affirm a binary gender expression (Spade, 2003: 18; Davy, 2015:1169). What is at stake here is the complex tension between a desire to resist the medicalisation of transgender bodies, while having to rely on diagnoses and other gatekeeper mechanisms of medical institutions to access health care, hormones, or surgeries. As Ulrica Engdahl (2014: 267) points out, even if the diagnoses emphasise the incongruence between the social assignment of gender and one's personal experience of gender, the notion of gender incongruence continues to rely on the discourses of being in the 'wrong body', rehearsing essentialist notions of an authentic gendered self, separate from a reified image of the body.

The most often cited reason for campaigning for trans depathologisation is the stigmatising impact of the psychiatric diagnosis and its attack on people's decisional autonomy. Moreover, transgender activists reject the label of mental illness, which continues to have cultural repercussions for the ability of transgender people to assert their humanity (Suess et al., 2014: 74). But as Josephine Krieg (2013: 44) argues, action geared towards depathologisation, owing to its stigmatising impact, can reproduce a medicalised understanding of mental health issues as pathological, without pointing to the societal causes of stigmatisation. The structures of compulsory able-bodiedness that place such a diagnosis in the realm of negativity in the first place are not commented on or are perhaps further entrenched in this move. Clare (2013: 262) echoes this sentiment when he writes: 'I often hear trans people [...] name their transness a disability, a birth defect. They say, "[...] I simply need a cure."'. Similarly, Mitchell and Snyder (2004: 6) note how the disabled body can serve as 'the raw material out of which other socially disempowered communities make themselves visible'.

In the medical regulation of gender, as well as in the trans activist responses to it, we can trace how ableism intersects processes of the pathologisation and the depathologisation of transgender identity alike. In the medicalised approach, the pathologisation of transgender experience is a process through which the transgender subject can re-assert able-bodiedness and able-mindedness by achieving normative gender congruence. Conversely, in the political project toward depathologisation, medical and psychiatric diagnoses remain a site of stigmatised disability that transgender subjects attempt to move away from. In both cases, structures of compulsory able-bodiedness remain intact.

Intra-actions of Disability, Queer and Transgender Subjectivity

Although it is a growing subject of scholarly work, the specific nexus of transgender and disability is under-researched. However, I locate precedents for this work in literature that examines how theories of the relationship between gender and the body have an affinity with disability studies, as well as literature that fuses queer theory and crip theory. In examining the relations between ways of understanding and theorising queer, transgender and disabled embodiment, it is important to recognise that not only might there be an overlap in theorising identities or the body, but more crucially, to understand the contested ways in which these sites as identity have been read through each other, where non-normative sexuality and gender expressions have been read as disabled, and vice versa. As Anna Mollow and Robert McRuer (2012: 1) observe, people with disabilities are often seen as somehow queer through associations of abnormal

68 *Theorising Cultures of Equality*

sexuality, be it marked as asexual or oversexual, if not ignored completely by virtue of rarely being regarded as desiring subjects or objects of desire. In addition, Kim Q. Hall (2015: 260) notes how normative configurations of gender are contingent on a particular appearance and capacity of the body that are potentially reconfigured by disability. Conversely, queer sexualities have often been considered a form of sickness, and transgender identity remains a site of ongoing medicalisation and pathologisation (McRuer, 2002: 94). Given the process of being positioned as disabled, most notably through medical diagnoses as well as cultural associations with mental disorders, transgender and genderqueer people have resisted the pathologising connection between non-normative gender expression and disability (Davy, 2015: 1173).

As the rubric of disability increasingly appears as part of the list of identity markers theorised and analysed in interdisciplinary feminist theory, the relationship between theories of gender and sexuality and theories of disability has taken varied forms. A central articulation of this relationship has been the integration of feminist theories of gender, body, and performativity, into disability studies as a tool to interrogate the instability of the category of 'disability' and the performative sedimentation of compulsory able-bodiedness. In taking up Judith Butler's theories of gender performativity, various scholars in disability studies have noted that, if the separation of sex and gender mirrors the distinction between impairment and disability, theories of gender performativity allow for a re-consideration of the presumed relationship between impairment as a bodily phenomenon and disability as a social phenomenon, as articulated in the social model of disability (Hughes and Paterson, 1997; Samuels, 2011). But as Ellen Samuels (2011: 68–70) points out, merely substituting the terms of gender performativity with disability obscures how structures of gender are different from disability, and how the performative sedimentation of gender at times leans on disability as the site of abjection.

Moreover, Butler's work on gender performativity and the heterosexual matrix has opened up investigations into how the maintenance of heteronormativity and ableism are entangled. For example, McRuer (2006: 10) proposes to resignify gender trouble as 'ability trouble', substituting Butler's terms of gender and sexuality for disabled embodiment, which results in a theory of how normative positions of able-bodiedness appear as a natural law, while remaining impossible actually embody. Crucially, connecting to Adrienne Rich's notion of 'compulsory heterosexuality', McRuer (2006: 2) points out how compulsory able-bodiedness and compulsory heterosexuality converge, so that successful heterosexual performances depend on able-bodiedness, and vice versa.

While these theories of queerness and gender in relation to disability also speak to transgender identity, much less theoretical work is available on the specificities of the possible affinities and dissonances of thinking disability and transness together. Using queer/crip theorising in understanding the entanglement of transgender and disabled experiences reaches a limit due to the continuing necessity for transgender people to undergo medicalising and pathologising diagnoses in order to get access to necessary health care. The erasure of

Entangled Theorising 69

homosexuality from the DSM in 1973 was considered a movement away from considering homosexuality as an illness, and while there are still cultural and ideological effects of this diagnostic and medicalised understanding of homosexuality, it did not have consequences for retaining access to health care today, such as the hormones or surgeries that transgender people might want or need to obtain. The reliance on access to health care in the case of transgender people limits the possibility of completely delinking gender recognition from medical diagnostic procedures. The biopolitical regulation of bodies under the medical gaze thus necessitates a rethinking of the experience of transness as one of debility – a formulation clearly articulated by Baril (2015).

Transness as Disability?

In his article 'Transness as Debility: rethinking intersections between trans and disabled embodiments', Baril (2015) proposes to consider transgender subjectivity as a form of debility, and I explore the implications of this argument in more detail here. In order to make the argument that transgender experiences are related to formations of disability, Baril (2015: 66) uses the conceptual tools from disability studies – the medical model and the social model – as a grid to map diverging approaches to understanding transgender embodiment. Transgender embodiment is positioned in different ways depending on these models of disability. Understood through the lens of the medical model, transness is positioned as a mental disorder or a sexual health condition, based on the diagnostic classificatory models offered by the DSM or WHO ICD. Conversely, understanding the activism and advocacy geared towards trans depathologisation as an enactment of the social model, transgender embodiment is, then, as Baril (2015 :66) writes, 'a neutral element to which stereotypes, prejudice and discriminatory attitudes are attached' in a society structured around normative gender dimorphism. Thinking of a third way – that is, an alternative to the medical model seeing transness as curable pathology, or the social model that views transness as a variation of sex/gender identity – Baril reclaims the experience of becoming trans as one which under conditions of social heteronormativity and medical gender diagnosis is inevitably debilitating.

In making this conceptual move, Baril follows critiques of the social model of disability, as proposed by Kafer, and for similar reasons. He argues that if we understand disability as exclusively social and/or political, we lack the tools to appreciate forms of suffering and pain related to, for example, experiences of chronic illness or mental health issues. In order to account for the phenomenological experience of disability, as well as give space for how disability and transgender experiences are connected, Baril articulates a 'composite model of disability' in which there is space for a 'complex disability politics of transness' (Ibid.: 70). What Baril wants to advance with this model is the possibility of considering transness as a disabling experience, rather than a neutral element that only becomes politicised in a social world. In his model of disability, transgender experiences are to be understood as related to social structures such as

70 *Theorising Cultures of Equality*

'cisgenderist oppression', but are also experiences of suffering and debilitation (Ibid.: 59). Baril asks why, despite the 'debilitating' conditions associated with transgender experiences, it is so unthinkable to consider transgender experiences as a legitimate disability, and finds cause for this in both a culture of cisnormativity in disability studies, as well as ableist strands of thinking in transgender studies (Ibid.: 61–63). He advances the proposition to consider transness as debility based on overlapping experiences, such as the distress resulting from relations to medicalisation, from the phenomenological experiences of dysfunctional or changing body parts and organs, and from social and political discrimination in various spheres of life (Ibid.: 63). Moreover, he argues that the exclusion of gender-related diagnoses from disability legislation such as the Americans with Disabilities Act points to a double standard. He writes: 'Although transsexuality is categorised as a mental illness, trans people do not, generally speaking, have access to the same rights and protections as other disabled people' (Ibid.: 62).

Baril's proposition to consider transness as a form of debility crucially resists the lingering ableist underpinnings of transgender depathologisation. In order to move towards thinking through the entanglement of 'transgender' and 'disability' without treating them as intersectional axes that are interchangeable, I want to make three contributions. Firstly, it is difficult to treat bodily experiences of pain and suffering as either universal aspects of transgender experiences, or as phenomena that we can know outside of cultural systems of gender regulation. In arguing against a social model, where transness would simply a neutral bodily experience that becomes entangled in social and political forms of oppression and medical forms of pathologisation, Baril argues that experiences of suffering related to transness would exist independent of structures of oppression of dimorphic gender normativity (Ibid.: 67) Turning the social model on its head, he writes:

> The lives of some disabled and/or trans people, however, are complicated by physical/mental suffering. Even if ableism and cisgenderism were eradicated, these people would still be affected by their conditions.
>
> (Ibid.: 69)

While I see the use of underscoring the physical and mental suffering that trans people experience, to conceive of the possibility of a transgender position, or any gendered position for that matter, outside of cultural structures risks circumventing the notion that how we understand bodily experiences such as suffering is always intertwined with, and mediated through, cultural formations of gender and bodies. In reviewing how 'sex' and 'impairment' have been assumed to be facts of bodily materiality, Kim Q. Hall (2015: 257) notes that 'it is difficult, if not impossible, to know what impairment and sex mean or how they are inhabited independent of the social and cultural context in which bodies are lived and assigned meaning'. By proposing that there is a reality of transgender embodiment outside of dimorphic gender culture, Baril creates a timeless notion of the transgender subject, leaving aside how 'transgender' is a historical and geopolitical formation as much as any articulation of gender.

Entangled Theorising 71

Secondly, I want to put pressure on the differences between arguing for 'transness as debility' or 'transness as disability', which Baril seems to use interchangeably. Puar's work on debility and disability offers tools here. In *The Right to Maim: Debility, Capacity, and Disability*, Puar advances a critical review of the vocabulary of debility and disability, and points to how these can, respectively, index the biopolitical regulation as well as neglect of bodies and bodily capacities, or the interpellation into categories of identity that match neoliberal identity politics as well as legal classifications of identity. She writes:

> I content that the term 'debilitation' is distinct from the term 'disablement' because it foregrounds the slow wearing down of populations instead of the event of becoming disabled. While the latter concept creates and hinges on a narrative of before and after for individuals who will eventually be identified as disabled, the former comprehends those bodies that are sustained in a perpetual state of debilitation precisely through foreclosing the social, cultural, and political translation to disability.
>
> (Puar, 2017: xiii)

What takes place in Baril's article is an apparently seamless shifting between 'debilitating aspects of transness', 'transness as disability', and 'transness as debility', but these articulates might have different stakes (2015: 67, 63). Building on how 'debility' is operationalised in Julie Livingston and Puar's work, Baril (2015: 61) understands it as a 'broad view of disability'. However, in her recent work, Puar (2017: xvi) theorises debility with a crucial distinction from Livingston, namely that debility does not encompass disability. Instead, her usage of debility points to how alongside of frameworks of disability inclusion there are processes of debilitation in which the subject category of disability remains out of reach. What I want to add to Baril's argument, then, using Puar's most recent work on debility, is the suggestion that a project of trying to include transness into the subject category of disability risks losing attention to how debilitation is a condition of structures of ableism that are not alleviated through disability rights frameworks, and that we need to pay attention to whom the category of disability is accessible.

Thirdly, the developing scholarship on the various connections between trans and crip politics might benefit from reflecting on how transness and disability might be entangled rather than coherent categories subject to intersectional theorising. As outlined above, I believe that it is highly significant at this cultural moment to resist ableist notions behind trans activism geared towards depathologisation, in which disability can remain an unquestioned site of 'negativity' to move away from, and Baril is one of the few scholars who are interested and invested in critically exploring these entanglements. However, there might be a difference between, on the one hand, proposing that transgender and disabled experiences are alike, or the same, owing to similar vexed relationships to medicalisation, and, on the other hand, pointing out how transgender emancipation is a process of entrenching structures of ableism. Put differently, this is a

72 *Theorising Cultures of Equality*

difference between understanding embodied experiences as similar and analogical, versus using the entanglement of trans/crip as a lens through which might complicate contemporary politics of identity categories. Part of what seems to be at play here are the limits of categorical thinking where 'disability' and 'transgender' are coherent categories that precede their potential meeting points. As Puar (2017: 176, n11) notes, what motivates her usage of 'assemblage' is a desire to 'methodologically move beyond the mutual interruptions of field X by field Y and vice versa'. Instead of formulaic thinking 'based on the assumption of the equality of each vector to the other and absence of each in the other', Puar (2017: 36) suggests moving from 'epistemological correctives' towards 'ontological multiplicity', where becoming trans and becoming disabled are implicated in the same assemblages of power that undo the fantasy of discrete categories. The epistemological coherence of transgenderism and disability as distinct identity markers and experiences, is both produced and maintained by power (institutional and discursive) and is the basis for a politics that either seeks to relate transgender embodiment and disability by analogy or overlap. Analogical theorising, in which trans and disabled experiences are separate entities which show similar or parallel characteristics, reinforces the stabilisation of identities. We can take insight here from Malini Johar Schueller's (2005: 72) critique of the function of analogy in feminist theory, where she argues that 'gender' and 'race' are deployed analogically to illustrate how sexist and racist structures of oppression operate similarly. She argues that this analogical equating of 'gender' and 'race' recuperates the potential disruption of racial difference into a safe notion of similarity that supports a political of liberal multiculturalism, writing:

> The seeming equivalence of the analogy and the horizontal seriality suggested by the commas often used by gender theorists to include concerns of race and class in routinely used phrases such as 'race, class, and gender' belie a hierarchy of ontologies that privilege whiteness.
>
> (Ibid.: 71)

The entanglement of trans/crip experiences and positions offers an opportunity to move beyond analogical theorising of identities, and to understand the specific material intra-actions that separate or consolidate trans and disability politics.

'Access' to Disability

By way of conclusion, I want to think of a way to navigate these difficulties that arise in theorising the connections between transgender and disability as identity categories, subjectivities, embodied experiences, or biopolitical regulations, through Spade's work on the legal regulation of gender nonconformity. As a US-based lawyer and activist working on transgender legal recognition in relation to the prison industrial complex, poverty, youth homelessness and developments in hate crime legislation, he founded the Sylvia Rivera Law Project in New York City, which provides free legal services to transgender, intersex and gender nonconforming people who are low-income and/or people of colour. While his perspective is focussed on practices in the context of the USA, his work brings forth important insights that help to understand how categories of 'transgender' and 'disability' coalesce. Spade points out that while disability legislation and policy, such as the Americans with Disabilities Act, often explicitly exclude transgendered and transsexual people from coverage, successful legal cases are still often based on a medical approach to transsexuality, where access to trans rights is contingent on medical evidence that indicates the presence of 'Gender Identity Disorder' or 'Gender Dysphoria' or 'Gender Incongruence'. As Spade (2003: 30) points out, by reaching claims for trans equality through this medical approach rather than through legislation for gender equality, transgender people might feel that there is a risk to be cast as disabled, and having their gender experience not validated but instead delegitimised as abnormal or defective. But the anxiety that being transgender is positioned as a disability is often underpinned by a notion of disability as a fixed site of stigmatisation. Understanding this response as an ableist gut reaction that reinforces notions of disability as lack or site of abjection, Spade (2003: 34) argues that this reaction can be resolved by pointing out the lessons from the disability rights movement, which indicate that disability inequality is a result of artificial social conditions which privilege certain bodies and minds over others. In rehearsing this social model of disability, Spade proposes to understand transgender rights in a similar register, writing:

> trans people could use the disability rights framework to argue that we are fully capable of participating equally, but for artificial conditions that bar our participation. Examples of such conditions include gender-segregated facilities or dress codes administered according to birth gender.
>
> (Ibid.: 34)

Hence, the problem with a medical understanding of transness through a gender-related diagnosis is not so much the 'risk' of suggesting that transgender people are disabled, but instead, Spade directs his critique on transgender-related diagnoses towards the regulatory regime of dimorphic gender that the diagnoses reinforce, and the limited access that people from low-income contexts, people of colour and gender nonconforming people have to receive the diagnosis. The coercive gender normativity assumed in the DSM, both in 'Gender Identity Disorder' and now in the diagnosis of 'Gender Dysphoria', leaves the diagnosis inaccessible for those not able or willing to adhere to a particular normative masculinity or femininity, or perform narratives of 'being in the wrong body' (Ibid.: 35). What Spade's work points to is both the contingency of when to understand and define transgender identity as a form of disability, and, crucially, that reaching a medical definition of transness through the diagnosis of the DSM is often a privilege in itself – a legal category of disability that many transgender people do not get access to even if they wish to. These important insights pertain to the difference between approaching trans/crip entanglements through shared experiences of

74 *Theorising Cultures of Equality*

debilitation or exclusion and the factors that influence the possibility of accessing 'disability' itself in order to get access to rights or recognition.

Notes

1 In the introduction, I use the term 'trans*' to refer to the various and diverse ways in which trans identities are lived and embodied. The usage of the asterisk does not denote an explicit flagging of an umbrella term that includes this diversity, a gesture that the prefix 'trans' in itself is sufficient for. Instead, taking inspiration from Eva Hayward and Jami Weinstein's writing on the 'fingery' asterisk, it denotes a desire to multiply what trans is or might be. Similarly, Marquis Bey suggests that 'trans*' highlights its own dehiscence, signaling the rupture of what was stitched together. The remainder of this chapter uses 'transgender' or 'transness' or 'trans' as they are the terms used in the literature discussed.
2 See the US based advocacy group 'PISSAR' (People in Search of Safe and Accessible Restrooms) for an example for such a moment of coalitional activism. See also, Kafer (2013) and West (2010).
3 'Crip is considered to be an inclusive term, representing all disabilities: people with vastly divergent physical and psychological differences. Crip represents the contemporary disability rights wave and is an "insider" term for disability culture.' Wright State University. Retrieved from www.wright.edu/event/sex-disability-conference/crip-theory

Bibliography

American Psychiatric Association. (2013). *Diagnostic and Statistical Manual of Mental Disorders* (5th ed). Washington, DC: American Psychological Association.

Barad, K. (2007). *Meeting the Universe Halfway: Quantum Physics and the Entanglement of Matter and Meaning*. Durham, NC: Duke University Press.

Baril, A. (2015). 'transness as debility: rethinking intersections between trans and disabled embodiments' *Feminist Review*, 111(1): 59–74.

Clare, E. (2013). *Body Pride, Body Shame: Lessons from the Disability Rights Movement* (A.Z. Aizura and S. Stryker, eds). New York: Taylor & Francis.

Davy, Z. (2015). 'The DSM-5 and the politics of diagnosing transpeople', *Archives of Sexual Behavior*, 44(5): 1165–1176.

Engdahl, U. (2014). 'Wrong Body', *TSQ: Transgender Studies Quarterly*, 1(1–2—Postposttranssexual: Key Concepts for a Twenty-First-Century Transgender Studies): 267–269.

Global Action for Trans Equality. (2013). '*Critique and Alternative Proposal to the "Gender Incongruence of Childhood" Category in ICD-11*'. Retrieved from https://globaltransaction.files.wordpress.com/2012/03/critique-and-alternative-proposal-to-the-_gender-incongruence-of-childhood_-category-in-icd-11.pdf.

Halberstam, J. (2017). *Trans: a Quick and Quirky Account of Gender Variability*. Berkeley, CA: University Of California Press.

Hall, K.Q. (2015). 'Gender'. In R. Adams, B. Reiss, and D. Serlin (eds), *Keywords for Disability Studies*:255–261. New York: New York University Press.

Hughes, B., and Paterson, K. (1997). 'The social model of disability and the disappearing body: towards a sociology of impairment', *Disability & Society*, 12(3): 325–340.

Entangled Theorising 75

Johar Schueller, M. (2005). 'Analogy and (white) feminist theory: Thinking race and the color of the cyborg body', *Signs: Journal of Women in Culture and Society*, 31(1): 63–92.

Kafer, A. (2013). *Feminist, Queer, Crip*. Bloomington, IN: Indiana University Press.

Krieg, J. (2013). 'A Social Model of Trans and Crip Theory', *Lambda Nordica*, 3(4): 33–53.

McRuer, R. (2006). *Crip Theory: Cultural Signs of Queerness and Disability*. New York: New York University Press.

McRuer, R. (2018). *Crip Times: Disability, Globalization, and Resistance*. New York: New York University Press.

McRuer, R., and Mollow, A. (2012). *Sex and Disability*. Durham, NC: Duke University Press.

Mitchell, D.T. and Snyder, S.L. (2004). *The Body and Physical Difference: Discourses of Disability*. Ann Arbor, MI: University of Michigan Press.

Puar, J.K. (2017). *The Right to Maim: Debility, Capacity, Disability*. Durham, NC: Duke University Press.

Samuels, E. (2011). 'Critical Divides: Judith Butler's Body Theory and the Question of Disability'. In K.Q. Hall (Ed.), *Feminist Disability Studies*: 48–66. Bloomington, IN: Indiana University Press.

Spade, D. (2003). 'Resisting medicine, re/modeling gender', *Berkeley Women's L.J.*, *18*(15).

Suess, A., Espineira, K., and Walters, P.C. (2014). 'Depathologization', *TSQ: Transgender Studies Quarterly*, 1(1–2—Postposttranssexual: Key Concepts for a Twenty-First-Century Transgender Studies): 73–76.

Transgender Europe. (2018). '*Joint Statement: Being trans is not a mental disorder anymore: ICD-11 is officially released*', 18 June. Retrieved from https://tgeu.org/joint-statement-being-trans-is-not-a-mental-disorder-anymore-icd-11-is-officially-released/

Waterlander, A. (2018). '*Drie UU-gebouwen krijgen genderneutraal toilet*', 1 May. Retrieved from www.dub.uu.nl/nl/nieuws/drie-uu-gebouwen-krijgen-genderneutraal-toilet.

West, I. (2010). 'PISSAR's Critically Queer and Disabled Politics', *Communication and Critical/Cultural Studies*, Vol. 7, Issue 2: 156–175.

World Health Organization. (2018). '*WHO releases new International Classification of Diseases (ICD 11)*', 18 June. Retrieved from www.who.int/news-room/detail/17-06-2018-who-releases-new-international-classification-of-diseases-(icd-11).

5 The (Re)production of (In)equality in Italy

Feminisms and reproductive labour in the era of populism

Elia A.G. Arfini and Beatrice Busi

Introduction[1]

Drawing on the history of the feminist movement and the contemporary Italian debate, this chapter reflects on the case of reproductive labour as a site for the production of political cultures of (in)equality. Historically, Italian feminism (Andall and Puwar, 2007; Bono and Kemp, 1991; Parati and West, 2002) has been organised around the concept of 'difference' rather than equality and has been, particularly during the 1970s, a mass social movement initiating profound societal and legislative transformations. However at the present time, Italy still ranks low in most measurable indicators commonly associated with the evaluation of gender equality (implementation of gender equality plans, gender pay gaps, gender-based violence, political and economic equal decision making, etc.) and is currently placed below the European Union-28 (EU) average on the Gender Equality Index for 2015 compiled by the European Institute for Gender Equality and in the lower ranks (24th place among the 28 states) in the domain of care activities.

By combining a genealogical perspective on Italian feminisms, current statistical data, and feminist political theory, here we look at reproductive labour as a paradigmatic case for a gendered reading of the crisis (Walby, 2015) in its intersection with class and racial inequalities. Reproductive labour has been a major area of feminist contestation since the 1970s, and has recently gained a renewed attention in feminist materialist analyses. Within Europe, Italian women spend the highest amount of time on domestic work (*Harmonised European Time Use Survey, 2005–2007*). Contemporary feminist struggles must work against the backdrop of the national political situation throughout the decade spanning the mid-2010s and into the 2020s, which has been characterised by a crisis of left-wing political parties and union organiaations and by the rise of sovereigntism, populism, nativism and conservative Catholic forces. Paired with the reduction in welfare spending and austerity measures, such a landscape has intensified both the neofundamentalist re-domesticisation of reproductive labour and its neoliberal externalisation to the racialised labour market of care work.

The chapter opens with a brief overview of the strand of Italian feminism known as the thought of sexual difference (*pensiero della differenza sessuale*) (Muraro, 1991; Diotima, 2003 [1987]), where we highlight the critical relationship

The (Re)production of (In)equality in Italy   77

of hegemonic Italian feminism with the concept of equality. In the second section we focus on a different and minoritarian strand of materialist feminism, inspired by Marxism, that first brought the issue of unpaid reproductive labour at the core of the analysis and struggle with the Wages for Housework campaign. The third section presents an overview of the political, legislative and institutional evolution of the country following the period during the 1960s and 1970s social movements and second-wave feminism, as well as the most significant current statistical data on paid and unpaid reproductive labour. In the final section, we provide a critical discussion of the concept of the feminisation of work and on contemporary feminist movements in Italy, with particular attention to their intersectional alliances and the transnational circulation of political cultures. We conclude by arguing that Italian feminist critiques of equality, which are understood as parity, inclusion, representation, protection of a minority or efficiency in the late capitalist project of economic growth, represent the distinguishing features of a feminist political culture that is currently under the pressure of populism and economic crisis, but also ambitious in its intersectional and radical scope.

Italian feminist difference

While a genealogy of Italian feminism is beyond the scope of this chapter, in this section we will provide a brief overview of Italian feminist thought in order to underline how – since the early 1960s – all of the most influential and transformative strands of Italian feminism have distanced themselves from the concept of gender equality. This stance was characterised not simply by the disinvestment from institutional forms of politics such as lobbying or parliamentary representation: a radical critique of the concept of equality served to articulate a revolutionary struggle against the patriarchy. In the politically charged task of telling feminist stories (Hemmings, 2011), feminism's relationships with the concept of equality is often employed as a narrative organizing tool:

> Western feminist theory tells its own story as a developmental narrative, where we move from a preoccupation with unity and sameness, through identity and diversity, and on to difference and fragmentation (Hemmings, 2015: 115–16).

Different understandings of equality organise feminist narratives in an orderly way that frames progressively complex theories of women's oppression and strategies to overcome it. The evolution of the concept of equality, in particular, proceeds from an aspiration to sameness to a struggle for the preservation of differences under equal social condition. A nuanced and advanced feminist theory would prove that equality does not mean sameness, nor the homologation of women to masculinity. Accordingly, in 1998 the Council of Europe clarified that:

> Gender equality is not synonymous with sameness, with establishing men, their life style and conditions as the norm. [...] Gender equality means

78 *Theorising Cultures of Equality*

accepting and valuing equally the differences between women and men and the diverse roles they play in society.

(Council of Europe, 1998: 7–8).

It is interesting to note how equality is defended here by reference to its effects on the individual dimension of existence. While gender equality has been, especially in the history of European gender mainstreaming, a guiding principle for policy making aimed at structural societal change, its validity and desirability are predicated upon an argument that rests on the effects of equality on individual gender roles and 'life style' (Ibid.: ivi.). We argue that the critique of equality put forward by Italian feminism bypasses the issue of role homogenisation or preservation of individual differences. Even when equality does not mean sameness, political cultures of equality still remain problematic in their consequences – or lack of thereof – at the structural level. For radical feminists, the question to be asked was not simply 'equal to whom?' but rather 'equal within what kind of society?'.

While in Italian language 'equality' and 'sameness' do translate with the same single word [*uguaglianza*], the work of Carla Lonzi demonstrates there was no slippage in the analysis. Lonzi, art historian and founding member of the Rivolta Femminile collective in Rome, contributed to the Manifesto (Manifesto di Rivolta Femminile, 1970) that appeared on the walls of the city of Rome in July 1970. The Manifesto is a bullet point summary of statements around which the largest part of feminist organising had and would mobilise in the country: the radical difference of women and their autonomy from men, the critique of marriage, but also of divorce ('Divorce is a grafting of marriages that ends up reinforcing the institution'—Ibid: ivi), the pivotal role of sexual freedom for a feminist politics of liberation, the struggle against unpaid care work, as well as the exclusionary nature of class struggle founded solely on the master–slave dialectic.

Within such a revolutionary framework, a struggle for equality is inadequate for a politics of liberation. In her seminal work *Sputiamo su Hegel*, Lonzi maintains that equality is 'a women's right to participate in the management of power following the recognition that she has equal capacity to that of a man' (Lonzi, 1970: 14). Thus, the critique of equality was not based on the incorrect conflation of equality with sameness, nor could it be put at rest by the clarification that diverse gender roles in society will still be valued once equality is achieved. For Lonzi and other feminists, the greatest feminist achievement and the foundational realisation of feminist liberation is the devaluation of the masculine world. For them, it was necessary not to struggle for the participation in existing structures of power, but to question those very structures, which were eventually entering a crisis. Why should women, Lonzi asks, 'deem [it] gratifying to participate in the great defeat of the man?' (Lonzi, 1970: 23). In this sense, a politics of equality is not only inadequate, but actually detrimental to the feminist project, because it reinforces the structural conditions of patriarchy, by glorifying them as the ultimate offering of the hegemonic group to the colonised and oppressed.

The anti-integrationist stance of the late 1960s feminist collectives clashed with the emancipatory politics of existing institutional groups, which were deemed to have insufficient autonomy from political parties and unable to deal with the profound transformations of post-war Italian society. A critique of equality politics was a unifying trait of many vanguard groups (such as Anabasi [Anabasis] in Milan) in the late 1960s, including the influential Milan-based group DEMAU (Demistificazione Autoritarismo) [Anti-Authoritarian Demystification], whose first programmatic point of their Manifesto was the 'opposition to the concept of integration of women in existing society' (DEMAU in Spagnoletti, 1971: 62 [1966]). By the early 1970s, alongside the widespread social turmoil of students' and workers' contestation initiated in 1968, the majority of feminist groups in Italy organised in separatist groups – intentionally kept small – around the practice of consciousness raising (*autocoscienza*). Relying on the understanding that the personal is political, the practice of consciousness-raising was based on the narration of personal experiences made together with other women (Fraire, 2002 [1978]). Influenced by French feminisms (in particular by the writings of Luce Irigaray and by the practices of the Politique et Psychanalyse group and its leader, Antoinette Fouque), these experiences would face complex internal evolutions and eventually form what is known as the thought of sexual difference (*pensiero della differenza sessuale*). This strand of Italian feminism had its epicentre in Milan and soon became hegemonic in the field. The theoretical and political capital produced in those years would influence Italian feminism to this day, elaborating experiences such as the practice of unconscious, philosophical proposals centred on the symbolic order of the mother, the practice of affidamento (literally 'entrustment' – a female mentorship model of relationship with a 'symbolic mother'), reflections on the ethics of care and the construction of a feminine philosophical system and literary canon, as well as the foundation of the Libreria delle donne di Milano (Milan Women's Bookstore) in 1975 and the philosophical community of Diotima in Verona in 1983. In 1987 the Libreria delle donne di Milano, an influential group, published a foundational book that recounts the experiences of local groups from 1966. It was translated into English in 1990. Contemporary reviews of the translation by Patricia Cicogna and Teresa de Lauretis, entitled *Sexual Difference: A Theory of Social-Symbolic Practice*, are critical of the fact that the book seemed not to take notice of the division between libertarians, radical, lesbian, or other strands of feminism, nor to the issues of race, class and disability (Green, 1992). In those days Italian feminist thought indeed escaped many canonical typologies of feminist narratives.

The concept of difference in Italian feminist thought, in particular, has resisted clear-cut categorisations, including its evaluation in terms of essentialism, but it fundamentally rests on the construction of a form of female autonomy in which equality has little value. Female autonomy, in this framework, is the space of freedom for a unified female subject, united under sexual difference and autonomous from men and male hegemony in parties and institutions. In this space, feminists came to the realisation that 'the prospect of becoming real equals with the opposite sex lost its attraction' (Milan

80 *Theorising Cultures of Equality*

Womens' Bookstore Collective, 1990: 52). Luisa Muraro, the most prominent intellectual associated with the Milan groups, claimed 'I am not against equality but against the kind of politics that makes equality its goal. I maintain that sexual equality is not a feminist goal' (Muraro, 2002: 77).

Notwithstanding the fierce distancing from equality politics, the 1960s and 1970s were years of profound reformation of legislative domains related to gender politics. 'Law 75', introduced in 1958 (Legge Merlin), for example, repeals all norms related to the state control of sex work, and the law on paid domestic work – which regulates the area to this day – was introduced in the same year by the initiative of Christian Democracy members of parliament. In 1963 women were admitted to careers in public offices; in 1971 contraception was legalised; in 1974 the referendum on divorce passed with 59% of the popular vote; and in 1975 the reform on family rights (Law 151) was passed, and Planned Parenthood (consultori famigliari) was instituted. Law 903 on the equal treatment ofmen and women in labour was passed in 1977, and in 1978 Law 194 was introduced to regulate access to abortion, which until then had been, according to the fascist-based penal code, a crime against the race.

Marxist feminism and the Wages for Housework network

The issue of female autonomy and refusal of emancipatory politics was also central in what is characterised as the second strand of Italian feminism. This group were inspired by Marxist readings of the female condition and emerged from the experience of extra-parliamentary radical left groups. The separation of these women's groups from the larger, mixed collectives was not without tension: female comrades were accused of being divisive, of detracting energy from the class struggle to privilege issues that were deemed either of minor importance or were cross-cutting class divisions, such as the issue of violence or abortion, which spoke to women of all classes. Indeed, Marxist feminists who would organise around the campaign of Wages for Housework (*Salario al lavoro domestico*) aimed, as we will see, at mobilising not only the working class housewife, but women in any household condition and type of relationships with men, including lesbians and sex workers.

Central to this strand of feminism was the construction of women's autonomy based on a materialist reading of the female condition. The achievement of autonomy would need to start not with the reconfiguration of the symbolic order but with economic autonomy. Marxist feminist analyses centred around the role of reproductive labour in the capitalist system: the labour force, upon which capital accumulation depends, needs to be produced and reproduced. Reproductive work is structured around and predicated on care-giving and domestic tasks, such as cleaning, cooking and child and elder care, which were provided by women but not remunerated. In order not only to transform women's condition, but to bring about a revolutionary class struggle, it is thus necessary to recognise reproductive work as productive work. Demanding a salary for the work of reproduction became the political perspective that organised Italian Marxist feminism from the early 1970s.

The(Re)production of (In)equality in Italy 81

The seminal group, Movimento di Lotta Femminile (Women's Struggle Movement), which quickly changed its name to Lotta Femminista (Feminist Struggle), was founded in Padua in 1971. Under the leadership of Mariarosa Dalla Costa, who had earlier been involved in the extra-parliamentary group Potere Operaio (Workers' Power), Dalla Costa's book *Potere femminile e sovversione sociale* (translated in English as *The Power of Women and the Subversion of the Community*), which includes writings by Selma James, was published in 1972 and quickly gained national and international attention. In July 1972 Lotta Femminista launched an international meeting in Padua, with the involvement of Selma James (United Kingdom), Brigitte Galtier (France) and Silvia Federici (USA) (Toupin, 2014; Federici and Arlen, 2017).

This was the founding assembly of the International Feminist Collective/Collectif féministe international/Collettivo femminista internazionale (1972–77) which, starting from 1974, adopted the Wages for Housework Campaign as an organisational strategy to lead or intersect the struggles against exploitation of women's labour, inside or outside the household. Issues addressed included family allowances and alimony payments; housing and social services, especially in the UK, Switzerland, USA and Canada; free abortion and women's health, especially in Italy; and the improvement of the working conditions of nurses and waitresses, especially in the UK and Canada.

In the following years, several collectives in Italy would organise around the campaign, including groups in Naples, Rome and Ferrara.

Wages for Housework, in fact, was not meant to be simply a campaign to introduce welfare provision, but rather a broader political perspective aimed at uncovering the role of reproductive work in capitalist accumulation and refusing the emancipative model centred on women's participation in the paid workforce. In this sense, this feminist Wages for Housework campaign was actually meant to be a campaign against housework and labour in general. This strategy reveals the affinity of the movement to Workerist thought, according to which class struggle has to be organised at the point of production and without the mediation of intermediary institutional actors such as conventional unions. Similarly of Workerist origin is the focus on increasing wages and reducing working hours as the most pressing issues of conflict. Perhaps the most important cultural politics that Wages for Housework shares with the Workerist movement is the refusal of labour. Contrary to the tradition of the institutional left, in which labour and work ethics are the source of positive identification for the working class, the Italian autonomous movement rejects the idea that waged work must be a pre-condition to access citizenship rights and social and economic justice. This theoretical approach would inform radical and innovative practices of political action – including insubordination, sabotage and strike actions in the factories – and, in general, to promote forms of self-organisation of workers in which immediate demands were always couched within a broader horizon of revolutionary liberation from work and the end of capitalism.

The refusal of work, and, specifically, the culture of disidentification from work, is particularly relevant for the Wages for Housework movement. Silvia

82   *Theorising Cultures of Equality*

Federici wrote an influential document in 1975 (Federici, 1975), which was translated into Italian in 1976 by the Neapolitan feminist chapter of the network. The strategy of drawing a parallel between waged labour and housework is central to the argument:

> They say it is love. We say it is unwaged work. / They call it frigidity. We call it absenteeism. / Every miscarriage is a work accident. [...] / Neuroses, suicides, desexualisation: occupational diseases of the housewife.
> (Federici, 1975: 1).

However, between housework and paid work there are also important qualitative differences. The role of the housewife is here seen as a peculiar form of alienation, originated by the necessity to naturalise reproductive work as a 'labour of love'. Constructing a natural feminine ethics of care as an essential attribute and aspiration, removes reproductive work from the public sphere and impedes the possibility of framing it into a negotiable, albeit unfair, form of social and legal contract under capitalism. The naturalisation of what others called the 'feminine mystique' (Friedan, 1963), has historically prevented women from struggling against it in a collective organised way: 'we are seen as nagging bitches, not workers in struggle' (Federici, 1975: 3). In this sense, Wages for Housework is not an economistic and utilitarian struggle, not simply because of its ultimately revolutionary goals, but also because it does recognise the affective and embodied dimension of care work in at least two ways. First in a negative sense, by unveiling how the socialisation to certain emotions and desires, including the desire to become mothers, is constructed in order to recruit women into their reproductive roles, and secondly in a positive sense, by foreseeing a new form of social and economic arrangement where care, desire and sexuality, are domains of life liberated from their oppressive consequences for everybody, including men.

Wages for Housework was thus innovative in its intersectional scope. Lesbian groups affiliated with the network grew after 1975 in San Francisco and Philadelphia in the USA, London in the UK and Toronto in Canada. Organised under the name Wages Due Lesbians, these groups worked at the intersection of gender, class and sexuality. Lesbians, they argued, were disproportionally unemployed and faced barriers in accessing better paid jobs, owing to homophobia in the labour market; those who had children from previous heterosexual relationships risked child custody rights after coming out; others could not leave their marriages for lack of economic independence. Wages Due Lesbians were particularly effective in exposing the economic injustice associated with homosexuality, understood lesbianism as a choice against patriarchy and capitalism and demanded compensation for 'the additional physical and emotional housework of surviving in a hostile and prejudiced society, recognized as work and paid for so all women have the economic power to afford sexual choices'.

The intersectional and transnational dimension of Wages for Housework also builds alliances with the sex workers' movement. The first organised group of sex workers was founded in San Francisco in 1973 under the name 'Coyote' (an acronym of Call Off Your Old Tired Ethics), and the English Collective of Prostitutes was formed in 1975. In the Italian context, the issue is documented as a point of discussion (Tatafiore, 1994: 2), but the first organised group – Comitato per i diritti civili delle prostitute (Committee for the civil rights of prostitutes) – was not founded until 1982, by Carla Corso and Pia Covre in Pordenone, which is a small town in the north-east of Italy where sex workers were particularly exposed to violence perpetrated by US military personnel deployed at the nearby Air Force base of Aviano. These groups focused mainly on the issue of rights for prostitutes and the decriminalisation of sex work, but also found in the Wages for Housework network an alliance around the strategy of work recognition. If reproductive sex was considered the central task of housework because it ensures the reproduction of the labour force, sex work performed outside the household demanded recognition as work too. These groups projected an empowering representation of sex workers as women who – despite suffering from oppression and specific forms of vulnerability – were not helpless victims of trafficking but working class women in search of economic independence.

Recognising care work as work would have been the tipping point of the revolution, by virtue of the profound impact that it would have on the relationship between the public and private sphere and the cost of labour on productivity and profit and on the relationship between the sexes. However, within the institutional and legislative domain at that time, further steps were being taken towards the politics of emancipation through work. The feminist movement in general, including Wages for Housework, remained relatively silent about the introduction of Law 903 on equal treatment between men and women in labour in 1977. Entering the workforce meant, at best, earmarking the salary earned to outsource care work or, at worse, working double shifts.

Gender care gap

Wages for Housework, although ambitious in its revolutionary, transnational and intersectional character, remained in a subaltern position to the hegemonic separatist strand of Italian feminism and eventually faded away by 1980. As we will see, once the radical wave of struggles lost momentum, the prevailing idea became that of emancipation and female accomplishment to be achieved through paid labour outside the household. A variety of systemic factors had been rapidly evolving. Economically, the so-called 'economic miracle' – launched by the USA's post-war Marshall Plan of foreign aid – ended in 1973 with the oil crisis. A phase of progressive impoverishment began, followed by a period of increase in prices, slow economic growth and high unemployment. Politically, the era of social movements of the 1970s suffered from a wave of state repression following the intensification of social conflict, including its armed variety into the early 1980s.

The bipolar political model – characterised by alternating governments of two coalitions led by the centre-left Christian Democracy or by the far-left Italian Communist Party – entered a crisis of legitimation and representativeness. The

84   *Theorising Cultures of Equality*

crisis of this institutional and political model exploded in the 1990s with the corruption scandal of Tangentopoli. The 'Second Republic' thus began with novel political forces and parties in the field, including the media entrepreneur Silvio Berlusconi and the separatist\federalist Lega Nord (Northern League) party. A crucial transformation for Italy took place at the European level: in 1997 Italy entered the Schengen area, and its economic politics have since then been accountable to the larger European system. In 2012, with public debt out of control and facing the risk of default, the Italian Constitution was modified in order to introduce the balanced budget amendment. This constituted the institutional backdrop for all further austerity policies, including reductions in public spending on welfare, education and healthcare. The political crisis trickled down to the trade unions, and a long era of unionised negotiation between workers and the entrepreneurial class ended.

During the Berlusconi premiership (1994, 2001–11), a novel form of political leadership emerged, based on the individualisation, spectacularisation and sexualisation of politics, aided by the emergence of private television first and social media later. Accordingly, the Italian feminism debate in those years focused mostly on the problem of representation of gender roles in the media (Gribaldo e Zapperi, 2012). The current political scenario is symptomatic of the crisis of the role of mediation of the political-institutional class and is characterised by the decline of left-wing political parties and union organisations and by the rise of sovereigntism, populism and nativism. The influencing role of the Church also appears to be transformed. On the one hand, Catholic moderate forces do not have a form of direct representation in the government since the dissolution of Christian Democracy Party; on the other, fundamentalist conservative forces are emerging with unprecedented radical force. Often in contrast to the moderate Vatican position and closer to neo-fascist groups, these neo-fundamentalist associations mobilise as a 'new minority' to be protected against abortion, marriage equality, same-sex parenting, lesbian, gay, bisexual, transgender and queer (LGBTQ) rights and the teaching of gender studies (Zappino, 2017).

In terms of the historical evolution of women's condition, emancipatory politics based on the equality framework – including those promoted by the EU – helped Italian women to enter the workforce. Overall, their formal participation rose from 26% in 1951 to 41% in 2011 (ISTAT, 2015). The model of dual-earning became hegemonic, and women entered the workforce in a variety of novel sectors, including the tertiary sector. Care work began to be outsourced to the market, in the form of services or domestic paid workers, often migrants (initially internal (female) migrants from southern Italy, but since the mid-1970s often employing a feminised foreign migrant workforce as the country entered positive net migration). Fertility rates dropped (from 2.65 children per woman in 1964 to 1.34 in 2016), and the population aged: Italy's ageing index is currently estimated to be the highest among EU-28 countries (168.7 elderly people for every 100 young people in 2018, compared with just 37.6 in 1960) (ISTAT, 2018b). Alongside the political, fiscal and financial crisis, the country entered a crisis of social reproduction.

The (Re)production of (In)equality in Italy   85

Current data on domestic work confirms the gendered nature of the crisis. Within Europe, Italian women spend the highest amount of time doing domestic work (*Harmonised European Time Use Survey, 2005–2007*). According to the latest data of the National Institute for Statistics on time use (ISTAT, 2016), the gender gap in housework begins at age 11–14, when girls begin to devote 13 more minutes per day to reproductive labour than boys. Data thus confirms the feminist interpretation of socialisation into stereotypically gendered roles during childhood. The gap consolidates between the ages of 25 and 64, when family work constitutes an average of 5 hours, 13 minutes of a woman's day compared with 1 hour, 50 minutes of a man's. The gap also persists in dual-wage households, albeit to a lesser extent. Men devote more time to waged labour, but women workers add to their day of work another 3 hours, 52 minutes of their time to reproductive labour, thus working – waged and unwaged –one hour more per day than men. Free time for working women is thus reduced to 13.5% of the day, as opposed to 17% for men.

In recent times (2009–14) the gender gap in total work has reduced, owing to the simultaneous contraction of male employment following the economic crisis and the stability of female employment (stable at about 50%). Based on 2014 figures, in couples of 25–44 years of age, with children and both parents employed, 67.3% of reproductive work is carried out by women. This represents an improvement in the gender gap, most of which is accounted for by childcare. Fathers are indeed increasingly taking care of their children and even surpass women in time devoted to playtime with the children. However, housework – cleaning and cooking – and care for the elderly is still done by women by 74%, or 3 hours, 1 minute every day, compared with 57% contributed by men.

Change is also unequally distributed along class and geographical lines. The gap is reduced in the north of Italy and among women holding a university degree, presumably owing to their higher leverage and capacity of negotiation. But it is also lower in working class families, where monetary and working hour limits do not allow families to outsource care work or reproductive labour, or for women to perform care work during their working hours, thus leaving men contributing to reproductive labour as the only viable option. Welfare provision for parental leave is among the most scarce in Europe: maternal leave is paid at 30% of salary, and the statutory paternal leave allowance just one day (plus two optional days). Other services for the reconciliation of life and work are largely provided by local services and in particular by municipalities. Public spending on elders and persons with disabilities is 40% lower than the European average. In terms of services to children, in 2002 the EU set the goal that childcare should be provided for one-third of children under three. Data from 2012 for Italy reveal a disproportionate coverage, ranging from 29% in the north-east area to 13.4% in the south and the islands.

Outsourcing carework is not an easily economically accessible option (CENSIS, 2013). According to the 2013 census, the majority of families would be interested in purchasing care services on the market, but do not, mainly for economic reasons (21.2% of respondents). The economic cost in these cases is

86 *Theorising Cultures of Equality*

outsourced to family caregivers, who either quit or reduce their paid work or cease looking for paid employment (about 20% of Italian families declare a dependant elder or person with disability in the household). In 90.4% of cases, this family caregiver is a woman. Despite the economic cost, the sector of domestic paid work has undergone a rapid expansion since the 1990s: between 1995 and 2013 it increased by fivefold, also following the increase in migration. According to the Ministry of Labour and Social Politics in 2018, more than 60% of paid domestic workers are currently non-EU migrants from Ukraine (22.9%), the Philippines (16.0%), Moldavia (10.7%), Peru (76.9%) and Sri Lanka (6.3%). In 2017 a total of 87.8% of paid domestic workers were women. In 2015–17 an estimated total of between 864,526 and 886,126 paid domestic workers were regularly employed, of whom 87% were women and 44% were from eastern Europe (INPS, 2018). Current labour regulation fixes salaries in four levels with retributions ranging from €4.54 to €8.07 per hour or from €625 per month to €1,373 per month for live-in care workers. However, sociological analyses point towards a massive incidence of off the book work, and ISTAT estimates that the weight of the unreported employment in care services is about 50% (ISTAT, 2018). Paid domestic workers are employed mostly in elderly care (21.4%), working in care for dependent elders (21.5%) and in childcare (21.8%), as well as in personal care to non-dependent adults (32.9%). Employers are largely (27.7%) couples without children (19.2%), with a net monthly income ranging from €2,000 to €4,000 (42.4%). Families choose to outsource reproductive labour mostly (57.8%) in order to reconcile life and work, and only to a lesser extent for the need of a special type assistance (16%) or for family tradition (7.3%) (CENSIS, 2013). For many families, outsourcing care work is not a luxury: in 2014 a total of 333,000 families used all their savings to pay for assistance for a dependant elder, 190,000 families sold their house to find the economic resources to fund this, and 152,000 families took out loans to pay for care (CENSIS, 2015).

Feminisation of work and the paradigm of reproduction

An overall assessment of data available on the gender care gap thus reveals a marked persistence of women's disproportionate involvement in reproductive work, increasingly segmented along racial and ethnic lines. Feminist debates on labour in Italy, however, left the issue relatively unaddressed until recently and focused instead on the issue of the feminisation of work. The concept of the feminisation of work emerged in the late 1990s, within analyses of the transformation of modes of production in post-Fordism, and gained popularity throughout the following decade, when readings of the transition towards neoliberalism and the precarisation of work became increasingly urgent. Despite its vast diffusion in the sociological, economic and policy literature, it remains a conceptual category marked by a problematic ambiguity. We can indeed trace at least two ways in which work is understood as to have become 'feminized': in a sociological sense, referring to the increase of women in the workforce and in traditionally male lines of job, the shrinking of industrial labour and the

The(Re)production of (In)equality in Italy   87

expansion of markets with a predominantly female workforce (e.g. care services, education, office work, nursing, human resources), which often pay lower salaries. Alongside these uses, there is eventually another, markedly political, use of the concept, promoted in particular by the Italian Post-Workerist or Neo-Workerist school. One of the most influential works by Italian feminists in the debate on the feminisation of work is Capital and Affects: The Politics of the Language Economy by the economist Christian Marazzi (2011). In this text, Marazzi discusses the centrality of the Marxist notion of 'living labour' (Marx, 1887: 163) in the post-Fordist era and identifies its ultimate expression in the relational aspects implied in domestic and care work. As Cristina Borderias argues:

> The concept of the feminization of work is increasingly used as the entry point into the new economy of capacities recognized as "feminine" (either "essential" or acquired as the result of "historical and cultural experiences"): "immaterial labour, cognitive, communication and relational skills" until now associated to jobs performed by women in the family and in the so-called "traditionally female sectors.
>
> (Borderias, 2006)

Many feminist scholars and activists have since adopted this reading (Ongaro, 2001; Nannicini, 2002; Morini, 2010) to point to a novel intersection between patriarchy and capitalism that takes place in the extension of the domestic sphere and of reproductive labour to society at large, and in the acceleration of processes of precarisation. Against an interpretation of the feminisation of work as a general downgrading of the quality of work, a further interpretation of the transformation of production is provided by the Milan Women's Bookstore on the pages of the issue-manifesto of the *Sottosopra* journal entitled *Immagina che il lavoro* (Imagine that work). Here, the traditional refusal of equality in the name of sexual difference becomes a 'double yes' to flexibility in the public work sphere and to maternity, which are seen as choices conducive of freedom and female self-accomplishment, valorising women's affective free labour as a measure for a new mode of development:

> We want to be able to say yes to labour and yes to maternity without feeling forced to choose. When we say yes to labour we say yes to an aspect of living that is the necessary money to buy food, clothes, housing. But it also means accomplishment, growth, invention, social project. We don't want to be excluded from this if we choose to become mothers.

We argue that the exclusive focus on the qualities of (re)productive labour and on the transformations of new modes of production and organisation of labour within the knowledge economy has paradoxically obscured the materiality of working conditions of women inside and outside the labour market, as well as the construction of new inequalities between men and women in the racial segmentation of domestic and care work.

88   *Theorising Cultures of Equality*

Responding to the European Commission's recommendations and directives, since 1992 Italy has introduced a variety of work-life balance initiatives. Most interventions focused on increasing flexibility (such as part-time working hours, reduced hours, telework schemes or job-sharing) and on rights for paid leave and parental leave, which were introduced in 2000 (Saraceno and Naldini, 2011). In the framework of a traditionally family-based welfare system, which is still heavily based on the male breadwinner model despite the increase of dual-earning families, these interventions are primarily focused on reconciling women's paid work and unpaid care work. For men, the main tool for the reconciliation of life and work is still represented by the unpaid work of social reproduction performed by women.

Centre-left governments in Italy (1996–2001, 2006–08, 2013–18) adopted a neoliberal approach to the socialisation of domestic labour that is based on the purchase of services on the market and the reduction of public spending on childcare and elder care services. Initiated before the 2007–08 global financial crisis, this route towards a neoliberal public gender regime (Walby, 2015: 148–9) has been paired with subsequent austerity measures that incentivised access to private solutions of outsourcing, often to low-paid undocumented migrant caregivers working off the books.

The more recent right-wing interpretations of work-life balance can be placed along this trend. The current populist wave rests on the cultural repertoire of traditional gender roles. The programmatic political document of the 2018 government, entitled 'Contract for a Government of Change' and signed by the Lega and Movimento 5 Stelle parties, mentions 'women' and 'mothers' in the section on 'Family and fertility politics':

> It is necessary to adopt effective family policies, to ensure that women can reconcile family and work time, also with the introduction of services and adequate income support. Moreover, it is necessary to program: the increase of maternity allowance, an economic incentive to women resuming their jobs after maternity leaves, tax reliefs for businesses that keep mothers at work after they have given birth.

Although there is no occurrence of the term 'gender', we find the word 'woman' mentioned once, in the section on a policy that would allow women aged 57–58 who have at least 35 years of pension contributions to retire earlier, with a pension reduced by 30%. This is an 'experimental' reconciliation policy that was actually introduced in 2004 during the second Berlusconi Government under the name the 'Woman Option' (*Opzione Donna*). The pension reform currently proposed by the government will favour men, in 90% of eligible cases: women will be disproportionately ineligible because they generally have lower wages and intermittent paid jobs and pension contributions.

Ironically, the concept of equality has only recently been mobilised by the government in order to promote an alarming family law decree (the 'Pillon Decree') on shared child custody. The Decree would introduce compulsory

The (Re)production of (In)equality in Italy 89

family mediation in all separation cases. The burden of paying for the mediation must be shared equally. The Decree also stipulates that the child must be guaranteed an equal dual-parenting arrangement, where maintenance is equally paid directly between the parties. Before legal settlement can be achieved, a child, even when a victim of violence, will be required to see the abusing parent. Disregarding the widespread inequality in labour conditions and women's disproportionate responsibilities in family care, the Decree fails to acknowledge economic inequality between the members of a couple; indeed, as Saraceno argues: 'promoted as a value that distinguishes "our culture" from that of "migrants", gender equality […] is used to avoid paying alimony checks' (Saraceno, 2018). The Pillon Decree met widespread opposition from a variety of civil society actors guided by anti-violence centres network and a (trans)feminist movement, Non Una Di Meno (Not One Less). However, regardless of the extent to which the decree will be implemented in future, it remains a bewilderingly specious use of equality that, in fact, provides an avenue for economic abuse, restricts access to divorce and exposes women and children to a greater risk of domestic violence. In summary, it is a paradigmatic example of how right-wing populism reinforces and renaturalises the racial and sexual boundaries of the 'nation' (Garbagnoli, 2018).

In the past few years, the feminist movement has organised in a new wave of global struggles, from the social and general strike promoted by the Argentinian Ni Una Menos (Not One Less) movement in 2017, to the #Metoo campaigns against gender-based violence. The structural character of male violence is considered by this movement as the core of the oppressive alliance between patriarchy, neoliberalism and racism. In this frame, the resurgence of feminist presence in the public sphere in Italy also demonstrated a renewed interest in the issues of production and reproduction and in the experience of Wages for Housework. Particular attention was devoted to the invention of feminist interpretations of the classic action of labour strike (Transnational Social Strike Platform, 2018), aimed at bringing strike actions to modes of production usually seen as private, natural, individual or immaterial, such as care work and emotional labour (Hochschild, 1983). Militant theoretical analyses of the centrality of unpaid reproductive work in the process of capitalist accumulation have become the guiding idea between feminisms in different contexts, together with the attention to working conditions of paid domestic workers (Federici, 2018; Segato, 2017).

We argue that these recent analyses underscore the centrality in contemporary feminist practices and theories of intersectional readings of male violence against women, the exploitation of reproductive work and migrant labour, as well as precarity and racism and their structural role in the architecture of late capitalism and its crisis. Surpassing individualised versions of hashtag feminism and a form of political subjectivation of women as only victims of violence, contemporary Italian feminism movements are engaged in an intersectional reading of gender-based violence. The #metoo hashtag has been turned into the #wetogether claim by a feminist movement that is attempting

90　*Theorising Cultures of Equality*

to expand the resonance of its scope and frame. An unprecedented and innovative intersection between trans and feminist standpoints has characterised the most recent grassroots mobilisations, in which gender-based violence is seen as a multi-faced form of violence that originates not simply from men, but from gender binarism itself. Pairing the classic sociological understanding of 'gender as a social structure' (Riesman, 2004) with a political understanding 'society as a gendered structure', contemporary Italian feminist movements continue to push beyond the concept of equality or to use it as a negative term of reference, in order to expand and radicalise their scope of action.

Conclusion

As highlighted by the Council of Europe, the EU is currently facing 'economic difficulties and subsequent austerity policies and measures, political uncertainties and raising inequalities at all levels of the society', in a context where the 'rising nationalism and populism and their attacks on women's rights' need to be confronted with a 'wider involvement of women in the economy' (Council of Europe, 2018: 3). In this chapter, we have looked at Italian feminist critiques of equality politics in order to put forward a gendered reading of the economic inequalities under neoliberalism and of the democratic crisis represented by the rise of right-wing populism. Within the paradox of both crisis and return of Marxist feminism, the case of reproductive labour has allowed us to show how neither the State nor the market – in their current forms – have been able to transform the deepest gendered structures of our society, as well as the limits of politics of equality aimed at the pacification of conflict or the reallocation of power within patriarchal structures.

Firstly, we have shown how the earlier second-wave Italian feminist critiques of equality politics were framed not as an opposition to sameness but as a broader political evaluation of the structural conditions within which equality would be realised. As Sylvia Walby (2015: 148) argues: 'there is not only a distinction between the domestic and public form, but also between different varieties of the public gender regime'. Italian feminism was thus founded on the assumption that escaping the isolation and oppression of the private sphere is not enough if the structure of the public sphere does not change simultaneously.

Secondly, we looked at the experience of the Wages for Housework movement as a case of materialist analysis of inequality that based its claim on the recognition of housework as work. Anticipating critiques of the so-called 'business case for equality' (Dickens, 1994; Noon, 2007; Lee, 2013), Wages for Housework exposed the trap of emancipation through paid labour when entering the workforce is not accompanied by a salary for housework or, to put it in more moderate policy language, by equal sharing of unpaid care work. Quantitative data presented in this chapter confirm a persistent gender care gap, increasingly segmented along racial lines.

Although minoritarian at its time, the experience of Wages for Housework has gained renewed attention in contemporary feminist militant analysis. In

The(Re)production of (In)equality in Italy   91

the current precarious, de-industrialised, gig-based and immaterial job market, qualities traditionally associated to women – flexibility, the capacity to multi-task, to cross and reconcile private and public roles, to resolve personal conflict and perform emotional labour, as well as their personal investment in the commodity produced – are nowadays associated with labour in general. However, we argued that the critique of the feminisation of work must not obscure a materialist reading of female labour that always existed and continues to exist, such as housework.

In our conclusive appraisal of contemporary transnational and intersectional feminist movements, such as the Ni Una Menos global campaign, with their renewed attention to materialist analyses and the feminist practice of gender strike, we argued that a gendered reading of the crisis represents the most comprehensive attempt to respond to the unprecedented and apparently contradictory alliance between neo-fundamentalist political cultures and neoliberal economic governmentality. At times when the concept of equality is used merely to sustain economic growth or even to justify conservative measures, such as in the case of the Pillon Decree discussed above, it becomes urgent to investigate, further theorise and possibly reclaim cultures of equality. The radical lesson of Italian feminism teaches that theorising cultures of equality against themselves can be an effective strategy for the construction of women's autonomy and the imagination of political actions for freedom and social justice.

Note

1 The authors of this chapter jointly contributed to the contents, the interpretation of data and drafting of the manuscript.

Bibliography

Andall, J., Puwar, N. (eds). (2007). 'Italian feminisms', Special Issue, *Feminist Review*, No. 87.

Bono, P., Kemp, S. (eds). (1991) *Italian Feminist Thought: A Reader*. Cambridge, MA: Basil Blackwood.

Borderias, C., Cigarini L., Nannicini, A., Bologna, S., Marazzi, C. (2005). *Tre donne e due uomini parlano del lavoro che cambia*. Milan: Libreria delle donne.

CENSIS, Fondazione ISMU (2013). Elaborazione di un modello previsionale del fabbisogno di servizi assistenziali alla persona nel mercato del lavoro italiano con particolare riferimento al contributo della popolazione straniera. Rome: CENSIS.

CENSIS. (2015). *L'eccellenza sostenibile nel nuovo welfare*. Modelli di risposta top standard ai bisogni delle persone non autosufficienti. Rome: CENSIS.

Council of Europe. (1998). *Gender Mainstreaming*. Conceptual framework, methodology and presentation of good practices. Strasbourg: Council of Europe.

Council of Europe. (2018). *Gender Equality Strategy 2018–2023*. Strasbourg: Council of Europe.

Dalla Costa, M. (1972). *Potere femminile e sovversione sociale*. Padua: Marsilio.

92 Theorising Cultures of Equality

Dalla Costa, M., James, S. (1973). *The Power of Women and the Subversion of the Community.* Bristol: Falling Wall Press.

de Lauretis, T. (1990). '*Upping the Anti in Feminist Theory*'. In M. Hirsch and E. Fox Keller (eds). *Conflicts in Feminism.* London: Routledge.

Dickens, L. (1994). '*The business case for women's equality: Is the carrot better than the stick?*', *Employee Relations*, 16(8): 5–19.

Diotima (1987). *Il pensiero della differenza sessuale.* Milan: La Tartaruga.

Federici, S. (1975). *Wages against Housework.* Bristol: Power of Women Collective and Fading Wall Press.

Federici, S. (2012). *Revolution at Point Zero: Housework, Reproduction, and Feminist Struggle.* Oakland, CA: PM Press.

Federici, S. (2018). *Reincantare il mondo. Femminismo e politica dei commons.* Verona: Ombre Corte.

Federici, S. and Arlen, A. (2017). *Wages for Housework: The New York Committee 1972–1977: History, Theory, Documents.* Chico, CA: AK Press.

Fondazione Moressa – Domina. (2017). *Il valore del lavoro domestico.* Il ruolo economico e sociale delle famiglie datori di lavoro. Rome.

Fraire, M. (ed). (2002). *Lessico politico delle donne: teorie del femminismo.* Milan: Franco Angeli [1978].

Friedan, B. (1963). *The Feminine Mystique.* New York: W.W. Norton & Company.

Garbagnoli, S. (2018). '*Matteo Salvini*, renaturalizing the racial and sexual boundaries of democracy', in OpenDemocracy. Retrieved from www.opendemocracy.net/can-europe-make-it/sara-garbagnoli/matteo-salvini-renaturalizing-racial-and-sexual-boundaries-of-dem.

Green, S. (1992). '*Reviewed Work: Sexual Difference: A Theory of Social-Symbolic Practice*', *Feminist Review*, No. 40: 109–111.

Gribaldo, A. and Zapperi, G. (2012). *Lo schermo del potere: femminismo e regime della visibilità.* Verona: Ombre Corte.

Hemmings, C. (2005). '*Telling feminist stories*', *Feminist Theory*, 6(2): 115–139.

Hemmings, C. (2011). *Why stories matter: The political grammar of feminist theory.* Durham, NC: Duke University Press.

Hochschild, A.R. (1991). *The Managed Heart: Commercialization of Human Feeling.* Berkeley, CA: University of California Press.

ISTAT. (2015). *Come cambia la vita delle donne 2004–2014.* Rome.

ISTAT. (2018). *Rapporto annuale 2018.* La situazione del Paese. Rome.

ISTAT. (2018b). *L'economia non osservata nei conti nazionali.* 2013–2016. Rome.

INPS. (2018). *Statistiche in breve.* Lavoratori domestici. Rome.

Lee, F. (2013). '*Show Me the Money: Using the Business Case Rationale to Justify Gender Targets in the EU*', *Fordham International Law Journal*, 36: 1471–1515.

Libreria delle donne di Milano. (1987). *Non credere di avere dei diritti. Come nasce la libertà femminile nelle idee e nelle vicende di un gruppo di donne.* Turin: Rosenberg & Sellier.

LIES Editorial Collective. (2012). '*All the Work We Do As Women*': *Feminist Manifestos on Prostitution and the State, 1977*', *LIES. A Journal of Material Feminism*, vol. 1: 217–234.

Lonzi, C. (1974). '*Manifesto di Rivolta femminile*', in Lonzi 1974, cit.

Lonzi, C. (1974). *Sputiamo su Hegel, la donna clitoridea e la donna vaginale e altri scritti.* Milan: Scritti di Rivolta Femminile.

Marazzi, C. (2011). *Capital and Affects: the Politics of the Language Economy.* Cambridge, MA: MIT Press.

The(Re)production of (In)equality in Italy 93

Melandri, L. (1997). *L'infamia originaria*. Milan: Edizioni L'Erba Voglio.

Melandri, L. (2000). *Una visceralità indicibile: la pratica dell'inconscio nel movimento delle donne degli anni Settanta*. Milan: Franco Angeli.

Milan Women's Bookstore Collective (1990). *Sexual Difference: A Theory of Social-Symbolic Practice*. Translated by P. Cicogna and T. de Lauretis, Bloomington, IN and Indianapolis, IN: Indiana University Press.

Ministero del lavoro e delle politiche sociali. (2018). *Ottavo rapporto annuale. Gli stranieri nel mercato del lavoro in Italia*. Rome.

Morini, C. (2001). *La serva serve. Le nuove forzate del lavoro domestico*. Rome: Derive Approdi.

Morini, C. (2010) *Per amore o per forza. Femminilizzazione del lavoro e biopolitiche del corpo*. Verona: Ombre Corte.

Muraro, L. (1991). *L'ordine simbolico della madre*. Rome: Editori Riuniti.

Muraro, L. (2002). '*The Passion of Feminine Difference.*' In Parati and West 2002, cit.

Nannicini, A. (2002). *Le parole per farlo. Donne al lavoro nel postfordismo*. Rome: Derive Approdi.

Noon, M. (2007). '*The fatal flaws of diversity and the business case for ethnic minorities*', *Work, Employment and Society*, 21: 773–784.

Ongaro, S. (2001). *Le donne e la globalizzazione. Domande di genere all'economia globale della ri-produzione*. Soveria Mannelli:Rubettino.

Parati, G., West, R., (eds). (2002*). Italian Feminist Theory and Practice: Equality and Sexual Difference*. Fairleigh, NJ: Dickinson University Press.

Risman, B.J. (2004). '*Gender as a social structure: Theory wrestling with activism*', in *Gender & Society*, 18(4): 429–450.

Saraceno, C. (2018). '*Maschilismo di governo*', *La Repubblica*, 5 November.

Segato, R. (2017). *La guerra contra las mujeres*. Madrid:Tinta Limón - Traficantes de sueños.

Spagnoletti, R. (ed.). (1971). *I movimenti femministi in Italia*. Rome: Samonà e Savelli.

Tatafiore, R. (1994). *Sesso al lavoro*. Milan: Il Saggiatore.

Toupin, L. (2014). *Le salaire au travail ménager: chronique d'une lutte féministe internationale (1972–1977)*. Montréal: Editions du Remue-ménage.

Transnational Social Strike Platform. (2018). Power upside down: Women's global strike, *Spring 2018 Journal*.

Wright, S. (2017). *Storming Heaven: Class Composition and Struggle in Italian Autonomist Marxism*. London, Pluto Press.

Zappino, F. (ed). (2016). *Il genere tra Neoliberismo e Neofondamentalismo*. Verona: Ombre Corte.

6 Cultures of (In)equality in Poland after 1989

Aleksandra M. Różalska

Introduction: Understanding Anti-Gender Movements in Poland after 1989

Drawing from the recent feminist scholarship on gender and far-right politics in Europe (Köttig, Bitzan and Petö, 2017; Tolz and Booth, 2005), as well as on the intersections between gender and nation (Yuval-Davis, 1997; Graff, 2008; Różalska, 2015), this chapter looks critically at the dominant cultures of (in) equality in Poland after 1989 in political/public discourses. I will analyse selected debates on, and popular depictions of, cultures of (in)equality in Poland concerning, for example, reproductive rights, equal pay, traditional gender roles in the context of recent changes in the Polish political landscape, i.e., the victory of nationalistic, anti-European Union (EU) and Christian-conservative parties in the 2015 presidential and parliamentary elections. The chapter concludes with an analysis of alternative narratives to, and social movements against, the dominant patriarchal order, specifically focusing on the example of the women's Black Protest against the total ban on abortion in 2016. I want to consider the Black Protest as an example of the widespread drive of Polish society toward a culture of gender equality that, despite significant political drawbacks and anti-feminist climate, has not been eradicated. In order to understand the circumstances in which the Black Protest was launched and the unique nature of this social mobilisation, the chapter explains the historical and national contexts of cultures of equality in Poland.

Theoretical reflection on the mutual co-construction of gender and nation with regards to growing nationalism in Poland allows for the understanding that neoliberal transformations of Poland's political and economic systems, under way since 1989, have not gone hand in hand with similar changes in the social sphere. Rather, xenophobic, racist, patriarchal and openly anti-feminist ideologies have been reinforced in Polish public and popular discourses in the post-communist era (Graff, 2003; 2009). Importantly, 'the human rights paradigm and the neoliberal stance on economy have come to be viewed as an inseparable package during the transformation in post-communist countries'; however, human rights were rather a 'powerless companion' to the process of introducing market economy and their scope was limited to 'individual political rights and civil liberties rather than economic and social rights of groups' (Gregor and

Cultures of (In)equality in Poland since 1989 95

Grzebalska, 2016: 13). Łapniewska underlines that although people were advocating for women's rights and certain issues, such as domestic violence, started to be discussed publicly, these discourses tended towards emphasising:

> 'the idea of a monolithic identity of women without taking individual differences into account, with gender regarded as superior to other components of identity (among others things, such as age, disability, rurality, ethnicity, and socio-economic location) and the neoliberal rhetoric of a 'self-made man' as the only progressive and proper course of development, was becoming more and more apparent'
>
> (Łapniewska, 2016: 24).

With no political representation and limited influence on legal regulations and with no support on the part of the newly elected government and a strong opposition on the part of the Catholic church, feminist agendas could not be enacted. In consequence, women's rights were neglected, and the patriarchal order has been consolidated since the transition period of the early 1990s, as reflected in the debate on reproductive rights that, despite massive protests and significant social mobilisation, resulted in the introduction of the Act on Family Planning in 1993, banning abortion (Szczuka, 2004). The very terms gender and feminism are misunderstood and perceived as 'an alien and undesirable ideology which, admittedly, does frequently challenge religious doctrine' (Łapniewska, 2016: 23). The so-called 'gender ideology' became a subject of public debate, discussed by politicians and church authorities, and of legal regulations that intervene in the private lives of Polish citizens and violate their basic civil rights. Interestingly, as Polish feminist scholars indicate (Grzebalska, 2015; Graff and Korolczuk, 2017), the politics of open anti-genderism started to be openly advocated for in around 2012, which points to both transnational and local contexts in which 'anti-gender' movements and initiatives should be analysed.

As for transnational context, first we need to acknowledge that, according to the European Institute for Gender Equality's *Gender Equality Index 2017*, 'progress towards gender equality in the EU-28 is rather slow. [...] Each Member State has room for improvement and faces particular obstacles to achieving gender equality' (2017: xiii). Not only is the progress slow, but it is also uneven in respective member states: "The picture is even grimmer in Visegrad countries [the Czech Republic, Hungary, Poland and Slovakia], which are lagging significantly behind older member states in terms of women's position, ranking around 10% below the EU average of 52.9%. But as recent conservative mobilisations across Europe alarm us, the progress that has been made in the field of gender equality has not only been rather stagnant and uneven, but also much shakier and easier to reverse than we had imagined' (Grzebalska, 2016).

The specific sociopolitical context is crucial to understand the popularity of anti-gender movements in Eastern Europe, where women's rights, gender equality ideals and gender mainstreaming as a set of tools to achieve equality are often associated with the EU, and so in the Polish public discourse they

96 *Theorising Cultures of Equality*

are perceived by conservative circles as foreign to our culture, imposed externally. This translates into two problems: first, 'mainly foreign donors and EU accession have influenced the agenda and strengthened the tendency to focus on a limited range of issues' and, consequently, 'gender equality is vulnerable as it is necessarily linked to attitudes about the EU' (Kovats, 2016: 7). The Polish example clearly shows that the anti-gender rhetoric is openly anti-EU, and the very word 'gender' is perceived as imposed by the European elites. For example, in Poland anti-gender campaigns 'initially focused on opposing the Istanbul Convention [on preventing and combating violence against women and domestic violence] as a carrier of "gender ideology", delaying its ratification by three years' (Grzebalska, 2016). The EU requires all member states to introduce gender-mainstreaming policies, for instance to appoint an office of the Ombudsman for Equal Opportunities, which operated in Poland between 2001 and 2005, and again from 2008. Since the 2015 elections, the conservative government has significantly cut funding for the Ombudsman, owing to accusations of promoting 'gender ideology' and established a new, façade office of the Ombudsman for Equality and Civil Society. Adam Lipinski, who was appointed to the body in 2016, voted against the Council of Europe Istanbul Convention (to combat gender-based violence) and declared that he will support Poland's withdrawal from this international agreement.

Other decisions of the conservative government are directed against gender equality and reproductive rights—both considered to be concepts imposed by the EU: withdrawal of the morning-after pill from pharmacies and hospitals, significant cuts in funding for non-governmental organisations (NGO) dealing with women's rights, lesbian, gay, bisexual and transgender (LGBT) rights and domestic violence, cancellation of the state-funded IVF programme, changes in perinatal care and withdrawal from school curricula of any kind of sex education or focus on issues of gender equality (Grzebalska, 2016).

Another reason for the popularity of anti-gender movements across Europe is related to economic disadvantage: 'The silencing of class conflicts over the nature of economic transition paved the way for the populist right to rearticulate the frustration and anger of those who have fallen victim to the erosion of basic social and economic rights' (Gregor and Grzebalska, 2016: 13). Furthermore, as Pankowski contends (2012: 8), 'socio-economic hardship provides a favourable breeding ground for extreme-right ideologies, but cultural factors are decisive when it comes to channeling socio-economic protest in Poland, which has routinely taken a far-right nationalist direction. Nationalist and populist tendencies in Polish politics have resulted from serious socio-economic tensions coupled with a political culture that prioritises national over social perspectives'.

Finally, anti-gender sentiments should also be linked to other sociopolitical phenomena: the crisis of the left in many European countries, the economic crisis and the failure of the EU as a neoliberal project, which feminist scholars have been pointing to within the last decade (Kováts, 2016; Ost, 2005). The consequences of a capitalist, neoliberal order, consisting of deepening social inequalities, economic discrepancies and disrespect for economic and

Cultures of (In)equality in Poland since 1989 97

social rights, all of which have a concrete gender dimension, have been neglected. As Gregor and Grzebalska (2016: 12) point out; '[t]he problems with gendered effects of austerity policies, feminisation of poverty, low income, inappropriate, exploitative and vulnerable working conditions, the double burden of women, difficulties of single female-headed households are also warning signs of the gendered face of neoliberalism and its consequences'.

As feminist research indicates, a backlash in cultures of equality and women's rights is particularly visible in moments of sociopolitical transformations and – real or imagined – national crises (Golańska, 2008). Within the 30 years of the Polish transition period, there have been several turning points: the collapse of the communist regime in 1989, the accession of Poland to the EU in 2004 or the presidential plane crash near Smolensk, Russia on 10 April 2010 with President Lech Kaczyński on board (Różalska, 2015). Sociopolitical tensions, the polarisation of the political arena and political instability triggered by these events have contributed to a strengthening of a conservative vision of gender difference, nation and nationhood, which are inextricably connected to both Catholicism and patriarchal order. Importantly, as the analysis of the recent situation in Poland shows, the key actors in the anti-gender campaign – most notably the Catholic Church, Christian-conservative politicians (who have constituted the majority in the Polish Parliament since 2015), right-wing journalists and publishers whose newspapers and television channels have been growing in popularity, pro-life and anti-gender NGOs and networks, conservative academics calling gender studies a pseudoscience, internet platforms and Facebook fanpages spreading anti-gender content – have successfully managed to create and mainstream a coherent patriarchal narrative.

Gender and Nation

Feminist scholars point to close relationships between the concepts of nation and gender/sexuality as they are 'both culturally constructed; moreover, they construct each other, via notions of what is 'natural' and what is "cultural." The negotiation of gender difference and the advancement of nationalism are parallel processes, because ideologies which naturalize gender tend to naturalize race and ethnicity' (Graff, 2007). Therefore, Polish nationalism is gendered and 'depends on the prior construction of gender difference' (McClintock, 1995: 353). Nationalistic attitudes intensify in moments of social unrest, economic instability and political tensions, which in the contemporary Polish context are inevitably connected with the ongoing and incomplete sociopolitical transformations initiated in 1989. As Dorota Golańska contends (2008: 170): 'Although recently there have been neither open nationalist conflicts nor ethnic wars in Poland [...] the country's situation during and after the transition period from the communist regime to a democratic system, as well as its integration within European structures, constitute a favorable ground for nationalistic rhetoric, since both are preoccupied with the issue of national identity'.

98 *Theorising Cultures of Equality*

Unlike Benedict Anderson's conception of 'imagined community', the Polish vision of the nation is based upon a collectivity called into existence by supernatural forces; a sacred community consisting of divine elements; or, alternatively, as a biological construct (Janion, 2006). Polish messianism involves a number of key elements: nation; God (Catholicism); suffering and sacrifice; and a sense of betrayal on the part of neighbouring countries and European allies. They contribute to the specific 'religion of patriotism', with Poland as the 'Christ of Nations' at the centre. Such messianic logic assumes that Poland repeatedly finds itself in a position of martyrdom by the will of God – it is chosen to suffer to be later saved. This attitude manifests itself today in the anti-EU rhetoric, which represents Poland as the last Christian, family-oriented nation in Europe that is supposed to serve as an example to follow by other members. The arguments that anti-EU sentiments are working against Poland's own interests in Europe and beyond are often disregarded.

As my research on the plane crash near Smolensk in 2010 demonstrates (Różalska, 2015), the messianic rhetoric re-emerged in the aftermath of this event and became the dominant vocabulary of conservative, right-wing Catholic circles. Not only have we witnessed an intensive eruption of nationalistic patriotism manifested both internally and externally that has fuelled the already existent sociopolitical conflicts, but also—in the words of Janion—'we are observing today [...] the old trope of the "God-and-country" stereotypes and Smolensk as a new messianic myth is to unite and comfort those harmed and humiliated' (Janion, 2016).

Consequently, the dominant patriarchal order and its vision of patriotism, influenced by both a messianic logic of thinking and the Catholic church, strengthens the construction of traditionally understood Polishness based upon concrete images of women and their responsibilities as mothers – 'bearers' of traditional family values and national identity (Oleksy, 2004; Graff, 2014), as well as of ethnic, religious and sexual minorities that are Othered and excluded from the public discourse.

Women's role in the Polish family is inevitably connected with the notion of motherhood, which for centuries has been glorified in Polish history, thanks to the famous archetype of the Polish Mother, which is still very strongly ingrained in the cultural consciousness. As Oleksy (2004: 162) states, 'In Polish cultural history, the ethos and moral identity of the nation was metaphorised as maternity. The Polish Mother was the personification of patience and altruism [...] The idea of Polish womanhood is, simultaneously, related to the religious cult of the Holy Virgin'. The idealised image of womanhood is crucial to national mythology and patriotism. As Maria Janion (2009) underlines, 'In this national drama the only role designed for women is the role of mother. [...] the Mother is the figure of an ideal womanhood, who safeguards male relations and male stories [...] There exists only one model of sexuality—heterosexual and oriented toward reproduction. Therefore, the woman-mother is needed. She becomes a guarantor of the national heterosexual community—its decency, its political and moral correctness'.

Cultures of (In)equality in Poland since 1989   99

Looking back at Polish post-1989 history, such rhetoric gains popularity in times of sociopolitical turmoil and during conservative turns that took place in 2005 – a year after Poland's accession to the EU – when a representative of a conservative right-wing Prawo i Sprawiedliwość (PiS) was elected president and his party formed a governmental coalition with two other ultra-Catholic and nationalistic parties (2006–07). The second outburst of nationalistic, anti-EU, conservative rhetoric dates back to 2015 when PiS won both presidential and parliamentary elections and was this time able to create a majority government. The Christian-conservative vision of nation and Polishness and strict propositions regarding reproductive rights and sexual education, as well as the anti-EU sentiments of regaining independence and 'getting up off our knees', dominated the election campaign. As Grzebalska (2015: 92) claims, 'The anti-neocolonial, Eurosceptic rhetoric used by the right played out loudly throughout the recent anti-gender mobilisation. In statements and discussions that accompanied the campaign, the discursive figure of the EU as a cultural coloniser, corrupting innocent Polish children and suppressing the Polish national culture, was used ubiquitously'.

In this context, one should not be surprised at how the metaphor of 'the messiah of nations' explained above resonates well with the current attempts to further restricting of the anti-abortion law in Poland, wherein Poland situates itself as the only advocate, the last hope for human life from the moment of conception in Europe. As Pietrzak and Fliger contend (2017: 301), 'The new extremely radical antiabortion law would show that Poles are the defenders of fragile unborn life, and in Europe, only Poles have the courage to do such, which ignores underground abortion, women's rights, freedom of belief, and freedom of choice'.

Women in Political and Public Discourses

Despite the fact that Poland is a member of the EU and that since 2004 certain EU regulations concerning women's rights, equal opportunities and gender mainstreaming were formally introduced, I would argue that a culture of equality has not been successfully created. Women's rights and gender equality have never truly been considered fundamental or important by any political party, even the so-called liberal, centrist or leftist political powers. Issues of equal opportunities have been used instrumentally and were included in political programmes merely as a rhetorical strategy. This is not to say that the role of the EU in implementing gender equality policies and practices in Poland was not significant, however, as 'these were introduced with resistance, at the last moment and often out of fear of financial penalties' (Grzebalska 2015: 92).

Both the lack of mainstreaming of women's rights and of political representation of women, together with anti-gender movements gaining increasing popularity, result in – to use Gaye Tuchman's words – 'women's symbolic annihilation' (1978: 8). This symbolic annihilation manifests itself in public and popular discourses that condemn, ignore or trivialise women, their rights,

100   *Theorising Cultures of Equality*

needs and interests, especially of those women who do not respect the dominant norms. This is especially visible in the media, which consequently ignore women's experiences and women voices. I have examined elsewhere television narratives of Polish women perpetuated by the media (Różalska, 2011), which showed that marginalising and stigmatising gender discourses are a norm and reflect the 'common sense' understandings of the public. Whatever goes beyond the dominant narrative is labeled deviant, abnormal or, at the very least, difficult to understand. Those who do not fit this norm, such as the single, unmarried, childless, divorced, feminist, gay or lesbian are Othered, marked as deviant and excluded from mainstream society. Consequently, non-normative family models or lifestyles are either absent or condemned in public debates and media narratives (Różalska, 2011).

Consequently, conservative patriarchal gender stereotypes relegating women to certain roles and duties remain strong within Polish society. Women are systematically deprived of the possibility of transgressing traditional social roles connected with motherhood, family and domestic life – roles that continue to be limited to the private sphere. It remains a non-negotiable fact that mothers are the only 'real' women (Graff, 2003: 246). Consequently, this normative biological essentialism significantly narrows the whole discussion about parenthood and parenting choices. Society reacts with shock, disbelief and condemnation if a woman openly declares that she does not want to bear children. The special relationship between mother and child also excludes fathers, and it remains rare for men to take paternity leave, especially beyond urban areas. If a father expresses a preference for his children over his career, this continues to be met with surprise and can lead to questions being raised about his commitment as an employee and indeed his masculinity. This narrow and essentialist approach to motherhood also negatively influences perceptions of and attitudes to adoption, IVF and homosexual partnerships, all of which are considered unnatural and abnormal. Significantly, as outlined above, the issues of IVF, abortion, LGBT rights and women's reproduction are those spheres of life in which the PiS government decided to intervene.

At the same time, other important issues, such as unequal pay, the feminisation of poverty, economic exploitation of women and violence against women are considered marginal problems. In this context, I argue in the subsequent section of this chapter that the Black Protest was successful partly because ignoring the reality of women's lives and experiences has served to raise levels of anger among Polish women.

Gender, Nationalism, Catholic Church

According to Rafał Pankowski (2012: 0), 'The majority of the Polish extreme-right groups subscribe to a Catholic fundamentalist ideology combined with a strongly radical ethnic version of nationalism including antisemitism. Their ideology is accompanied by a very traditionalist view on family and gender roles and concerning foreign policy marked by an opposition to the EU'. The

Cultures of (In)equality in Poland since 1989   101

mainstreaming of fear of 'gender ideology' was undertaken by the Church in the now infamous Bishops' pastoral letter entitled *Threats to the Family Stemming from the Ideology of Gender* that was read in all Polish churches in December 2013 (Sierakowski, 2014). The letter reads: 'Gender ideology results from many decades of ideological and cultural changes rooted in Marxism and neomarxism promoted by some feminist movements and from sexual revolution. Genderism [...] claims that biological sex does not have any social significance and what matters is gender, cultural sex, which can be developed and defined irrespective of biological circumstances. According to this ideology, one can freely choose whether to be a man or a woman; one may also select their own sexual orientation' (List Pasterski, 2013).

The letter was probably the first official and mainstream anti-gender statement by church authorities preceded by a set of controversial interviews in the Catholic press with a priest, Father Dariusz Oko, about, among others, gender education and sexualisation of children. On numerous occasions he – similar to other actors in this anti-gender campaign – equates the term 'genderism' with Marxism and relates it to hubris, lies, violence, lack of respect for others and aggressiveness (Cichobłazińska, 2013). Of course, in his opinion it is impossible to reconcile 'genderism' and Christianity.

The public debate about gender ideology as the main enemy initiated by the church was quickly joined by politicians, and the voice of Father Oko, which was initially marginal, became mainstream. Beata Kempa, a popular right-wing PiS politician and the main protagonist in the Polish 'war on gender', used very similar words to Oko in reference to the 'gender threat': 'Gender is the same as any other ideology, Marxist or communist: it leads to totalitarianism [...] Why do we have to achieve equality by demolishing the traditional family?' (Pawlicka, 2014: 32). Kempa implies that both gender ideology and homosexuality are threatening the fabric of society and harming Polish children: 'Gender ideology is nothing more than an attempt to imprint in children's minds that homosexual marriages are a norm' (Pawlicka, 2014: 32). In just one interview in *Newsweek*, Kempa makes 'gender' responsible for many social phenomena that she considers pathological and dangerous, including divorce, diminishing family values, the acceptance for non-normative models of family, the demoralisation and sexualisation of children through sexual education, promoting homosexual lifestyles and even psychological disorders. Evidently, as argued by Grzebalska (2016), anti-genderism is 'a "symbolic glue" which connects various progressive issues under one umbrella term, and unites different conservative actors in a much bigger quest to change the values underlying European liberal democracy. As such, anti-genderism is not "just" a feminist issue, but rather one threatening liberal democracy—a Trojan horse for making much broader and deeper changes to our political system.'

'Gender ideology' became such a mainstream term, and the need to investigate its social consequences so strong among conservative-Christian politicians, that in 2014 Kempa formed a Parliamentary Committee named 'Stop Gender Ideology!' in order 'to combat the negative influence of gender ideology on the Polish family and education of children' and 'to work towards

102   *Theorising Cultures of Equality*

introducing legal regulations protecting the rights of traditional family and supporting pro-family policies' (*Parlamentary Zespół*, 2014). Although the activities of the Committee were more for show and were largely contested by less conservative politicians and mocked by the mainstream liberal media, the language of Oko and Kempa, with its patriarchal, homophobic and anti-EU rhetoric, permeated public discourse.

Moreover, 'gender ideology' was directly addressed in the programs of Christian-conservative parties and pictured as a foreign-imposed threat to traditional family and national identity (Grzebalska, 2015). Whereas other, more liberal, parties declared their commitment to women's rights – e.g., maintaining the 'consensus' over the anti-abortion bill, and combating violence against women – these issues have been at the margins of their programmes. Although the Istanbul Convention to combat gender-based violence was finally signed in 2015,advocates for cultures of equality 'did not exactly succeed in overcoming the language of cultural wars and building bridges between the adversaries' (Grzebalska, 2015: 98) and the strong anti-gender narrative that was successfully constructed and perpetuated by the consolidated anti-gender movement.

#BlackProtest

Here I argue that the anti-gender narrative analysed above has been successfully contested and altered by the Black Protest, which I consider a manifestation of Polish society's commitment to ongoing struggle for culture of gender equality. In what follows, I critically reflect on the Black Protest and All Women's Strike organised in Poland in the autumn of 2016 to protest against further radicalisation of the anti-abortion bill. The anti-abortion law proposal, presented by a radical pro-life organisation, Ordo Iuris, assumed a total ban on abortions (even in the case of fatal damage or genetic disorder of the foetus, the pregnancy being a result of rape or incest or when the life and health of woman is under threat) and the penalisation of doctors and women alike in cases where abortion is performed. The draft of the bill was presented in Parliament, which started discussion on its implementation. The direct outcome of the Black Protest was Parliament eventually rejecting the project to tighten the abortion law.

The plan to introduce an even stricter anti-abortion bill was a wake-up call and triggered massive resistance (both active and passive) by Polish society. People started to mobilise through the Facebook page 'Czarny Protest' ('Black Protest') and on 21 September 2016 the first protests were organised in Warsaw in front of Parliament. Between 21 September and 3 October 2016 hundreds of protests were organised across Poland, including outside big cities: 'For the first time in many years, Polish women [and men] united in a way and in numbers that had not been expected' (Pietrzak and Fligel, 2017: 298). The mass mobilisation culminated on 3 October on so-called Black Monday: 'More than one hundred thousand people in over sixty cities across the country took to the

Cultures of (In)equality in Poland since 1989   103

streets [...] Even the European Parliament in Strasbourg spoke of the rights of Polish women just one day after Black Monday. Something that seems for many people in Poland and Europe to be completely private became completely public' (Pietrzak and Fligel, 2017: 298).

Activists and feminist academics alike enthusiastically approached the protests, and in their analyses of the movement they evaluated favourably its uniqueness in terms of organisation, social scale and use of technology: 'The protests against the abortion ban can be interpreted as an example of an organisationally enabled network, in which women's organisations coordinated some national initiatives, provided social technology outlays and produced a body of knowledge [...] which allowed for creating and sharing messages that were both individualised and well-embedded in the narratives referencing the fight for Poland's independence and resisting the oppressive state' (Korolczuk, 2016a: 108).

Let me quote a few statements that will illustrate feminist scholars' approach to the 'women's revolution', which often refer to affective aspects of shared experiences. In the words of Ewa Majewska, a feminist scholar and philosopher, 'On September 21, 2016 feminism began in Poland. Not an exclusive movement of middle-class women from metropolitan elites, but a nation-wide, and then also international, mobilisation of women in favor of our rights' (Majewska, 2016). Agnieszka Graff, a feminist scholar and activist, pointed out that 'The protest was bigger than anyone expected. People were astonished. Warsaw was swarming with women in black. It was amazing to feel the energy and the anger, the emotional intensity was incredible' (Davies, 2016). Pietrzak and Fligel underlined that 'The phenomenon of the Black Protest as well as all activities taken in the last year show that Polish women are demanding the right to their own bodies and fertility and that draconian laws will not stop them from having an abortion, if they need it. This request was shouted out loudly in the Black Protest, which was a manifestation of a real civil society' (Pietrzak and Fligel, 2017: 302).

Mass protests came as a surprise to virtually everyone: the government, the Catholic church, the media (both liberal and right-wing) and wider society, as well as to feminists and women's activists themselves (Korolczuk, 2016b: 31). Previous mobilisations like this, except for protests in 1993 against the introduction of the anti-abortion law, did not attract significant attention from such diverse groups of women and men from different parts of the country and of different backgrounds. The fact that protesters were diverse in terms of gender, class, religion, education, profession, political views (or lack thereof) and geographical location, undoubtedly contributed to its success. Many, if not all commentators underlined – some in emotional statements – that the Black Protest brought about 'a chance for women's agreement independently of class divisions. All of us, regardless of social class, are treated as childish, promiscuous, and animalistic. All of us, regardless of social class, should be treated as adult and responsible people. All of us should have freedom of choice' (Kubisa, 2016).

104   *Theorising Cultures of Equality*

Paradoxically, the sociopolitical conditions in Poland after 2015 facilitated mobilisation on such a scale and the overcoming of certain differences among the protesters because under the new political regime mass street protests started to be socially acceptable and drew the attention of more supporters. However, the Black Protest was distinct from other protests that have typically been associated only with certain social classes or professional groups, such as miners, nurses and, recently, young medical doctors. According to Korolczuk (2016b), such forms of resistance became normalised, as protests and strikes were a common way of protesting under the communist regime between 1945 and 1989, and this expectation of resistance found a resurgence

Similarly, the new political circumstances contributed to huge interest on the part of the mass media in the Black Protest and associated events. This comes as a surprise to critical media discourse scholars because it is unprecedented that the mainstream media pays so much attention to abortion and reproductive rights; indeed, thus far this topic has been, to say the least, marginal and largely ignored. There was also a new approach to media coverage in that debates were shaped by inviting experts, academics and activists – people who actually have knowledge about the reality of women's experiences – whereas previously the media would cover abortion as an ethical, church-related issue or as a marginal problem for a small number of women, usually leading to trauma or health problems (Różalska, 2011). Furthermore, what contributed to the media's more professional approach to the Black Protest, was, paradoxically, the successful mainstreaming of pro-life, anti-women, anti-gender, anti-IVF, anti-sexual education and anti-contraception messages by Christian-conservative parties and press, the Catholic Church and pro-life organisations. The mainstream media, which were under attack from the current government, which aims at limiting freedom of press and broadcasting in Poland, wanted to situate itself in opposition to the dominant power. I have no doubt that the media interest and active engagement in covering women's protests are superficial and impermanent. Certainly, the media did not suddenly start to support feminist claims to liberalise restrictive abortion law. Rather, in that particular political climate, supporting women meant being anti-authority and anti-PiS. So women and women's issues were, again, instrumentally used to advance a certain political agenda, but this time, I think, feminists and women's activists also strategically used the opportunity to be present in the mainstream media to convey their messages.

The Black Protest, unlike any other protest in post-1989 Polish history, was able to represent reproductive rights not solely as a women's issue but as an important aspect of all citizens' lives. Majewska (2016) writes about the simplicity and universality of the Black Protest: 'Women's reproductive rights, part of which is the right to access to safe and legal abortion, is an issue concerning the whole of society, not only women of reproductive age. A reductionist approach to these rights, making them a claim of the narrow margin of young women who *de facto* want to enjoy them, completely ignores a complicated network of social relations, which make the problems of my daughter, granddaughter, mother, wife, student, employee, friend or neighbour, my problems.

Cultures of (In)equality in Poland since 1989   105

Luckily, such reductionist logic was not applied in case of #blackprotest, which makes it universal.'

The universality of the protest was possibly due to the fact that it was not inspired and organised exclusively by so-called 'elitist' feminists, who are often accused of not understanding the needs and problems of 'ordinary' Polish women, or by educated middle- and upper-class women from big cities. In fact, as mentioned above, feminists were amazed by the scale of the protest and multiplicity of undertaken activities. Instead, many #blackprotest initiatives were grassroots, spontaneously organised and attended by women often admitting that they had not been activists before, but determined that 'enough is enough,' and with some support on the part of celebrities (Korolczuk, 2016b). For this reason, the movement was very inclusive. It invited acts of 'resistance of the weak' (Majewska 2016) and gave 'the weak' the possibility to redefine their agency and subjectivity. Therefore, the strength of the Black Protest lies in its spontaneous 'resignation from the hierarchical dichotomy strong/leader vs. weak/participant. Here each of us had a sense of identical agency' (Majewska, 2016) as all initiatives and all methods to express protest were equally important, and together they served to fulfill massive, common and universal goals.

In other words, the protests were decentralised, networked and unhierarchical, and they had multiple sources – local and situated (Korolczuk, 2016b: 39–40). Feminist sociologist Elzbieta Korolczuk calls this phenomenon the 'new logic of mobilisation', using new means of expression and communication, often outside of traditional movements and NGOs. (Korolczuk, 2016b: 39). In addition to the hundreds of thousands of people who attended marches and gatherings, the Black Protest was accompanied by huge support from wider society, expressed more passively through social media (sharing information, creating memes, posting photos wearing black, etc.). Such a sense of community was built in an untraditional way – in the exchange of highly personalised, emotional messages, rather than through interpersonal contacts or building formal organisational structures (Korolczuk, 2016b: 40).

Importantly, this sense of community was built across society and despite significant political differences. It was possible precisely because it was a grassroots movement, perceived by many of its participants as apolitical. Some activities engaged in at the protests actually openly advertised their initiatives as located outside of traditionally understood politics and outside of the traditional party system. This was because political parties are often perceived as corrupt, unable to speak for women, not sufficiently interested in representing women's rights and issues and simply failing to be advocates for pro-women agenda (Korolczuk 2016b; Grzebalska 2015). What started as an apolitical movement and culminated on Black Monday will of course have consequences, both short- and long-term: 'The main outcome is awakening of women's activity with regards to abortion and their political empowerment. From now on whoever wants to make any decisions about abortion, it cannot be done over the heads of women' (Gdula, 2016).

106 *Theorising Cultures of Equality*

Although the main focus of the protest was the anti-abortion law, the scope of the protests went beyond the issue of abortion. In a more general way, it referred to different dimensions of women's rights – freedom, dignity, equality. (Korolczuk, 2016b: 35). Among other issues that were brought up were: different dimensions of violence against women, women's health (e.g., during pregnancy and childbirth), sexual education, IVF, access to contraception and problems with child support claims. Some of the slogans from various protests read: 'No women, no kraj' ('kraj' = 'country'), 'Boję się żyć w tym kraju' ('I am scared to live in this country'), 'Mocy zamiast przemocy' ('Power instead of violence') or 'Edukacja seksualna zamiast represji' ('Sexual education instead of repression').

The participants also underlined that 'the battle for the right to have an abortion is not about the good of children or about protecting life. It is about misogyny—the hatred toward women' (Kubisa, 2016). Therefore, many slogans referred to human free choice: 'Bóg dał nam wolną wolę, kim jesteście, że chcecie nam ją odebrać?' ('God gave us free will, who are you to take it away'), 'Myślę, czuję, decyduję' ('I think, I feel, I decide'), 'Wolny wybór' ('Free choice'), 'Żyję w wolnej Polsce. Mam wolny wybór' ('I live in free Poland. I have free choice'), 'Wybór należy do mnie' ('The choice is mine') and 'Żaden polityk nie ma prawa decydować o prawach kobiet' ('No politician has the right to decide about women's rights').

Women participating in demonstrations and the slogans they promoted also reflected a great amount of anger against misogyny that the Black Protest mobilised – 'Mordercy, fanatycy, sadyści' ('Murderers, fanatics, sadists') or 'Jesteśmy wkurwione' ('We are pissed off') being just some examples of messages that were conveyed. This was the first time in post-1989 Polish history that anger, fear and the sense of danger led women to the streets on such a massive scale. These emotions were widely shared, and therefore many different movements, organisations and activist groups became engaged and created a wide coalition of support. This power of emotions, and these affective, spontaneous reactions to the protests were stimulating, but also to a certain extent surprising to women (Korolczuk, 2016b). According to Majewska, 'a sisterly bond between different women, their solidarity and being together despite difference made the protest possible' (2016).

Summing up these considerations about the Black Protest, which I want to see as a way to build a more stable and sustainable culture of equality, there is one last thing to consider: Was it a feminist protest? Is it important and productive to ask such question? Clearly, the scope of women's concerns and rights brought up was wide. However, as far as the very issue of abortion is concerned, there was no agreement among the protesters and supporters about it. Some women protested against the further limiting of abortion possibilities and wanted to leave the law as it is; others pointed to economic and class aspects, as well as the medical aspects of terminating pregnancy illegally. Some women were advocating for liberalising the law and permitting abortion until the 12th week of pregnancy. Korolczuk claims that what linked the conflicting views together 'was not the support for a certain type of legal

Cultures of (In)equality in Poland since 1989   107

solution (or lack thereof) but rather women's discord about the state forcing women to sacrifice (their health, their life) and resistance against the compulsion to give birth' (2016b: 38). But is it possible to reconcile claims about women's free choice and free will with postulates to allow for abortion only on certain conditions? Is then the demand 'My body, my choice,' promoted by so many women, just a slogan, when in fact both the body and the choice are subject to restriction? In my opinion, respect for women's choice should be unconditional; there should be more debate on education, contraception, gender awareness, conscious motherhood and parenthood than on penalising abortions. Enthusiasm and a feeling of common agency evoked by the Black Protest was a shared experience. However, women's stories about abortions and support for liberalising the anti-abortion law were not welcomed so enthusiastically, especially when the confessions did not concern pregnancies terminated for health reasons (of either mother or foetus or both), but for economic reasons or because the pregnancy was unwanted.

Scholars have different approaches to this dilemma. Korolczuk (2016b) claims that despite these conflicting viewpoints on abortion and a lack of common ground, women acted together against the total abortion ban. This was the main point and the main goal of the protest, and only some participants wanted to manifest their pro-choice stance, to bring up the issue of the so-called 'abortion compromise' and the 'consciousness clause' that often prevents the law to be put in practice.

Kubisa (2016), however, underlines that most protesters and slogans accompanying their marches were not only against the ban, but openly about liberalising the current bill. Women demanded, among others, 'Politycy precz od mojej macicy' ('Politicians, keep your hands off my vagina'), 'Rząd taki gibki, że wchodzi nam do cipki' ('Government is so slick, it gets into our pussy'), 'Od macicy wara' ('Stay away from my vagina'), 'Oprócz macicy mamy mózgi' ('Besides vaginas, we've got brains'), 'Nie jestem za aborcją. Jestem za wolnym wyborem' ('I am not for abortion. I am pro-choice'), 'Rząd nie ciąża usunąć można' ('Government unlike pregnancy can be gotten rid of'), 'Nie! Dla robienia z kobiet biologicznych pojemników' ('No! For making women biological containers'), 'Martwa dziecka nie urodzę' ('Can't deliver a baby when I am dead'), 'To nie kompromis, to kompromitacja, jedna droga: liberalizacja' ('This is not a compromise, this is disgrace, the only way is to liberalise'). These slogans clearly emphasised freedom, free choice, and dignity of women (Kubisa, 2016).

Scholars also underline that regardless of women's particular stances towards abortion, one needs to acknowledge that the Black Protest was not based on one shared (feminist) identity but rather on shared emotions (anger, compassion, empathy and fear) and common political goals, i.e., stopping further work on tightening the abortion law. The movement had an unhierarchical, hybrid, open and inclusive structure that encouraged 'ordinary people' to participate, and it facilitated a different way of communicating—bottom-up forms of personalised cultural memes that invited multiple interpretations and reactions. The organisation of the Black Protest, or lack thereof, contributed to its scale, but

108　*Theorising Cultures of Equality*

participants could engage on their own terms and only in those actions that were consistent with their viewpoints, possibilities or competences. Understood in this way, mass mobilisation does not require resources or formalised structures, as it is spontaneous and flexible (Korolczuk, 2016b: 40). On the one hand, this excluded fragmentary postulates, prevented internal divisions, and ensured some sort of flexibility, but on the other, this could also be a source of dissatisfaction with such postulates being insufficient, conservative and not feminist enough.

Conclusion

I would argue that one of the most important outcomes of Black Protest was a shift in the dominant understanding of social resistance, i.e., its deheroisation and altering the meaning of the concept of strike (Kubisa, 2016). Korolczuk compares the Solidarity strikes of the 1980s and the All Women's Strike of 2016, stating that: 'while the former is constructed around specific figures of heroes and the imperative of self-sacrifice, the latter coalesce around collective effort and solidarity between women who refuse to be sacrificed for the greater good—be it God, the Nation or just higher fertility rates' (Korolczuk, 2016a: 105). Similarly, Majewska praises the Black Protest for contesting the type of heroic resistance so frequently present in Polish history consisting in glorification of its leaders, necessary sacrifice (of freedom or of life) and rejecting other alternative models of social protest. The 2016 women's protests were completely different largely because they referred to 'resistance of the weak and helpless, which values solidarity over sacrifice, cooperation over heroism, and ordinariness over uniqueness' (Majewska, 2016).

The second significant contribution of the Black Protest was the mainstreaming of women's rights in public discourse, the media and among elites who, although they may consider themselves liberal or even leftist, nonetheless often neglect the needs and freedoms of women, disregarding or diminishing them. For politicians, the issue of abortion has always remained on the margins of what is considered politically significant (Korolczuk, 2016b: 35). The support of certain politicians, celebrities and media outlets should be considered with suspicion and limited trust. Noneheless, as the Black Protest proved, used strategically and instrumentally, it can help to mainstream certain feminist claims that 'there is no democracy without women's rights, there is no liberalism without minorities rights, no social justice without gender equality and equality among women' (Korolczuk, 2016b: 35).

Finally, let me come back to earlier considerations in this chapter about the link between neoliberalism, anti-genderism and nationalism. As Grzebalska (2016) rightly contends, '[T]he neoliberal, market-driven democracy that we currently see in Europe, structurally excludes a huge number of people from social participation, pushing them into insecurity if not outright poverty. It is in this context that conservative protest movements create a space for these people to vent their fears and insecurities, voice their anger and dissatisfaction with politics and claim a sense of agency and empowerment that European liberals and social democrats once promised—but failed to deliver'.

Cultures of (In)equality in Poland since 1989 109

Without addressing a whole range of issues, including growing economic disparities, the feminisation of poverty, insufficient funding for social benefits, the gender pay gap in almost all professions, unemployment and poor working conditions, emigration owing to economic hardship, the malfunctioning health care system, to name just a few, a genuinely transformative culture of gender equality in Poland remains a distant aspiration.

Bibliography

Barbieri, D. et al. (2017). *Gender Equality Index 2017. Measuring gender equality in the European Union 2005–2015. Report.* [online] Available at: http://eige.europa.eu/rdc/eige-publications/gender-equality-index-2017-measuring-gender-equality-european-union-2005-2015-report [Accessed 10 January 2018].

Cichobłazińska, A. (2013). 'Gender – ideologia totalitarna', *Niedziela Ogólnopolska*, 24, 40–43. [online] Available at: http://m.niedziela.pl/artykul/106423/nd/Gender—ideologia-totalitarna [Accessed 10 January 2018].

Davies, C. (2016). 'Poland's abortion ban proposal near collapse after mass protests', *The Guardian*, 5 October. [online] Available at: www.theguardian.com/world/2016/oct/05/polish-government-performs-u-turn-on-total-abortion-ban [Accessed 10 January 2018].

Gdula, M. (2016). 'Dzień gniewu i godności', *Krytyka Polityczna*, October 4. [online] Available at: http://krytykapolityczna.pl/kraj/gdula-dzien-gniewu-i-godnosci/2016/ [Accessed 10 January 2018].

Golańska, D. (2008). 'Intimate Citizenship: The Intersection of Gender and Nationalism in Polish Discourses on Abortion and EU Enlargement'. In: D. Golańska and A.M. Różalska, ed., *New Subjectivities: Negotiating Citizenship in the Context of Migration and Diversity*, Łódź:Łódź University Press: 169–186.

Graff, A. (2003). *Świat bez kobiet. Płeć w polskim życiu publicznym*. Warsaw: W.A.B.

Graff, A. (2007). 'The Land of Real Men and Women: Gender and E.U. Accession in Three Polish Weeklies', *The Journal of the International Institute*, Vol. 15, issue 1. [online] Available at: https://quod.lib.umich.edu/j/jii/4750978.0015.107?view=text;rgn=main [Accessed 10 January 2018].

Graff, A. (2008). *Rykoszetem. Rzecz o płci, seksualności i narodzie*. Warsaw: W.A.B.

Graff, A. (2014). *Matka feministka*. Warsaw: Krytyka Polityczna.

Graff, A. and Korolczuk, E. (2017), 'Worse than Communism and Nazism Put Together: War on Gender in Poland'. In: D. Paternotte and R. Kuhar, ed., *Anti-Gender Campaigns in Europe: Mobilizing against Equality*. London and New York: Rowman & Littlefield International: 175–193.

Gregor, A. and Grzebalska, W. (2016). 'Thoughts on the contested relationship between neoliberalism and feminism'. In: E. Kováts, ed., *Solidarity in Struggle Feminist Perspectives on Neoliberalism in East-Central Europe*. Budapest: Friedrich-Ebert-Stiftung.

Grzebalska, W. (2015). 'Poland'. In: E. Kováts and M. Põim, ed., *Gender as symbolic glue. The position and role of conservative and far right parties in the anti-gender mobilizations in Europe*. Budapest: Foundation for European Progressive Studies: 83–103.

Grzebalska, W. (2016). 'Anti-genderism and the crisis of neoliberal democracy', *Visegrad Insight*, 7 March. [online] Available at: http://visegradinsight.eu/why-the-war-on-gender-ideology-matters-and-not-just-to-feminists/ [Accessed 10 January 2018].

110   *Theorising Cultures of Equality*

Janion, M. (2006). 'Moje herezje antynarodowe', *Gazeta Wyborcza*, 26 May. [online] Available at: http://wyborcza.pl/1,75478,3374302.html [Accessed 25 March 2013].

Janion, M. (2009). 'Solidarność – wielki zbiorowy obowiązek kobiet', *Krytyka Polityczna*, 24 June. www.krytykapolityczna.pl/Opinie/Janion-Solidarnosc-wielki-zbioro wy-obowiazek-kobiet/menu-id-197.html (accessed 20 December 2010).

Janion, M. (2016). 'Mesjanizm to przekleństwo. List Marii Janion do Kongresu Kultury', *Gazeta Wyborcza*, 10 October. [online] Available at: http://wyborcza.pl/7,75410,20813344,mesjanizm-to-przeklenstwo-list-marii-janion-do-kongresu-kultury.html [Accessed 10 January 2018].

Korolczuk, E. (2016a). 'Explaining mass protests against abortion ban in Poland: the power of connective action', *Zoon Politikon*, 7, 91–113.

Korolczuk, E. (2016b). 'Bunt kobiet AD 2016: skąd się wziął i czego nas uczy?' In: A. Czarnacka, ed., *Przebudzona rewolucja. Prawa reprodukcyjne kobiet w Polsce. Raport 2016*. Warsaw: Fundacja im. Izabeli Jarugi-Nowackiej: 31–42.

Köttig M., Bitzan R. and Petö A. (2017). *Gender and Far Right Politics in Europe*. New York: Palgrave Macmillan.

Kováts, E. (2016). 'Preface: Overcoming false dichotomies—Reclaiming feminist politics in a neoliberal age'. In: E. Kováts, ed., *Solidarity in Struggle Feminist Perspectives on Neoliberalism in East-Central Europe*. Budapest: Friedrich-Ebert-Stiftung: 5–10.

Kubisa, J. (2016). 'Odzyskajmy Polskę dla kobiet!', *Krytyka Polityczna*, 10 October. [online] Available at: http://krytykapolityczna.pl/kraj/odzyskajmy-polske-dla-kobiet/2016/ [Accessed 10 January 2018].

(2013) List pasterski na Niedzielę Świętej Rodziny 2013 roku. December 29. [online] Available at: http://episkopat.pl/list-pasterski-na-niedziele-swietej-rodziny-2013-roku/ [Accessed 10 January 2018].

Łapniewska, Z. (2016). 'First-world aspirations and feminism translocation: In search of economic and leftist alternatives'. In: E. Kováts, ed., *Solidarity in Struggle Feminist Perspectives on Neoliberalism in East-Central Europe*. Budapest: Friedrich-Ebert-Stiftung: 21–31.

Majewska, E. (2016). 'Słaby opór i siła bezsilnych. #czarnyprotest kobiet w Polsce 2016', *Praktyka Teoretyczna*. [online] Available at: www.praktykateoretyczna.pl/ewa-majewska-slaby-opor-i-sila-bezsilnych-czarnyprotest-kobiet-w-polsce-2016/ [Accessed 10 January 2018].

McClintock, A. (1995). *Imperial Leather. Race, Gender and Sexuality in the Colonial Context*. London: Routledge.

Oleksy, E.H. (2004). 'Women's Pictures and the Politics of Resistance in Poland', *NORA—Nordic Journal of Women's Studies*, 3: 162–171.

Pankowski, R. (2012). *Right-Wing Extremism in Poland*. Berlin: Friedrich-Ebert-Stiftung.

Parlamentarny Zespół. "Stop ideologii gender!" Regulamin. [online] Available at: http://orka.sejm.gov.pl/opinie7.nsf/nazwa/zesp_stopgender/$file/zesp_stopgender.pdf [Accessed 10 January 2018].

Pawlicka, A. (2014). 'Beata Kempa i spółka, czyli młot na gender', *Newsweek*, 27 January. [online] Available at: www.newsweek.pl/polska/stop-ideologii-gender-i-beata-kempa-na-newsweek-pl,artykuly,279041,1.html [Accessed 10 January 2018].

Petö, A. (2016). 'Feminism and Neoliberalism: Peculiar Alliances in the Countries of Former "State Feminism"'. In: E. Kováts, ed., *Solidarity in Struggle Feminist Perspectives on Neoliberalism in East-Central Europe*. Budapest: Friedrich-Ebert-Stiftung: 108–111.

Cultures of (In)equality in Poland since 1989   111

Pietrzak, E., and Fligel, A. (2017). 'Black Protest. Abortion Law in Poland in the Context of Division into Private and Public Sphere'. In: S. Bohn and P. M. Yelsalı Parmaksız, ed., *Mothers in Public and Political Life*. Bradford, ON: Demeter Press: 287–306.

Różalska, A.M. (2011). 'Gender and Family Discourses in Polish Television Series in the Context of Catholic and National Values'. In: D. Golańska and A.M. Różalska, ed., *Gender and Diversity: Representing Difference*. Łódź: Łódź University Press: 59–77.

Różalska, A.M. (2015). 'Pop-Messanism and the Politics of Death in Days of Honor: Feminist Critique of the Dominant Polish Historical Memory'. In: E.H. Oleksy, A. M. Różalska and M.M. Wojtaszek, ed., *The Personal of the Political: Transgenerational Dialogues in Contemporary European Feminisms*. Newcastle upon Tyne: Cambridge Scholars Publishing: 145–166.

Szczuka, K. (2004). *Milczenie owieczek. Rzecz o aborcji*. Warsaw: W.A.B.

Tolz, V. and Booth S. (2005). *Nation and Gender in Contemporary Europe*. Manchester: Manchester University Press.

Yuval-Davis, N. (1997). *Gender and Nation*. London: SAGE Publications.

7 Why We Need Literature, Art and Fantasy

Susan Stanford Friedman

Introduction

What do literature and the arts – and the study of them – have to contribute to gender and cultures of equality? In today's world, with its push toward STEM fields (science, technology, engineering and maths) the arts and humanities are under threat, regarded by many as the icing on the cake of real education – a luxury for the privileged but an expensive distraction for the many. Some Republican governors in the United States have urged public higher education to promote STEM majors that lead to jobs, denigrating and even penalising majors in the humanities (Klebnikov, 2015). Even President Barack Obama – surely a stronger supporter of education than his successor, Donald Trump – dismissed the value of humanities majors in his efforts during 2012–15 to encourage more STEM majors, even at one point recommending a national rating system for public universities based on the income of students in the first five years after their graduation (Jaschik, 2014). In Japan about a dozen universities eliminated their humanities curriculum entirely in 2015, leaving only the most elite universities with humanities offerings (Jenkins, 2015). Worldwide, there is increasing pressure on universities and colleges to produce metrics on concrete, even monetary value for the arts and humanities to justify their existence relative to the economically measurable values of STEM fields.

Imagination, creativity and fantasy—they are not in themselves hard facts, policy initiatives or political programmes. And their value is difficult to quantify or measure. But they can help to make new futures, often through creative engagements with the past: a recycling of temporalities. 'Stories matter', writes Stephen Greenblatt (2017) in his defence of the 'collective fictions' and cults that play out in holiday seasons like Christmas – such as Ebenezer Scrooge, the Nutcracker or Santa Claus. After Trump's election in the United States, sales of George Orwell's Animal Farm surged on Amazon.com. Once again, American nativism and know-nothingism reawakened to create a new age of 'fake news' and 'alternative facts' (Anbinder, 1994). The playful fantasy of Lewis Carroll's *Through the Looking Glass, and What Alice Found There* seems to be more real than ever, as we relive Alice's shock at a world turned upside down – a crazy world normalised. 'When I use a word', Humpty Dumpty scornfully tells Alice, 'it means just what I choose it to mean — neither more nor less'. 'The question is', said Alice, 'whether you can

Why We Need Literature, Art and Fantasy   113

make words mean so many different things'. 'The question is', said Humpty Dumpty, 'which is to be master – that's all'' (Carroll, 1871 [2007]: 2167, [1871: 205]). Fantasy has a way of naming reality and making the unreal, real.

As Hanna Meretoja (2018) points out in *The Ethics of Storytelling*, narrative can be mobilised for both good and evil (see also Meretoja and Davis, 2017). The question that I explore in this chapter is the ethical and political potential of the imaginative arts and storytelling to contribute positively to the gender and cultures of equality. My focus is on the way that they can re-engage with the past to suggest new pathways into more equitable futures, not only in terms of gender but also for all dimensions of equality, including race, class, sexuality, religion, national origin and embodiment. Recall Sheila Rowbotham's prescient observation in 'Through the Looking Glass', chapter three of her classic second-wave feminist text, *Women's Consciousness, Man's World* (1973). Echoing Carroll, she writes that 'All revolutionary movements create their own ways of seeing' (1973: 27). She does not say seeing new things, but rather creating their own ways of seeing – a phrase that implies new or alternate frameworks or paradigms for seeing the old. Her revolutionary call echoes Adrienne Rich's 1971 essay 'When We Dead Awaken: Writing as Re-Vision'. 'Re-vision', Rich writes, 'the act of looking back, of seeing with fresh eyes, of entering an old text from a new critical direction – is for women more than a chapter in cultural history: it is an act of survival.... . We need to know the writing of the past, and know it differently than we have ever known it; not to pass on a tradition but to break its hold over us' (1985: 35). Here Rich, in her early feminist theoretical writing, sees tradition in binary oppressor/oppressed, male/female terms, not yet articulating the intersectional feminism evident in her writings of the late 1970s and 1980s, essays like 'Notes toward a Politics of Location'. But the concept of re-vision – of looking back to look forward – is compatible with today's more complex feminist theory.

Here and now, in the 21st century, as I suggest in this chapter, Rowbotham's creating our own ways of seeing and Rich's re-vision find regenerated forms in the new temporalities of the contemporary. Influenced by early 21st-century revolutions of multifaceted mobilities, time is increasingly theorised not as linear, chronological or objective but rather as subjective, multilayered, multidirectional, multidimensional and palimpsestic (Agamben, 2009; Burges and Elias, 2016; Friedman, 2019; Rothberg, 2009). More specifically, I examine feminist discourses of recycling in storytelling and performance that re-make the old into the new. With the example of multi-media artist Kabe Wilson's recycling of a feminist classic, Virginia Woolf's *A Room of One's Own*, I will consider ways in which contemporary feminists might re-mix prior feminisms into ones suited for the intersectional feminism of the 21st century that envisions broadly conceived cultures of equality.

Kabe Wilson's "The Dreadlock Hoax"

Picture it. 2014. A Bloomsbury drawing room like the one that Virginia Woolf once occupied, the scene of "The Dreadlock Hoax," where performance and

114 *Theorising Cultures of Equality*

installation artist Kabe Wilson dressed up as Virginia and read an essay about writing his novel that begins: "'Of One Woman or So" is a book, written by putting every single word of *A Room of One's Own* in a new order. Now that is not easy. It took five years, and day to day the words would offer some different obstacle." With his grey-dusted dreadlocks passing as Virginia's ageing hair and his clothing signifying the act of cross-dressing, Wilson's performance called to mind the controversial Dreadnought Hoax of 1910, when Virginia and her Bloomsbury companions dressed up in blackface as Abyssinian royals and boarded the British Navy's warship, the *HMS Dreadnought*, pulling off the performance and thereby piercing the patina of invincibility upon which the British Empire was founded and maintained. Wilson, as a British subject of half-Ethiopian/half English heritage, performed Woolf in his natural 'blackface', so to speak, thereby joining the chorus of those who have criticised the Dreadnought Hoax for re-inscribing the imperial and racist power even as it subjected that power to mockery.

However, Wilson's Dreadlock Hoax represents a much more complex relation to the British past than the binarist notion of writing back to the racism of empire. He performs Virginia not as parody, not even as Bhabhaian colonial mimicry. Instead, he develops what he calls in an hour-long video interview a relationship of 'recycling' between the present and the past – one that requires a mix of gender and racial passing. 'The question of old living beside new is emphatically what the novels about', he explains in 'The Dreadlock Hoax' performance. 'The words remain on minds and lips as if they are new, and because they seem so fresh they are useful for our craft'. Wilson means this literally, revealing at the end of the 2014 Dreadlock Hoax performance that every word that he has just read has been recycled from Woolf's short 1937 essay 'Craftsmanship'. Cut to pieces, nothing wasted, just 'shuffled', reordered. Made into something 'new'. An even more elaborate hoax, his novel, *Of One Woman or So*, by Olivia N'Gowfri, is a reordering of every word and only every word of *A Room of One's Own*, cut to pieces and re-used to tell the story of an angry, biracial, queer scholarship student at the University of Cambridge who attempts to burn down university libraries and stops just short of burning the manuscript of *A Room of One's Own* on display at one of the college libraries as part of its exhibit on women in education, called Rooms of Our Own. Wilson's term – 'recycling' – borrows simultaneously from 21st-century environmental discourse and from the musical practice of the 're-mix'.

Wilson's novel was some five years in the making –impossible, he explains in the interview, without the computer, digital resources and technical collaborations that allowed him to ensure that he used every word and only every word in *A Room of One's Own* the exact number of times that it was used in Woolf's essay. In its very body, the novel's cut-up pieces can be recycled only with the technologies of the 21st century. Once completed, however, Wilson returned to his novel and made it into an art installation – a process of literally cutting up each word of *A Room of One's Own*, then gluing each onto a lengthy scroll in the order of the words in his novel and finally displaying his novel in a 2014 showing at the University of Oxford. Unlike the novel, the art installation took a relatively short time to produce – about 4–5 weeks instead of years. Close-ups of sections give tangible testimony to the recycling process of the text's construction – both as words on a page and as signifiers reordered into a re/newed pattern of meaning.

Recycling as Revolution and Re-Mixing: The Past into New Futures

Recycling is something of a miracle: taking apart the old into its component parts enables the making of something new. Sometimes, old paper just becomes new paper: a repetition of sorts, but in a new time/space, deployed for new uses. But sometimes, the old becomes fully new: a metamorphosis of sorts, like the transformation of plastic water bottles into polyester clothing. Recycling also partakes of creation, of making one thing out of other things: quilt designs made of used scraps; found art made of objects dis-placed or re-placed anew; found poems made of words set in different spaces; re-mixed music made of prior tones and rhythms; art made of trash; use made of waste. Not creation *ex nihilo*: the creative act as a form of recycling implies a transformative, transactional relation between the old and the new.

The discourse of recycling is more than a cliché of contemporary environmental ethics and activism – though it is that, most certainly, a word for the 21st century facing the crises of a shrinking planet amid drastic climate change, a word that conjures virtue for those who sort and moral castigation for those who do not. Recycling brings us back to the Latin prefix re-, meaning again or backwards, and then to the earliest meanings of revolution, whose first usages in English, in about 1300, meant a turning, specifically a turning-back, a re-turning, as in the revolution of the sun, moon, stars and planets, as in a cycling through time and space: a repetition, a revolving (Oxford English Dictionary, 2019). By the 15th and 16th centuries, English usage of the word 'revolution' included additionally the notion of a recurrence of a point or period in time, an epoch (Oxford English Dictionary, 2019). By the 17th century, the word 'revolution' had acquired a new meaning, the one we predominantly associate with it today: 'a complete overthrow of the established government in any country or state by those who were previously subject to it' (Oxford English Dictionary, 2019). Revolution as overthrow, as explosive change, as complete rupture: these are the meanings that took on added ideological, nationalist and internationalist associations with the advent of revolutions from the early 18th century until the early 20th century in the Americas, Europe, the Caribbean, Africa and Asia. In the 1960s and 1970s, in the United States and elsewhere, the discourses of revolution permeated the cultural, social, sexual and political upheavals of the times, reflected in the marches and movements and in the popular music of the day—e.g., the 'Revolution' hits of the Beatles, Bob Marley and Jimi Hendrix, among others. Revolution as radical change in every aspect of life spread, especially through mass culture. By the 21st century the Digital Revolution signalled revolutionary changes in knowledge production and dissemination. The word 'revolution' has

116 *Theorising Cultures of Equality*

repressed its earlier meanings of turning back to suggest a longing for and often dashed hopes of liberation, emancipation and change as freedom from the old, and then all too often, or in bleaker moments, like Orwell in *Animal Farm*, the reassertion of the old political and social orders in new forms.

To achieve cultures of equality, revolution is a concept dear to our hearts and activisms. But I am suggesting here that we rethink the meanings – even the strategies and tactics – of revolution away from absolute rupture with the past and towards notions of creative engagement with the past. This revolutionary temporality looks to the future through transformative recyclings of the past, in Wilson's sense of the term. Recycling as a recurrence that is not absolute repetition, but repetition with a difference, with the creation of something new-out-of-the-old, with a deployment that is distinctive for its own time and place. A revolutionary recycling that involves re-, that is, again, backwards as the precondition for the formation of the new: that is, re-new.

Thinking about revolution as recycling renewal, a turning back as precursor to turning into the new, suggests a range of additional words, all of which involve some form of intertextual encounter: Rich's re-vision, but also related to more contemporary terms like re-mixing, repurposing, reversioning, revisiting, signifying on, sampling, and shuffling. All these terms emphasise how artists and writers are always already embedded in pre-existing signifying systems. Creations of the new – even radically new – recycle the old, anew, renewals with a difference. The more startling the difference, the more transformative the act of recycling appears to be, but recycling it remains, from trash to treat.

The contemporary musical terms are particularly suggestive: re-mixing, sampling and splicing. The re-mix (sometimes spelled without the hyphen) is a word in contemporary music signifying a kind of recycling, a genre with its roots in Jamaican dancehall culture of the 1960s and now widespread in hip hop and rap music. First appearing in print in 1969, 're-mix' involves a 'reinterpretation or reworking, often quite radical of an existing recording' (*Oxford English Dictionary* [online], 2019). Now a highly technical digital procedure, re-mixing reworks, revamps and remakes prior musical forms into new ones: the new built digitally out of recombinations of old musical phrases and rhythms. Sampling involves lifting a portion of a prior tune or beat or song to place it into a new musical piece through splicing, the lifting of a portion of another's tune or beat or song to re-place it into a new musical piece. Increasingly, the term 're-mix' has broadened to encompass more than musical forms: -videos, photographs, poems and novels. As all creative forms are new arrangements of at least some pre-existing forms, what distinguishes a re-mix is often its degree of self-conscious, or metafictional, awareness of its recycling of what has come before to create something new. Samples and re-mixes assume a before and a now – a temporal recycling. But in the context of intensified global circulations of cultural forms, they also contain a spatial displacement: the re-use of a cultural form from elsewhere into the here and now. Wilson dubs this spatial recycling as '(T)here'. (*Of One Woman or So*, 2014: 5). The revolutions of recycling and re-mixing involve the mobilities of time and space alike.

Why We Need Literature, Art and Fantasy 117

Re-mixing A Room of One's Own

Queer Theory has been obsessed with temporality, especially futurity, at least since the publication of Lee Edelman's *No Future: Queer Theory and the Death Drive* in 2004, with its attack on normative temporalities that assume a kind of reproductive futurism. Wilson's re-mix of *A Room of One's Own* also attacks normative futurism, but his emphasis is on race, class and origin rather than sexuality or reproduction. The novel's title – *Of One Woman Or So*, by Olivia N'Gowfri – is an anagram of *A Room of One's Own*, by Virginia Woolf, mixing up Woolf's letters to skew the by-now tropic status of 'a room of one's own', thereby putting the emphasis on an indeterminate woman instead of a room. The author's name – Olivia N'Gowfri – is ambiguously part of the novel's title and creolises the English-sounding name 'Olivia' with a vaguely African-looking name, 'N'Gowfri'. The title page itself anticipates the re-mix to come, blending echoes of 'Chloe liked Olivia' in A Room and Shakespeare's Olivia in *Twelfth Night* with the Afro-Caribbean heritage of the novel's protagonist. What we learn in the course of the novel is that queering *A Room of One's Own* involves the story of Olivia's alienation as a scholarship student among the privileged classes and a bi-racial woman who is confronted with virulent racism when she attends the exclusive Shakespeare Society to which she had hoped to gain admittance as a member through her literary knowledge and sharp wit.

As with recycling in general, the process by which Wilson re-mixed *A Room of One's Own* merits as much attention as its final product. An exhibit in 2009 featuring the manuscript of *A Room of One's Own* at Lucy Cavendish College, a women's college founded in 1965 at the University of Cambridge, led Wilson to select *A Room of One's Own* for recycling. In the interview, Wilson recalls that he had been a fan of Woolf's since high school and that through his Cambridge years, he retained 'great affection' for her work. But he also wanted to bring out a certain critical 'tension' as well – one based around issues of race and class. His re-mix of *A Room of One's Own* began in some sense, he notes, with one of Woolf's throw-away sentences – an idea that remains undeveloped in *A Room of One's Own*, but is foundational for his 21st-century novel: 'It is one of the great advantages of being a woman that one can pass even a very fine negress without wishing to make an Englishman of her' (Woolf, 1929: 50). Like Alice Walker in her essay 'In Search of Our Mothers' Gardens', Wilson was put off by Woolf's emphasis on the need for money and a room of one's own in order to write. As in Walker's splicing of black women into Woolf's story of Shakespeare's sister, Wilson returns to Woolf's 'very fine Negress' to make race the wedge that breaks open *A Room of One's Own* in order to renew it for the 2st century. As he explains in the interview, he wanted to 'satirise' elements in *A Room of One's Own* at the same time that he performed his ongoing affection. What allows for this doubled relation to *A Room of One's Own* is Wilson's literalised practice of recycling: taking each and every word in Woolf's text and only those words and mixing them up anew, to re-new them for the 21st century: a revolution, that is, a turning back to turn forward. 'A New World Order', the novel begins: 'Refresh from the word. Go' (Wilson, 2014: 2).

118 *Theorising Cultures of Equality*

In what he calls his 'collaboration' with Woolf, Wilson developed the storyline of his novel by beginning at the level of words rather than plot or theme. Rereading *A Room of One's Own*, he first made a list of particularly interesting or unusual words. Then he reviewed that list to locate words that might mean something quite different in a contemporary context—like 'Negress', for example, or 'black'. He found nine instances of the word 'black', but he did not waste the word by putting it next to 'coat', he explains. Instead, he conjoined 'black' with 'power' to recycle these words into something new: 'Black Power'. Names like Henry James and Mary Carmichael got 'shuffled' – one of Wilson's synonyms for 'recycling' – and came out as C.L.R. James and Carmichael, as in Stokely Carmichael, a Trinidadian-born immigrant to the United States who co-founded Students for a Non-Violent Coordinating Committee and then co-led the Black Panther Party. These new combinations of Woolf's words and the associations that they spawned suggested the outlines of a plot that featured Olivia, the mixed-race girl of partly West Indian heritage, who discovers the books of James, Carmichael and H. Rap Brown in the University Library. Carmichael and Brown in particular become her guides, helping her to reject the university's appeal for her to assimilate fully along with its underlying racist dismissal of her difference. Their radicalism inspires her own, her acts of arson that 'satirise', as well as show an admiration for the extremes of the Black Power movement, as Wilson explains in the interview. Wilson's 'hoax' is a double sword, cutting both ways – against both Woolf and Black Power – even as its recycling compositional process simultaneously honors the usability of the old in the new.

The novel's re-mix of *A Room of One's Own* is as doubled-edged as the process by which it was made. *Of One Woman or So* has six chapters that uncannily ghost the six chapters of *A Room of One's Own*, patterned after the fiction of October days that structure Woolf's narrative. Like *A Room of One's Own*, Wilson's progression of chapters first establishes the institutional and ideological power that Oxbridge represents: the material conditions and traditions of a patriarchy that for Olivia are also riven by race and class privilege. But Wilson's re-mix becomes a subtle dialogue with its precursor, including a rejection of *A Room of One's Own's* advocacy of 'androgyny', which Olivia finds old-fashioned and out of step with contemporary queer identities (Wilson, 2014: 45). Olivia finds a key basis for rejecting *A Room of One's Own* with her discovery of James's *Letters from London*, written shortly after he arrived in London from Trinidad in 1932 and reflecting on his experiences with Bloomsbury intellectuals. Olivia recycles James, who recycled Woolf in writing: 'whatever you do the loneliness of the room is dreadful. When you lock the door you are in a world of your own' (2014: 14). For the migrant and racial other, far from home, a 'room of one's own' is a mark of loneliness, isolation. Wilson's re-mix of *A Room of One's Own* turns Woolf's prescription of a room of one's own into description of the alienation that Olivia feels as a scholarship student at Cambridge based on her mixed race, class and queerness.

Olivia's alienation deepens as she wonders if going to Cambridge might not make her into one of 'them': 'Perhaps', she worries, I am 'more like them

Why We Need Literature, Art and Fantasy 119

than I thought. [...] Aspiring to end up in power. Or with it. With ease [...] One more woman of note from the factory of famous men... . Not a real feminist [...] The logic of masculinity, for men, by men. [...] I become part of the problem, for women. Leaping through any glass ceiling to spend my time talking to men with power' (Wilson, 2014: 12–13). Olivia's rejection of the future that Cambridge promises anticipates Woolf's own development of her feminist theory in *Three Guineas*, which explicitly warns educated women NOT to enter the processions of privilege, but rather to join the Outsider Society, indeed to 'burn' the words 'tyrant' and 'dictator', and even the old-fashioned word 'feminist' (120–22). In *A Room of One's Own*, there is little hint of Woolf's later pacifist radicalism, and Wilson's re-mix focuses steadfastly on her earlier essay.

Olivia's direct experience of overt racism at the Shakespeare Society (in Chapter 4) transforms her self-doubting alienation into a rage that finds full confirmation in the memoirs of Carmichael and Rap Brown and their call for a separatist, even violent Black Power revolution, specifically in Carmichael's *Black Power: the Power of Liberation* and Brown's *Die Nigger Die!* (in Chapters 5 and 6). Re-mixing Woolf's exploration of gender difference in Chapter 5 of *A Room of One's Own*, Wilson's Chapter 5 ratchets up the discourse of difference by having Olivia exude the rage that Woolf suppresses. Like Rich's argument in 'When We Dead Awaken' that women 'must go through that anger' (1971) instead of trying for Woolf's 'detachment' (Rich, 1971: 48–9), Olivia embraces her anger and identifies with Black Power by plotting to burn down Cambridge libraries, especially the University Library and those of Newnham and Fernham, the women's college of *A Room of One's Own*. 'A sanctuary for women of money', she thinks, 'is unprofitable to the liberty of all women' (Wilson, 2014: 128), as she sets the fire at Newnham. The fire-setting scenes are chilling, invoking the long history of state and mob violence threatening both knowledge and vulnerable people, most recently the Nazi burning of Jewish books in 1933 and al-Qaeda's burning of Timbuktu's ancient Islamic texts in 2013. *Fahrenheit 451*, Ray Bradbury's dystopia of burning books (1953), hovers in the background of Olivia's decision. Destroying knowledge, even knowledge that oppresses and threatens freedom of thought. Olivia's anger burns bright, a retaliatory terror. She believes that in burning books, especially *A Room of One's Own*, she will succeed in burning her bridges into the elite world that Oxbridge represents. The climax is to be her burning of the manuscript for *A Room of One's Own*: 'I must set light to the original', she thinks, 'that life manual of Our Own. Because that woman is not my hero [...] Which is why I embark alone. I, the Woman of October. Summoning the courage to complete a war against fiction, for a hundred thousand women, or so, by an army of one woman, or so. Or s [...] I had my help. Two men' (Wilson, 2014: 130; second ellipsis in original).

Olivia's revolutionary burnings come to an abrupt halt when she actually picks up Woolf's manuscript, only to see her flame mysteriously go out. She determines to tear up the manuscript: 'But she could not do it' (Wilson, 2014: 131). The actual feel of the old manuscript in her hands sets in motion a new train of thought – one that returns to the original meaning of revolution, a turning back

120 *Theorising Cultures of Equality*

as precondition to moving forward. *A Room of One's Own*, Olivia realises, 'had asked questions that she had had to answer herself, as those of the writer had been inadequate. Its value was its inquiry, not its conclusion' (2014: 131). Rejecting the kind of violent revolution that Carmichael and Brown call for, Olivia instead thinks: 'The words were right, they were just in the wrong order' (2014: 131). She will re-mix Woolf to make 'The right words in the right order' (2014: 131). She still believes that *A Room of One's Own* 'is not poetry. Or truth as I know it […] But, it could be […] If I were to mend it […] Cut it up and put them in a different order […] Tampering with the shape of what there is. If the trouble is not with words but with their use' (2014: 131; ellipses in original).

Olivia articulates the poetics that govern the novel of which she is the protagonist. The new, she thinks, is remade from the old: 'I will give her another go […] I will write her again. For the new now'. (2014: 131; ellipses in original). This is the 'New Word Order', she says, a re-mix of a new world order. These reflections give Olivia a new way to say her name: Olivia N'Gowfri—the anagram of Virginia Woolf—becomes 'I-live-here, an'-go-free', (2014: 132), her book a 'memoir of a fortnight, An Olivia of My Own' (2014: 132). In the end, she recognises that the letters of her memoir are 'Our letters', that is, 'by Olivia and by…'. The unnamed Woolf resides in the ellipsis; she is Olivia's interlocutor, the one with whom she shares words – cut up in pieces and reordered, but nonetheless shared in a cycle of ends and beginnings – a revolution in which the echo of Shakespeare's *All's Well That Ends Well* in the final lines of the novel provides the ultimate commentary on the collaboration of old and new:

> Because we share them, and write the sequel together in conciliation, once
> morning has broken…
> Autumn into spring…
> …I had to. But this is not the end. The very beginning…
> ***
> 'that can such sweet use make of what they hate'
> (Shakespeare, 135; ellipses in original)

Conclusion

The end as a new beginning that reversions the old builds on the subterranean meaning of revolution: that is, a turning back to start anew. As Wilson himself writes about revolution-as-turning: '"revolving" is a fantastic word to anchor it all around, it's such a beautiful image, the embrace of being dizzy, of going backwards as well as forwards and not needing to know exactly when and where we are at every moment."

A dizzying break, a refresh, a re-mix: this is what imagination, fantasy, creativity bring to our efforts to promote cultures of equality. And to the visionary pleasures and mysteries of the arts, we can add the importance of

Why We Need Literature, Art and Fantasy   121

the disciplines that study literature and art as well as philosophy, history, geography, cultural anthropology and linguistics; that is, all the pillars of the humanities. I argue here not for the greater importance of the humanities than the sciences and the social sciences. Rather, I promote the complementary and mutually necessary modes of knowing – from sciences and social sciences to the arts and humanities. We need to be asking: what is it that each mode of knowing can uniquely teach that others do not teach as much or as well? How can we build bridges among these modes of knowing that allow for crossings, connections and mutual enrichments while still retaining their distinctiveness? These are pressing questions for universities in their institutional structures if they hope that to turn departmental barriers into bridges, for researchers who want to cross those bridges, and for students who must cross those bridges in their multidisciplinary curricula. Integrating these different modes of knowing has been integral to women's and gender studies from the beginning. Let us make sure that the heavy push for practical knowledge and measurable results in today's world does not erase the power of fantasy and creativity, as well as the necessity for non-metrical, non-quantifiable and non-empirical modes of knowledge in service of the cultures of equality.

Bibliography

Agamben, G. (2009). *"What Is the Contemporary?" What Is an Apparatus? And Other Essays.* Transl. D. Kislik and S. Pedatella. Stanford, CA: Stanford University Press: 39–54.

Anbinder, T.G. (1994). *Nativism and Slavery: The Northern Know Nothings and the Politics of the 1850s.* Oxford: Oxford University Press.

Bradbury, R. (1966 [2012]). *Fahrenheit 451.* New York: Simon and Schuster.

Brown, H.R. (1969). *Die Nigger Die!: A Political Autobiography.* Westport, CT: Lawrence Hill Books.

Burges, J. and Elias, A., eds. (2016). *Time: A Vocabulary for the Present.* New York: New York University Press.

Carmichael, S. (1971 [2007]). *Stokely Speaks: Black Power Back to Pan-Africanism.* Chicago, IL: Chicago Review Press.

Carmichael, S. and Hamilton, C.V. (1967 [2011]). *Black Power: The Politics of Liberation.* New York: Vintage.

Carroll, L. (1871 [2007]). 'Chapter VI: Humpty Dumpty'. *Through the Looking Glass: and What Alice Found There. Complete Works* (Illustrated). Phoenix Classics. New York: Barnes & Noble.

Edelman, L. (2004). *No Future: Queer Theory and the Death Drive.* Durham, NC: Duke University Press.

Flood, A. (2014). 'Virginia Woolf's A Room of One's Own Remixed to Form a New Story', 26 September. [online] Available at www.the guardian.com/books/2014/sept/26/Virginia-woolf-a-room-of-ones-own [Accessed 27 February 2015].

Friedman, S.S. (2019). 'Recycling Revolution: Re-mixing A Room of One's Own and Black Power in Kabe Wilson's Performance, Installation, and Narrative Art'. In

122 *Theorising Cultures of Equality*

Contemporary Revolutions: Turning Back to the Future in 21st Century Literature and Art. Ed. Susan Stanford Friedman. London: Bloomsbury Academic Press.

Greenblatt, S. (2017). 'Why Our Stories Matter', *The New York Times*, 21 December.

Jasehik, S. (2014). 'Obama vs. Art History', *Inside Higher Ed*, 31 January. [online] Available at www.insidehighered.com/news/2014. 18 January 2018.

Jenkins, N. (2015). 'Alarm over Huge Cuts to Humanities and Social Sciences at Japanese Universities', *Time*, 16 September. [online] Available at www.time.com/4025819/japan-university-liberal-arts-humanities [Accessed 1 January 2018].

Klebnikov, S. (2015). 'Liberal Arts vs. STEM: The Right Degrees, the Wrong Debate', *Forbes*, 19 June. [online]. Available at www.forbes.com/sites/sergeiklebnikov [Accessed 18 January 2018].

Lee, H. (1999). *Virginia Woolf.* New York: Vintage.

McIntosh, M. (2014). Video Interview with Kabe Wilson, 25 April. [online] Available at www.youtube.com/watch?v=AzOPxa2y8aQ. [Accessed 11 September 2015].

McIntosh, M. (2014). 'Re-writing Virginia Woolf'. [online]. Available at www.dreadlockhoax.co.ulk/Eng_newsletter.jpg. [Accessed on 11 September 2015].

Marcus, J. (2004). 'A Very Fine Negress'.In *Hearts of Darkness: White Women Write Race.* New Brunswick, NJ: Rutgers University Press:24–58.

Marosevic, Z. (2014). 'Woolf's A Room of One's Own Rewritten as Of One Woman or So', 22 September. [online] Available at www.mhpbooks.com/woolfs-a-room-of-ones-own-rewritten. (Accessed on 2 November 2015].

Megill, A. (2014). 'The Creativity of Limits'. 26 September. [online] Available at www.annamegill.com/blog/2014/9/26/creastivity-within-limits. [Accessed on 2 November 2015].

Meretoja, H. (2018). *The Ethics of Storytelling: Narrative Hermeneutics, History, and the Possible.* Oxford: Oxford University Press.

Meretoja, H. and Davis, C., eds. (2017). *Storytelling and Ethics: Literature, Visual Arts and the Power of Narrative.* London: Routledge.

Oxford English Dictionary. (2019). Oxford: Oxford University Press. [online] Available at www.oed.com. [Accessed 5 April 2019].

Orwell, G. (1934). *Animal Farm.* London: Secker & Warburg.

Rich, A. (1984). 'Notes toward a Politics of Location'. In *Blood, Bread, and Poetry: Selected Prose, 1979–1985.* New York: W.W. Norton & Co, 1985. 447–459.

Rich, A (1971) 'When We Dead Awaken: Writing as Re-Vision'. In *On Lies, Secrets, and Silence: Selected Prose, 1966–1978.* New York: W.W. Norton & Co., 1978: 35–50.

Rothberg, M. (2009). *Multidirectional Memory: Remembering the Holocaust in the Age of Decolonization.* Stanford, CA: Stanford University Press.

Rowbotham, S. (1973). *Women's Consciousness, Man's World.* London: Verso.

Small, H. (2013). *The Value of the Humanities.* Oxford: Oxford University Press.

Walker, A. (1974). 'In Search of Our Mothers' Gardens'. *In Search of Our Mothers' Gardens: Womanist Prose.* New York: Harcourt Brace Jovanovich, 1983: 231–243.

Wilson, K. (2014). 'The Dreadlock Hoax', *Studies in the Maternal*, 6(1). [online] Available at www.dreaklockhox.co.uk/the-dreadlock-hoax. [Accessed on 11 September 2015].

Wilson, K. *Of One Woman or So*, O. N'Gowfri. 2009–2014. Unpublished. PDF available from Kabe Wilson.

Wilson, K. (2015). *Of One Woman or So*, O. N'Gowfri. Installation at the Weston Library, Special Collections Library of the Bodleian, Oxford University.

Woolf, V. (1937). 'Craftsmanship', British Broadcasting Corporation series, 'Words Fail Me'. Broadcast 20 April. [online] Available at www.youtube.com/watch?v=E8czs8v6Pul. [Accessed on 6 November 2015].

Woolf, V. (1942). 'Craftsmanship', 1937. *The Death of the Moth and Other Essays.* New York: Harcourt Brace: 198–207.

Harcourt Brace, 198–207 (1929 [1957]) *A Room of One's Own.* New York: Harcourt Brace Jovanovich.

Harcourt Brace, 198–207 (1938 [2006]) *Three Guineas.* Annotated and with introduction by Jane Marcus. New York: Mariner Books.

8 Translating Homosexuality

Urbanism and the masculine *bakla* in Severino Montano's *The Lion and the Faun*

J. Neil Garcia

Introduction

In the Philippines, one of Americanisation's most enduring effects is the socialisation of Filipinos into modern modes of gender and sexual identity formation. This process was instituted and 'naturalised' through a variety of biomedical discourses (public hygiene, guidance and counselling, psychology, psychiatry, feminism and AIDS, among many others), and it has resulted in the entrenchment of the 'homo/hetero' dichotomy as the key organising principle in the increasingly *sexually freighted* lives of educated Filipinos, many of whom reside and work in the Philippines' expanding urban centres, where Westernised knowledges are increasingly the norm.[1]

The globally cathected city, being the centre of knowledge dissemination, is therefore the privileged location of 'perverse implantations' of global genders and sexualities, and indeed, it is to these self-same processes that the Philippines owes the reality of local gay and lesbian culture as well as, in more recent times, lesbian, gay, bisexual and transgender (LGBT) politics and identities. Even as the metropolis in many other places around world has functioned in more less the same way, there are many encouraging narratives that the mostly urban-based sexualisation of Filipinos has engendered, and these are the narratives of cultural hybridity and appropriation, which may also be read – using a different kind of analytic optic – as post-colonial narratives of resistance. The perspective that enquires into the issue of resistance is different from and possibly runs counter to that being offered by cosmopolitanist theorisings, which tend to elide the agonistic questions of neo/colonial power, by and large.

More specifically, we can say that these narratives include LGBT activism itself, which, as Filipinos espouse and practice it, is certainly not reducible to the same political 'thing' that it arguably is, elsewhere in the globalised world. While we must accept the fact that it was colonial modernity's sexological regime that pathologised the Filipino LGBT community in the first place (Ramos Suarez, 2017),[2] as the present-day example of increasingly politicised Filipino gays, lesbians and transgender people illustrates, we must also recognise that it was precisely this very stigma that also, paradoxically, enabled them, in all sorts of interesting and unpredictable ways.

Translating Homosexuality 125

In this chapter I perform a broadly post-colonial reading of Severino Montano's unpublished novel, *The Lion and the Faun*, paying critical attention to the ways in which the various translocal spaces of the city are conceptualised not only as privileged locations for sexual self-realisation, affording the sexual 'exile' structures for community-formation and support outside the traditional family, but also as ambivalent habitational tropes (for both global and national gay 'belonging') that are at once welcoming and alienating, precisely because of the city's own inescapable contradictions, as the site of knowledge-dissemination and subject-formation.

Of course, more crucially, the city can do all this because it in fact provides the literal and conceptual space within which the homo/sexualisation of the local effeminate identity of the bakla takes place – most efficaciously – in the Philippines. Needless to say, in the Philippines as elsewhere, the city is where traditional understandings of gender have come to confront, dialogue with and syncretise the homo/hetero distinction that the unfinished project of modernity continues to bequeath.

The 'post-colonial' signifier remains an entirely useful rubric within which to understand the textual productions of Filipinos, especially where they are in English – a language that continues to occupy an ambivalently dominant place in the lives of many in our corner of the Global South. This seems a necessary qualification, despite or precisely because of the emergence and increasing 'popularity' of cosmopolitanism – a theory sourced from social anthropology that has come to subsume the more *culturalist* aspects of globalisation, of which it is generally uncritical. Cosmopolitanism pertains to the inter-disciplinary academic 'movement' currently gaining currency in increasingly cosmopolitan locations around the world, and at its heart is a social theory that attempts to address the question of modernity. The genealogy of this theory is undeniably Western – drawing, for its key concepts, from ancient Greek and Kantian discourses. This genealogy itself problematises cosmopolitanism's essentialist claims, and its most important idea – of a supposedly universal attitude of, or competence for, 'openness' supposedly to be observed in all cultures – not the least because this genealogy in many parts of the world has actually coincided with the history of imperialism (Delanty, 2006).

In other words, the various cases of attitudinal or even affectional investments into acts of cross-cultural détente and/or 'translation' by various peoples around the world may need to be distinguished from the cosmopolitanist imagination (as such), and flagged accordingly, especially when such investments have been and are being made by colonised peoples. Openness itself as an ideal cannot be made innocently normative across all cultural locations where it apparently manifests itself, for as we all too painfully know, the fact of territorial subjugation has actually forced the colonised to translate themselves – their own lives, their own identities – into the cosmopolitan languages of their colonisers.

While it is true that cosmopolitanist theorising arguably addresses questions of global seriousness and import, as well as national 'self-problematising' in view of increasing global pressures to connect and dialogue across cultural

126 *Theorising Cultures of Equality*

borders, the 'politics' that this kind of sociology betokens must remain suspect, precisely to the degree that it seems to assume that the playing field between Self and Other is now all of a sudden amicable and 'equal'. Despite its *translatedness,* insisting on the resistant and post-colonial – as opposed to cosmopolitanist – character of contemporary Philippine literature is not only more historically precise; it is also more politically and ethically 'responsible'.

At this point, there are a few conceptual clarifications we need to make. We begin with the idea that gender is analytically separable from sexuality: male/female, masculine/feminine are gender distinctions; while homo/hetero/bi are sexual categories. They do not necessarily converge or line up neatly. As we by now all too acutely know, both are nothing if not social constructions.

To be specific, we need to see that the most popular local term for the male homosexual – the word *bakla* – started out as an ungendered adjective to denote a state of confusion or fear. Then, during the Spanish period, it slowly became synonymous with the local gender terms for womanish or feminine men, except that unlike the words that it eventually came to eclipse – examples of these precolonial words for gender-crossers are *bayoguin, binabae,* and *asog* – it carried with it the force of macho insult.[3]

With Americanisation, upon the arrival of the psychological and psychiatric style of reasoning – that, among things, implanted sexological categories – *bakla* was slowly but securely 'homo/sexualised', so much so that it is now understood as a synonym for 'male homosexual'' although in most cases, as it occurs in popular culture, it still carries with it the earlier ideas of effeminacy and even transgenderism.[4] The *bakla* is therefore only a partly homosexualised identity – partial because only he and not his love object (the 'real man') gets imputed with the orientation, despite their mutual indulgence in – and enjoyment of – homosexual sex. We might say that gender identity in the Philippines is mostly premised on a concept – actually, an article of faith – that privileges depth, psychospiritual plenitude, core-ness or *kalooban*; external acts can be countervailed by the primacy of this interiority.[5]

The 'sexualisation' of local concepts of gender accompanied English-based education in the Philippine colony at the beginning of the last century (Lagmay, 2000). Since then, Filipinos have been increasingly socialised in Western modes of gender and sexual identity formation, courtesy of a sexualisation that rode on different but complementary discourses (Tan, 1994).[6] This has resulted in the deepening of sexuality's 'perverse implantation' into the local soil, characterised by the discursive escalation and naturalisation of the 'homo/hetero' distinction.

Severino Medina Montano (1915–80) was the moving force in Philippine theatre before the outbreak of the Second War and for some time after that (Cultural Centre of the Philippines, 1995).[7] After finishing his degree in the University of the Philippines, he left for the USA on a scholarship in 1940, receiving his MA in Fine Arts from Yale University, and his MA in Economics from the American University in Washington, DC, where he also finished his PhD in public administration in 1949. During the Second World War years, he did research and wrote for the Philippine government-in-exile in the USA.

Shortly thereafter, he travelled all around Europe on a number of Rockefeller grants to pursue his love of theatre. Upon returning to the Philippines, he became dean of instruction at the Philippine Normal University, where he established the Arena Theater, 'to bring drama to the masses'. He wrote, managed, acted and directed for this theatre company, which ended up staging almost 200 performances of four ensemble plays, all penned by him. Montano received the Presidential Award of Merit in 1961, and for his 'nationalist endeavors' he was posthumously accorded the Cultural Center of the Philippines Centennial Honor for the Arts in 1999.

Montano was posthumously declared a National Artist in 2001. His work in Philippine theatre in English was extensive, and in terms of his staging innovations and the sheer scale and 'reach' of his productions, undeniably significant and path-breaking. But he did write an unpublished novel, a self-consciously homosexual novel titled, *The Lion and the Faun*, a photocopy of which I had the good fortune of acquiring about fifteen years ago. This work, written well before his death in 1980, provides yet another interesting example of how the city-centred sexualisation of gender identities in the Philippines has ironically produced an abjected homosexual identity that can be seen to embrace its abjection and to speak *of* and *for* itself. As was likewise the case with the first Filipino gay author, Jose Garcia Villa (who wrote the earliest gay texts in the Philippines' literary tradition), what seems to have occasioned this undeniably voluble speech was the lived reality and experience of the colonial centre (that is to say, the USA) itself.

In the text that I have acquired and read, it is clear that Montano's novel means to present itself as a provocative and largely autobiographical *roman à clef*. Reading the existing biographical accounts of Montano's life, and juxtaposing them against this novel, I must say that this angle does seem, rather intriguingly, to hold water. In other words, comparing the known facts about Montano's life with those of his main character's – Dr Diosdado Medalla's – the reader is indeed encouraged to carry out a 'biographical interpretation' of the text, which effectively parodies and satirises the shallow and hypocritical lives of Manila's *culturati* and even makes broad hints at a possible romantic dalliance between Medalla, whose nickname is Dadong, and his famous dearest friend, the late Philippine President, Ramon Magsaysay.

Magsaysay (1907–57) was the third president of the Philippine republic after the Second World War. The year that he died in a plane crash on the central Philippine island of Cebu, the trustees of the Rockefeller Brothers Fund based in New York City, with the consent of the Philippine government, established the Ramon Magsaysay Award in order 'to commemorate the late president of the Philippines and to perpetuate his example of integrity in government, courageous service to the people, and pragmatic idealism within a democratic society'. It needs, however, to be said that no account other than Montano's exists – that I know of, at least – that imputes homosexuality to this famous former Philippine president. In a typically soap operatic passage in this novel, Monching (Magsaysay's nickname) and Dadong are shown sharing an intimate conversation

128   *Theorising Cultures of Equality*

while taking a long leisurely walk in the garden of the latter's palatial and newly constructe house, tenderly holding each other's hand as they do so.

Nonetheless, despite the gossipy subplots and rather crass intrigues, the main story of this novel is still Dadong's relationship with the younger Amihan, an Army major stationed at the Reserve Officers' Training Corps office of the university where Dadong teaches, and where he has founded a theatre company. Despite the novel's numerous interesting distractions involving well-known socialites and celebrities, including Cielo Madriaga, whom the reader may recognise as a thinly veiled fictional stand-in for the multimillionaire and shipping heiress, Chito Madrigal, this is still, in the main, a love story (as we shall see, a rather unremittingly syrupy one).

Dadong's background is interesting. Like Montano, for whom he is a fictional representation, he had lived and studied in large urban centres in the West – chiefest of which is Washington, DC, where he resided for several years before coming back to the Philippines to teach and do theatre, as well as privately practice a kind of 'vulgar' psychoanalysis. While in the USA, he had a romantic relationship and cohabited with a German-born American, an economist for the State Department by the name of Leonard Blumenthal. Despite this candid revelation, however, the novel takes pains to paint a 'masculine' and 'bisexual' picture of Dadong as a suavely intelligent and eminently eligible bachelor, who is admittedly homosexually oriented but can swing the other way just as effectively. In the opening chapter we are told that he was 'raped' by their mulatta maid one drunken evening, an incident that convinces him that he can bring himself to 'like' women too, although it is important to note that they have to be extremely intelligent, sexy, talented and menially devoted to him first, before they can ever hope to catch his fancy. Anyway, once back in the Philippines, he is pursued by all manner of desperate, vicious and big-breasted women, with whom he is hopelessly bored. After all, being a well-travelled Renaissance man, he aspires to loftier things… And so, to amuse himself, he quickly puts his mind to building his magnificent 'mansion of love', Villa Bello, one of whose many gardens he plants with bamboo in memory of his beloved friend, the charismatic Philippine president Magsaysay, whose life was unexpectedly cut short in a plane crash outside Cebu City.

Still in mourning, Dadong meets Amihan at a play that he is directing for the university. They quickly hit it off, fall desperately in love and wistfully call each other 'faun' and 'lion', respectively. Dadong fancies himself both as a shrink and a mentor to his beloved, whom he compares, Pygmalion-like, to a rough slab of marble from which he intends to carve his own marvellous sculpture of David. Amihan is unhappily married to a scheming first cousin, who seduced him and thus forced him to marry her. Needless to say, by the time Amihan and the abundantly talented theatre director meet, the former is practically buried under a mountain of pesky and malnourished children and feeling utterly oppressed by his empty marriage – a dismal fate that the latter, needless to say, is determined to redeem him from.

In the course of psychoanalysing his lover, Dadong discovers all the perversions that occurred throughout the latter's astonishingly amoral youth,

Translating Homosexuality 129

including his incestuous attachment to his mother's milk-giving breast, his regular homosexual encounters with a colonel in the Philippine army and countless other men in the anonymous darkness of movie houses, sexual escapades with a number of female cousins, etc. Toward the end of the 500-page novel, Dadong succeeds in convincing Amihan's wife to share her husband with him, for this is the only way – as he seriously impresses upon her – that they can save him from impending insanity or even, heaven forbid, suicide. To her mind, it is all quite fine as long as her husband stays in the mood when it is her turn. Liberated from the exclusivity of his marital obligation, the lion makes love to his faun in the elegantly appointed bedroom of the latter's magnificent mansion.

The novel is flawed, needless to say. The glaring problems of narrative inconsistency, shallow characterisation, crass sentimentalism, belabored and hackneyed poeticism and disorienting shifts in point of view admittedly detract from the novel's overall fictive effect. Other than the controversial nature of its subject, this lack of formal merit (and polish) could have been one of the main reasons that this text never did see the light of publishing day. Nonetheless, my interest in this novel is not really its formal excellence (or woeful lack thereof), but rather its representational content, especially as concerns the issue of homosexual identity and/or consciousness, which it is the first to narrativise in novelistic form in the Philippines (and for this reason alone commends Montano as an important artist indeed, in its national literary tradition). It is likely that Montano had been writing this novel on and off for three or more decades before his death – a fact that was told to me, sometime in the middle of 1993, by my professor in Comparative Literature, the late Angelito Santos, who introduced me to Montano's unpublished novel – which, according to him, had been turned down for publication by several local presses in the 1960s and 1970s and allowed me to photocopy it. Thus, it is entirely plausible to say that Montano at the time simply had no access to the more sophisticated and affirmative and feminist-inspired gay liberationist literatures that would not have mandated a misogynistic attitude toward women in the project of articulating gayness and militating for its emancipation. Montano's appalling anti-woman attitude is all too evident everywhere in the text, from the unflattering description of the 'loose' and 'smelly' genitalia of Lucing, Amihan's grubby tubercular wife, to the unfair characterisation of women as grasping, pathetic and sex-starved gold-diggers.

To Montano's mind, it must have proved necessary to put down women in general in order to destroy the feminised and feminising stereotype that afflicted the Philippine *bakla* – an identity strangely missing in or perhaps deliberately 'evacuated' from the novel. However, precisely because Montano has exiled all traces of effeminacy (or *kabaklaan* in Tagalog) from his text, we are forced to read the *bakla* as being in fact a central force in his articulation, for in repudiating this identity he could only have made it all the more foundational, in the end. Indeed, despite its main characters' testosterone-powered, ambisexually potent machismo, the novel's casting aspersion on women and conceiving them as vicious 'competition' for the attention and affection of men are, finally, very *bakla* things to do.

130   *Theorising Cultures of Equality*

This clearly attests to the fact that Montano, following his attempt to at once *cosmopolitanise* and homo/sexualise the *bakla* – to acquaint this identity with the gender-intransitive and masculine tradition of homosexuality as orientation (rather than gender), which he doubtless encountered in the urbane knowledge systems of the West – the resultant representation could not help but bear traces of the very identity and the very culture he wanted to supplant and supersede. To the degree that the *bakla* is a feminised identity whose object of desire, as with a woman, is a *lalake* or 'man', it is only logical that he should function as a woman's rival every now and then, as indeed Dadong does in relation to his partner's 'uncultured' and 'wretched little wife'. It is important to note, however, that as represented in the novel the beloved man's sexual preference admits to both male and female erotic objects, although it is also clear that the genitally male lover (Dadong) needs to put in extra work, as well as to help out, financially and emotionally, in order to compete viably with the woman who, by the sheer privilege of her anatomy, gets to become the man's sad and ignorant wife.

Montano's cosmpolitanism in this text aspires to celebrate gayness: he mentions the word gay only once, but it is enough to give the reader an awareness of his political agenda. *The Lion and the Faun*, while less successfully poetic than Villa's self-indulgent short fiction, does manage to register its politically aware 'homosexual' quality in a slightly more obtrusive way. That he chooses to play down effeminacy and *kabaklaan* and to focus instead on the gender-intransitive aspect of male homosexuality that may be evidenced in his masculine-comported and behaviourally bisexual yet affectively homosexual characters, can only be seen as a 'naive reactionism', on his part: indeed, how can a novel about male-to-male affection set in the Philippines not implicate the discourse and reality of effeminate homosexuality, embodied most forcefully in the ubiquitous persona of the swishy and slavishly fascinated *bakla*? How could Montano have even believed that he could create a novelistic portrait of the Filipino gay man as masculine and non-*bakla*, when he intended this very same portrait to be 'realistic' – which is to say, recognisable – as Filipino, in the least?

As Michael L. Tan (1998), a Filipino anthropologist, has argued, the local discourse on male bisexuality in the Philippines weaves in and out of the discourse on and by the *bakla*, who are both its apparent subject and its object, and whose anxiously disavowed presence must therefore haunt it in a constitutive way. Indeed, because of this decision to forego openly implicating the *bakla* in the world that it attempts to fictionally capture, Montano's text ends up languishing in phony Graeco-Roman mythologising – a project that he must have known would necessitate the maligning and devaluation of women, who indeed were second-class citizens in these classical worlds.

Also, if his plays are any indication, he would seem to have held highly dubious, conservative and plainly pre-feminist beliefs regarding women in general, who are depicted as happily immolating themselves in at least his two most popular plays, for the sake of their unrequited love for men. I am referring here to the popular plays, *Sabina* and *The Love of Leonor Rivera* – centrepieces in Montano's theatrical oeuvre. In the former, after learning of her

American boyfriend's infidelity, the main character commits suicide by shooting herself; in the latter, Leonor Rivera dies after giving birth to her first and last child by her British husband, but not before she professes, in a poetic soliloquy, her deathless devotion to her one and only love, the ill-fated national hero, José Rizal (Montano, 1958). Needless to say, precisely because this novel denies the empirical facticity of the *bakla* within the local setting to which the *bakla* inescapably belongs, it ends up being fantastical in more senses than one. Fantastical and sentimentally overwrought, to be precise.

We can only guess how Montano's own colonial urbanity – his residency and advanced studies in America for more than a decade – exposed him to the homoerotic histories of ancient Greek and Roman civilisations – histories that proffered a distinctly masculine narrative for the kind of homosexual love story that he subsequently set out to narrate. His knowledge of Freudian psychoanalysis, although shallow and mostly egregiously pretentious, indicates the allure and power that American psychosexual discourse and American erudition in general wielded over his consciousness, and these arguably helped him to make better sense of his own lived homosexuality.

However, it is these very same influences that caused him to reject the bakla-specific effeminacy of his own social formation as a homosexual man in the Philippines, and this could possibly be because the flamboyant persona of the shrill and effeminate 'queen' was likewise being rejected and supplanted by the 'healthier' and 'more mature' masculine gay identity in the initial literary productions of the American gay culture that he must have personally experienced during his residency in the USA, and on any of his extended trips to cosmopolitan centres in Europe shortly thereafter.[8] This is clear in the novel. In the early parts, it is carefully insinuated that the 'very masculine' Dr Medalla went out looking for equally masculine if not more masculine partners in the cruisy areas of Washington, DC. In other words, it appears that Montano did not particularly fancy effeminacy – at least, not in his primary characters, nor in their multiple objects of desire.

Montano illustrates, hence, the simultaneously coercive and 'enabling' effects of modern sexualisation – necessarily urban in its locality – which stigmatised the local *bakla* identity but also made available a discourse and thus a discursive 'position' from which the homosexualised *bakla* may now speak, and from which he may come to know of and to challenge his own subjection. While leaving more to be desired, especially as regards its displacement of abjection from the anguished homosexual man to the uselessly long-suffering or rapacious heterosexual woman, Montano's text does represent one memorably full step toward a kind of empowered self-consciousness for the homosexualised *bakla*. Thankfully, more political and 'fully flowered' manifestations of this self-consciousness may be found in the works of succeeding generations of Filipino gay authors – for example, Tony Peres, whose novella, *Cubao 1980,* is set in Metro Manila's famous 'armpit', in the western portion of Queson City (Perez, 1992), and the many poets, fictionists, essayists and dramatists whose avowedly gay works first came out in the landmark anthology series, *Ladlad* (Garcia and Remoto, 1994).

132 *Theorising Cultures of Equality*

As I have hopefully sufficiently described, *The Lion and the Faun* is a sprawling narrative about a gay, upwardly mobile, suavely urbane, globally travelled and American-educated theatre director, who practices psychotherapy, and his tempestuous love affair with a much younger, less worldly and behaviourally bisexual officer of the Philippine army. Written in English, the novel's text problematises the sexual definitions of its main characters and uses the narrative pretext that the director, who is the narrator, is a psychoanalyst, in order to accomplish this otherwise dour and expository project. Needless to say, this fictive endeavour eventuates in the mooting of the local understandings of gender – namely, that the *bakla* is homosexual, while the 'real man' or *tunay na lalake* whom he loves is not – and the novel ultimately adopts the Western perspective on the issue and basically declares them both to be homosexuals.

This attempt to translate the masculine or gender-intransitive discourse of orientation into the local setting does not entirely succeed, of course: on one hand, as I have earlier argued, its misogynistic subplot specifies its sexual politics as agonistic and peculiarly gender-inflected; on other hand, despite the novel's textual insistence on their comparably masculine comportments as well as the mutuality of their desire, the material disparity – or inequality – between the genteel, well-off and supremely cultured (and domestically skilled) unmarried older man (Dadong) and the economically burdened, handsome and married younger one (Amihan) is tellingly familiar, for it calls to mind popular culture representations of *bakla* love (for the *lalake*) as financially transactional and therefore ultimately 'non-reciprocal'. Indeed, it is easy to see that the good doctor invests more in this so-called love between equals. This text actually deconstructs its own claim regarding this love: its profession comes in the form of spoken dialogues as far as Dadong is concerned; but again and again, it is merely indirectly reported or narrated in the case of Amihan.

We can say that the earliest examples of the gay theme in Philippine writing demonstrate the defining role the city – as the privileged site of modern subject-formation – has played in the history of Philippine sexual identities. Comparing, for example, Montano's text with another famous work, *Hanggang Dito na lamang at Maraming Salamat*, the celebrated one-act play of Orlando Nadres (Maniquiz, 1994)[9] (likewise written sometime between the late 1960s to early 1970s), we readily see the role that location plays in the way that these writers handled and depicted the 'homosexual' question.

In Nadres' text (set, mostly likely, in his hometown of Tayabas, Queson), the protagonist, also an older man who is in love with a much younger man, while acceding to the point that the closeted *bakla* can sometimes look masculine (to his own internal turmoil), simply accepts the *bakla/tunay na lalake* ('real man') dualism, and more or less endorses the idea that the *bakla* needs to reconcile himself to his ultimately sad fate, as the *lalake* he is attracted to (and slavishly fascinated with) will have to end up getting married to a real woman, and becoming a father, as these are what solidify the realness of his masculinity, in the first place. The setting of these fictional worlds – Washington DC, New York and Manila, in Montano's novel, a small and unnamed town in the southern Tagalog province of Queson, in Nadres' play – clearly spells a difference, as does the choice of language, in the treatment of the gay subject matter in these texts.

The expatriate nature of Montano's autobiographical novel, and the fact that its main character, like Montano himself, resided, studied and became sexually self-aware and empowered in the USA, establish, rather blatantly, the American connection in the Philippines' gay literary tradition. This is a connection that had been established earlier on, in fact, in what may be the 'first' Filipino gay texts: four stories by the legendary and exiled poet, José Garcia Villa.[10] These stories are called 'autobiographical' by the American editor and literary power-broker, Edward O'Brien, who functioned as Villa's literary benefactor, in his preface to the collection, *Footnote to Youth*, in which they first saw print (published by Scribner in Chicago in 1933). In these stories, Villa narrates his consuming attraction to and love for two American boys, David and Jack, who were his schoolmates at university in Albuquerque, New Mexico, where he first resided, after leaving the Philippines more or less for good in the late 1920s (Garcia Villa, 1933; 1973).[11]

Apart from detailing the racialised and unrequited nature of these attractions, Villa's stories also propound a psychoanalytic understanding of homosexuality, as an orientation that supposedly derives from an unresolved Oedipal complex, which results in an 'arrested psychosexual development'. This is something that is clearly suggested by Villa's own confessional passages concerning his tormented familial circumstances, characterised by an aversion toward his stern and unloving father and a tender affection for his mother and aunts, who doted on him. In these stories, the city is evidently American modernity itself, with its future-looking secular knowledges, its comfortable anonymity and, yes, its irrevocable distance from the stifling judgment of the natal past, embodied most painfully by the image of the harshly intolerant patriarch, whom Villa left behind in the 'backward' Philippines, but whose ghostly presence haunts his early attempts at fiction, and certainly his poetry, as well.

In both Villa's and Montano's texts, the use of English arguably facilitated the broaching of the otherwise unseemly and unspeakable topic of homosexuality, although it is more likely that this language did not so much render this topic simply *sayable* as made it experientially real, to begin with: colonial education was the vehicle upon which the homo/hetero distinction (and sexological thinking, in general) rode, and it was inexorably conducted in English – the medium through which Filipinos were sexualised and, in the main, continue to be sexualised. It is only to be expected, therefore, that the earliest and more explicit literary representations of homosexuality in the Philippines were in its anglophone texts. This is simply of a piece with the fact that this literature is also where the first critical questionings of long-kept traditional values and depictions of perversions – like incest and paedophilia – were made.

In this final section, I would like to refer to my previous statement that the lack of formal merit in Montano's novel is fairly easy to see. Unlike any of the 'modernist' novels of Nick Joaquin, N.V.M. Gonzalez or Bienvenido Santos,

134 *Theorising Cultures of Equality*

who together formed the triumvirate of exemplary Filipino novelists in English at this time, Montano's *roman à clef* is, admittedly, incoherent even on the 'literal' level. Strangely enough, his language is figurative most of the time, which makes for some additional difficulties. Focalisation, or point of view, is awry, for every so often epiphanies are being undergone by *all* the characters. Because even the minor characters are granted the privilege of explaining their motives – through the omniscient narration – motivation and the behaviour that it prompts is mostly fictionally unearned. Consequently, a lot of the action is reflected upon, thereby exposing the author to the danger of false characterisation and giving one the impression that, in effect, there is only one mind behind all the characters. There is also very little texture in the dialogue, and this results in rather shallow characterisation, with all of them speaking in the same way, and, in light of the novel as a whole, thinking the same way too, fatally. Narrative progression is simplistic and unengagingly linear, save for the first and only flashback in the first scene.

But it is precisely because the novel is 'badly written' that its politics never got the chance to be articulated institutionally, and presumably, Montano wrote the novel with his institutional peers as his audience. I assume this to have been the case because Montano's stand-in, Dadong (or Dr Medalla), works in the academe, and his friends are mostly writers and theatre people, and, more significantly, the way that he describes himself is defensively arrogant. By the way that Dadong explains himself, by the reflections that he makes on his past and present action, by the way that the novel as a whole feels like one gigantic excuse to slap Dadong/Montano's own back, I can almost conclude that the novel was written to veritably redeem its author.

Redeem Montano from what? The reproach of his peers, presumably, for this is a novel that dares to expose its author as a homosexual, a practicing homosexual, a homosexual with wife, children and female lovers all of a piece. Did the real Montano do, and was the real Montano, all that? I for one cannot say for sure. An exercise in literary self-championing, this novel may not be relied on, after all, to impart any clear sense of objectivity.

Finally, we can see that because the novel is unpretentiously personal – with 'gut-feel poetry' invariably cropping up without any warning, and seeping into its very structure – any of the charges of sloppiness that may be levelled against it are really just stating the obvious (as well as nitpicking). To a certain extent, I have decided to read the novel as a kind of autobiography, and specifically as a kind of homosexual autobiography, and the responsibility that comes with a political reading such as this is the responsibility of contextualisation.

Montano was working under the ideological and aesthetic ensign of Humanism, which derives directly from the institutional Christian religion and the political ideology of his milieu. Indeed, arguably all local writers at the time were humanists, too, their fictional, poetic, and dramatic universes revolving around the concept of an essential, universal human 'Self'. For Montano, this Unconscious, this specific 'cryptoarchive', manifested itself as Dr Medalla, the globally urbane and all-around Renaissance Man whose homosexuality is but a small part of his multifaceted personality, is God-given, and, therefore, natural and good. Furthermore, Montano seemed to be constrained to locate his novel in the figurative settings of Greek mythology, thereby imputing its *telos* in the well-known fact that ancient Greek society exhibited institutionalised homosexuality (more accurately, pederasty). Or perhaps he saw poetic confabulation as a means to escape precisely the reproach of having written a scandalous homosexual love story.

It is relevant that we remember, at this point, the fact that for a long time Montano was a canonical figure in Philippine theatre. Up until the 1980s, his more famous short plays were regularly staged in many Philippine high schools and were cited in academic forums as early examples of local anglophone dramaturgy. The difficulty that Montano obviously encountered in writing the novel could therefore be traced to a translational problem, not just of linguistic competence, but of genre-shifting as well. In theatre, every character is granted the opportunity to explain himself/herself, for indeed theatre is both presentation *and* representation. Hence, the problem of focalisation or point of view that appears to be the most serious flaw in *The Lion and the Faun* could well be just an unprocessed theatrical convention that Montano deployed, predictably to a fault, in his novel. For when, in a novel, the third person 'selective omniscient' point of view engages in an interior monologue about another character, he/she is doing it as just another participant in the novel's story and is, therefore, neither infallible nor all-knowing, but is rather biased and 'limited' – and the reader knows this, at once. By contrast, in a play, each character is there on the stage himself/herself, fully present to make himself/herself known to the audience. Indeed, all the characters in this novel seem to talk in soliloquys, unmindful of the possibility that they are all mouthing what in effect are identical lines that could have proceeded only out of a single mind.

Furthermore, looking at the plays that in this period were being written in English by playwrights such as Jesus Peralta, Jose Flores and Antonio Bayot, all of whom were at one time or another apprentices to Montano, or even at the works of Montano's successor as the foremost champion of Philippine theatre in English, Wilfrido Ma. Guerrero, the problem of 'cultural impunity' – or the guiltless, unmediated use of English to refer to Filipino cultural phenomena – was very clearly not a problem at all at this time. Or at least, not to the playwrights themselves or their audiences at large. It seems that the verisimilitude of this brand of theatre rested not on language, but rather on other modes of expression and theatre conventions like the melodrama, the 'arena' method of staging, etc. Nonetheless, looking at Montano in particular, the plays that his theatre group produced were promoted all over Luzon island, but always under the auspices of the public schools of the regions concerned. This presumably implies that the aesthetic mode of the Arena Theater was shared by a large part of the public educational system at the time.

Of course, even with these 'qualifications,' it is still possible to say that the novel is *defective,* without even batting an eyelash. Normally, a novel's narrative language is different from its language of dialogue, thereby implying a

136 *Theorising Cultures of Equality*

split between interior and exterior speech, which also suggests a split in the levels of consciousness, between the 'outside world' of setting, time, etc., and the 'inner world' of the main character's psyche. In an English novel – that is to say, a novel written in English – the difference is not as profound if the reality that it refers to, or if the characters who speak in it, are also (in) English.

Working with alternative modes of storytelling, new literatures in English (indeed, new literatures in *englishes*), however, have needed to develop sundry ways and means to circumvent this problem of disparity between linguistic and extralinguistic content by inventing an alloy tongue: a general language of narration and dialogue characterised by hybridised, pidgin, or patois *english*. Montano's novel, however, exhibits no such obviously 'ethnic' appropriation that should have decentred or upset the proper English usage and therefore effected a semantic sabotage of the colonial tongue. Instead, the novel simply pretends that English is the language that these characters actually speak and think in.

Such a formal gesture toward (in this case, sexual) universalism does not, of course, mean that his text is not post-colonial: like the other texts comprising the tradition of Philippine anglophone literature, Montano's novel can be said to perform its post-coloniality by negotiating the plurality of cultural and linguistic registers and ideas of the Philippine reality and encoding them in/as English, which of course is localised and transvalued in the very act of its being used. Even the universal, as an aspiration, 'register', or idea, is one such 'meaning' that has been translated by and in Filipino writers' works (Garcia, 2014).[12] Pedagogically, our task when we teach Philippine literature in English must therefore be post-colonially to interpret its seemingly universal themes, images and textual gestures, by translating them back into the specific conditions and situations that framed and engendered them. However, we must maintain that evidence of this *translatedness* does not always have to be inscribed visibly in the text, but necessarily attends the writing and reading contexts that frame it.

In other words, our 'universal-sounding' anglophone texts, despite being devoid of post-colonial ethnic 'particularity', and seeming to be 'at home' in the neocolonially endowed English language, do finally lend themselves to a post-colonial reading that reveals how complicated and uneasy this interpretive arrangement – its intentions, affects and rhetorical effects – truly is. The universal, in the hands of the post-colonial subject, is nothing if not a translated or translational universal, and for this reason it cannot be remotely coincident with – or even performatively comparable with – the universal of colonial Humanism (Bhabha, 1993). We can even say that the more oppositional forms of post-colonial writing are not easily contained in their extraordinary foreignness, but rather subvert and reinscribe transgression from within.

The Philippines' anglophone tradition represents local realities by translating them, both in the technical and cultural senses of the word. If, within a monocultural context, realism is already the translation from imitation to 'creation', then in the linguistically plural situations of post-colonial societies this already fraught process – of verbal mimesis – can only be even more

Translating Homosexuality 137

complex and confounding. As translational, Philippine literature in English negotiates the plurality of cultural and linguistic registers and ideas of local realities, and encodes them in/as English. The critical task, then, is to *post-colonially interpret* its seemingly self-evident themes, images and gestures, by translating them back into the specific conditions and situations that generated them. We must, however, maintain that evidence of this *translatedness* does not always have to be inscribed visibly in the text, but necessarily attends the writing and reading contexts that frame it.

On the other hand, to Montano the choice of standard English makes perfect sense not just because situated in his specific historical context, there was hardly any question about which language to employ for a relatively new, equally foreign form as the novel, but also because the delicacy of the subject that he chose to explore in a way only required it. Simply put: there is something very attractive about the idea of appropriating 'external' things, if what it means is that one may avoid (if not undo) what one's own culture calls one's very self: in Montano's – and our own – case, *bakla* and others too awful to mention. Following this notion, we may perhaps also say that 'one's own' is not always good and can even be at the root of one's very anguish and oppression.

Montano must have intimately known this, too. By choosing to write the way that he did, he was possibly unconsciously trying to escape from the sexual constraints or the close-minded 'conservatism' of his own culture, primarily by appealing to the relative urbane openness and 'liberalism' of another. Hence, the unbridled use of English in this novel, which was the medium through which Filipino culture was sexualised on one hand, but, by the same token, also the medium through which a discursive space was made possible for the subjects that this self-same process has abjected to reimagine, speak and affirm themselves.

In sum, Montano's attempt to displace prevailing categories and to translate the gender-intransitive discourse of orientation into the local setting ended up being problematic, at best. On the one hand, its misogynistic subplot specifies its sexual politics as agonistic and peculiarly gender-inflected; on the other, despite the novel's textual insistence on their comparably masculine comportments as well as the mutuality of their *same-sexual* desire, the material 'inequality' between the genteel, well-off and supremely cultured unmarried older man and the economically burdened and married younger one is tellingly familiar, for it calls to mind popular culture representations of *bakla* love (for the 'real man') as financially transactional and therefore ultimately 'non-reciprocal'. Indeed, it is easy to see that the good doctor invests more in this so-called love between equals. This novel actually 'self-deconstructs' here: the profession of this love comes in the form of spoken dialogues as far as the benefactor-lover is concerned; but is merely indirectly reported or narrated in the case of the beloved.

And yes, finally, we need to realise that like all the other mother tongues in the Philippines, Tagalog, the language of the world that this novel is set in, is gender-neutral. While seemingly inconsequential to Philippine anglophone criticism, the fact is that realistically, these local characters would not have been a 'she' or a 'he'. Thus, gendering these characters' identities and lives –

138   *Theorising Cultures of Equality*

from the Tagalog 'source' to the English 'target' – is and can only be ironic, to the degree that what the latter takes to be fundamentally binary is to the former, to all intents and purposes, unitary (Quindoza Santiago, 2007).[13] An immense slippage takes place when one translates the pronoun *siya* to either 'he' or 'she'. Hence, despite the anatomical dimorphism of modern biomedicine, on which the homo/hetero binary rests, as translated into the Philippine linguistic context, this binary is far from coherent and simplistically assured. Montano's ignorance of this translational dynamic caused him to mistakenly believe that erotic equality can only be achieved in the supersession of the *bakla* identity, which is to say, its 'masculinist homosexualisation'. As we know, this is a project that can only fail, even as in his text it did generate interesting albeit mostly ruinous effects.

The realist project in anglophone writings requires cross-cultural dialogue – a practice of 'double translation' that involves both the representational movement across cultures and the transcultural movement across realities. As I have attempted to rehearse here, the post-colonial reclaiming of referential anglophone texts by Filipinos requires tracing the trajectories of this double or hybrid movement, with the view of proposing various modes of 'post-colonial resistance' – as made possible by the metonymic gap between *mimesis* and *poeisis* that cleaves all translational acts (Garcia, 2016)[14] – particularly as they involve the reading of seemingly simple and 'universal' representations.

Notes

1 An early version of the foregoing summary of the history of homosexuality in the Philippines (which is also, viewed from a slightly different angle, the history of heterosexuality therein) first appeared in my introduction, 'Reading Auras,' to be found in: J. Neil C. Garcia, Aura: the Gay Theme in Philippine Fiction in English (Manila: Anvil Publishing, Inc., 2012): 10–15.

2 The history of the sexual medicalisation – or the medical sexualisation – of the Philippines is the subject of an MA thesis in Gender Studies. See Kiel Ramos Suarez, 'The (Post)colonial Medicalization of the Filipino Homosexual,' MA in Gender Studies, Central European University, Budapest, Hungary, 2017.

3 The more important Spanish colonial accounts about indigenous 'gender crossing' in the Philippines include: Francisco Ignacio Alcina, Historia de las islas e indios de Bisayas (1668), Part I, Book 3, translated by Paul S. Leitz (Chicago: University of Chicago, Philippine Studies Program, 1960), quoted in Evelyn Tan Cullamar, Babaylanism in Negros: 1896–1907 (Manila: New Day Publishers, 1986): 18; Marcelo de Ribadeneira, Historia de las islas del archipelago Filipino (Madrid: Imprenta Saenz, 1947); Domingo Perez (1680), Relation of the Zambals, The Philippine islands, 1493–1898, ed. Emma Blair and James Robertson (Cleveland: Arthur H. Clark, 1903–09), Vol. 7; Juan de Plasencia, Customs of the Tagalogs, Blair and Robertson, Vol. 7: 300; Antonio de Morga, Sucesos de las islas Filipinas, ed. Jose Rizal (Paris: Garnier, 1890), in Blair and Roberts: 16, 130; Francisco Combes, Historia de las islas de Mindanao (Madrid: 1667) ed. W.E. Retana (Madrid 1897), translated in Blair and Robertson, Vol. 40: 150; 'The manners, customs, and beliefs of the Philippine islands of long ago; being the chapters of a late 16th-century Manila manuscript,' translated by Carlos Quirino and Mauro Garcia, The Philippine Journal of Science, Vol. 87, No. 4 (December 1958): 374–75; Pedro Chirino, 'Relation of the Filipinas islands and what has there been accomplished,'

Translating Homosexuality 139

(1601–04), Blair and Robertson, Vol. 12: 260; and Juan Francisco de San Antonio, Cronicas (Manila 1738–44), in Blair and Robertson, Vol. 40: 340–45.

4 For a longer and more 'scholarly' version of this history, see Part One of my Philippine Gay Culture: Binabae to Bakla, Silahis to MSM (Hong Kong: Hong Kong University Press, 2009).

5 What facilitated the process of sexualisation in the Philippines was the existence, among the Tagalog-Filipinos especially, of a 'psychospiritual' discourse of gendered interiority and exteriority: namely, loob and labas. For a cogent explanation of this concept of the sexually defined 'inner self,' see Albert Alejo, S.J., Tao Po! Tuloy! (Quezon City: Office of research and publications, Ateneo de Manila University, 1990). For my own analysis of the loob/labas dynamic, especially as it figures in the history of homosexuality in the Philippines, see my Philippine gay culture: 120–30.

6 The Filipino anthropologist, Michael L. Tan, makes this point clear in his study of the pathologisation of homosexual, effeminate identity and behaviour in the Philippines. See Michael L. Tan, 'Sickness and Sin: The Medical and Religious Stigmatization of Homosexuality in the Philippines,' in Ladlad: An Anthology of Philippine Gay Writing, ed. J. Neil C. Garcia and Danton Remoto (Pasig City: Anvil Publishing, 1994): 202–19.

7 For a short biography of Severino Montano, see the Cultural Center of the Philippines' Encyclopedia of Philippine Arts, vol. 4: Literature, ed. Nicanor Tiongson (Manila: Cultural Center of the Philippines, 1995), Vol. 7, 355–56.

8 For an interesting account of the masculinising imperative that seemed to function as a requirement for the depathologisation of (male) homosexuality in the USA, see Eve Kosofsky Sedgwick, 'How to Bring Your Kids Up Gay,' in Fear of a Queer Planet: Queer Politics and Social Theory, ed. Michael Warner (University of Minnesota Press, 1993): 69–81.

9 According to the Cultural Center of the Philippines Encyclopedia of Philippine Art, Nadres' Hanggang Dito na Lamang at Maraming Salamat has been presented all over the country over the past 20 years, often to full houses of appreciative mixed audiences. See M.L. Maniquiz, 'Hanggang Dito na Lamang at Maraming Salamat,' in Cultural Center of the Philippines Encyclopedia of Philippine Art, ed. Nicanor G. Tiongson (Manila: Cultural Center of the Philippines, 1994), vol. 7: 196.

10 José Garcia Villa (1908–97), National Artist for Literature, is known as the Father of Filipino Literary Modernism. A medical student in the American-founded University of the Philippines, he was suspended in 1929 because of the explicit sexual content of his poetry that appeared in the school paper which he edited. After winning in a national literary competition, he left for the United States, where he ended up residing for the rest of his life. He did manage to visit the Philippines for a few times after that, usually to teach for short periods or to receive some award or other. The foremost champion of the 'art for art's sake' cause, Villa continued to exert tremendous influence over the development of Philippine poetry in English up until the early 1960s. His poetry has been described as Blakean and avant-garde, and it was accorded the American Academy of Arts and Lettters Poetry Award and the Shelley Memorial Award in the 1950s. Villa was also the recipient of the Guggenheim, Bollingen and Rockefeller Fellowships. He was the first writer of Asian descent to have been given such distinctions in the United States. On the other side of the Pacific, among numerous recognitions, he received the Commonwealth Literary Award in 1940, the Republic Cultural Heritage Award in 1962, and an honorary doctorate from the University of the Philippines in 1973, which was the same year he was named a National Artist in Literature. See the Cultural Center of the Philippines Encyclopedia of Philippine Arts, vol. 4: Literature, ed. Nicanor Tiongson (Manila: the Cultural Center of the Philippines, 1995): 772–73.

11 José Garcia Villa, Footnote to Youth: Tales of the Philippines and Others (New York: Scribner, 1933): 'Wings and Blue Flame': 69–130; 'Song I Did Not Hear': 243–62. In 1973 a 'slimmer' version of this book by Villa, Footnote to Youth, was

140 *Theorising Cultures of Equality*

published in the Philippines under Alberto S. Florentino's Storymasters series. It excluded, predictably enough, the original collection's three most revealing, 'autobiographical' stories. See José Garcia Villa, Footnote to Youth (Manila: Alberto S. Florentino, 1973).

12 This has been my point in a number of studies, the most extensive of which has been the following: J. Neil C.Garcia, 'Translation and the Problem of Realism in Philippine Literature in English'. Kritika Kultura: A journal of literary/cultural and language studies, Ateneo de Manila University, Number 22, August 2014.

13 Filipino feminists have long reflected on the implications of this grammatically unitary notion of gender in Philippine languages. For the most forceful of these reflections, see Lilia Quindoza Santiago, Sexuality and the Filipina (Quezon City: University of the Philippines Press, 2007): 72–79.

14 This postcolonial gap – related but not reducible to the metonymic – in all translational moments in post-colonial writing is the subject of my ongoing critique of Philippine anglophone literature. A recent demonstration of this approach may be found in: J. Neil C. Garcia, 'Translating the Real: Rethinking Resistance in Philippine Postcolonial Literature,' in Myth and Writing: Occasional Prose (Quezon City: University of the Philippines Press, 2016).

Bibliography

Bhabha, H.K. (1993). *The Location of Culture.* London: Routledge: 45.

Cultural Center of the Philippines. (1995). *Cultural Center of the Philippines Encylopedia of Philippine Arts*, Vol. *4:* Literature, ed. Nicanor Tiongson;and Vol. 7: 355–356.

Delanty, G. (2006). 'The cosmopolitan imagination: critical cosmopolitanism and social theory', *The British Journal of Sociology*, Vol. 57 Issue 1: 25–47.

Garcia, J.N.C. (2009). *Philippine Gay Culture: Binabae to Bakla, Silahis to MSM.* Hong Kong: Hong Kong University Press.

Garcia, J.N.C. (2012). *Aura: the Gay Theme in Philippine Fiction in English.* Manila: Anvil Publishing, Inc.: 10–15.

Garcia, J.N.C. (2014). 'Translation and the Problem of Realism in Philippine Literature in English', *Kritika Kultura: A journal of literary/cultural and language studies,* Ateneo de Manila University, No. 22, August.

Garcia, J.N.C. (2016). 'Translating the Real: Rethinking Resistance in Philippine Postcolonial Literature'. In *Myth and Writing: Occasional Prose.* Quezon City: University of the Philippines Press.

Garcia Villa, J. (1933). *Footnote to Youth: Tales of the Philippines and Others.* New York: Scribner.

Kosofsky Sedgwick, E. (1993). 'How to Bring Your Kids Up Gay'. *In Fear of a Queer Planet: Queer Politics and Social Theory*, ed. Michael Warner. Minneapolis, MN: University of Minnesota Press: 69–81.

Lagmay, A.V. (2000). 'Western Psychology in the Philippines: Impact and Response'. In *Journey of a Humanist.* Quezon City: College of Social Sciences and Philosophy, University of the Philippines: 163–180.

Montano, S. (ed.). (1958). *The Prize-winning plays of the Arena Theater of the Philippines*, Manila: Phoenix Press.

Perez, T. (1992). *Cubao 1980 At Iba Pang Mga Katha: Ang Unang Sigaw ng Gay Liberation Movement sa Pilipinas.* Manila: Cacho Hermanos.

Quindoza Santiago, L. (2007). *Sexuality and the Filipina*, Quezon City: University of the Philippines Press: 72–79.

Ramos Suarez, K. (2017). *'The (Post)colonial Medicalization of the Filipino Homosexual'*, Unpublished Master's dissertation, MA in Gender Studies, Central European University, Budapest, Hungary, 2017.

Severino Montano, S. *The Lion and the Faun*, Parts 1 and 2, unpublished manuscript.

Tan, M.L. (1994). 'Sickness and Sin: The Medical and Religious Stigmatization of Homosexuality in the Philippines'. In *Ladlad: An Anthology of Philippine Gay Writing*, ed. J. Neil C. Garcia and Danton Remoto. Pasig City: Anvil Publishing: 202–219.

Tan, M.L. (1998). 'Silahis: Looking for the Missing Filipino Bisexual Male'. In *Bisexualities and AIDS*. Peter Aggleton (ed.). London: Taylor & Francis: 207–226.

9 The City Animated by the Spirit of Patriarchy

Jimmy Turner

Introduction

In this chapter I will seek to understand a series of ethnographic encounters which transpired in the southern Brazilian city of Florianópolis, the capital of the state of Santa Catarina in the far south of Brazil, which is a relatively small and affluent city in Brazilian terms. These ethnographic encounters between me, a number of middle-class Brazilian women and the material fabric of the city revealed the gendered inequalities experienced by these women in their urban lives and the role played in this inequality by the concrete tables and chairs that are set into the pavement in the city centre (see Figure 1). I would like to emphasise at the outset that the inequalities of the city are intersectional, with racial, class and sexual dominance(s) vivid and equally important, as explored, for example, by Moura, Fernández and Page elsewhere in this volume. As with all Brazilian cities, patriarchy exists alongside white supremacy, heteronormativity and bourgeois dominance, but my aim here is not to explain or account for urban inequalities in general, but certain ethnographic encounters in particular. My intention in discussing these encounters is not to seek to represent either the city or the women who participated in my research, but rather to seek to represent the ethnography as I experienced it. Through this process of attempting to elicit meaning, I hope to develop an understanding of these encounters that corresponds with my experiences, in a similar methodological manner to that gestured to by Ingold (2013: 7) when he describes a method that aims:

> not to describe the world, or to represent it, but to open up our perception to what is going on there so that we, in turn, can respond to it [...] Anthropology, I believe, can be an art of inquiry in this sense. We need it in order not to accumulate more and more information about the world, but to better correspond with it.

This ethnography, while of course located and particular, will also be brought into correspondence with the large body of academic work on gender, space and the city. Gendered inequalities in putatively 'public' spaces are a concern that has been expanded theoretically in line with broader developments across the social

Figure 9.1 Concrete street furniture on the Rua Felipe Schmidt, central Florianópolis
Image author's own

sciences, humanities, geography and beyond. In just the past 40 years we have seen multiple and expanding ways of understanding how and why gendered inequalities are encountered in cities across the world, most often proceeding from a feminist analysis of the classification of public space as masculine and private/domestic space as feminine, wherein:

> in all human societies sexual asymmetry might be seen to correspond to a rough institutional division between domestic and public spheres of activity, the one built around reproduction, affective, and familial bonds, and particularly constraining to women (Rosaldo, 1980: 397).

From this universalising starting point, we have seen a number of stages of theorisation and increasingly nuanced understandings, including, for example: Spain's (1992) theorisations of gendered inequalities in particularly urban settings; Bondi and Rose's (2003) nuancing of the universalising tendencies in

144 *Theorising Cultures of Equality*

many of these earlier works; and, increasingly, many works which describe challenges, contingencies and contestations of this urban gendering of space, from notions of queer space (Oswin, 2008) to the work of activists to subvert patriarchal control of space, for example in Perry's (2004; 2013) ground-breaking intersectional analyses of Afro-Brazilian women's urban activism. The above examples barely scratch the surface of the work produced, but rather than attempt to account for them all, I will turn now to the more specific context of the ethnographic encounters to which I referred above.

The Gendered Street in Brazil

The gendered division of the city in Brazil has been subject to a sizeable body of research, anthropologically and beyond, but I would argue that one of the most influential theorisations remains that of Roberto DaMatta (1991). He theorises that in Brazil's cities there is an important division between 'a casa e a rua', the 'house and the street', a division Carla de Meis (2002: 4) summarises neatly when she writes that:

> DaMatta believes that the universe of the house is hierarchically organized and is built on relationships with kindred and friends that are characterized by warmth and affection. The universe of the street, in contrast, is a place of distrust, anonymity, incomprehension, and "salve-se quem puder," or "every man for himself," the law of the jungle. Accordingly, the symbolic space of the house is orderly and peaceful, while the street is a dangerous place characterized by its lack of rules.

The street is categorised as a risky and dangerous domain – one where the model colonial woman, respectable and moral and subjected to the 'concepts of passivity, withdrawal and reserve' (Quintas 2007: 51; my translation), would not linger. It is fundamentally a masculine space and one where I repeatedly encountered men lingering at leisure.

One of the clearest examples of men at play on the street was found at the central square Praça XV de Novembro, where the scene depicted in Figure 2 was typical. Large groups of men would congregate on most days to sit together at the concrete tables and stools which are sunk into the pavement and play cards, dominos, and socialise together. The majority of the men on any given weekday would be retirees, and one day, while watching a particularly animated game of dominoes contested by four elderly men, whose rapid fire and clattering place-ment of their tiles was creating a high degree of excitement among a growing crowd of spectators, I asked a fellow bystander, Felipão, how often he came here. He replied that as long as it was not raining too heavily and was not too cold when the *vento sul* (south wind) would blow in the winter, he would take a bus down from the nearby neighbourhood of Trinidade four or five times a week, to spend a few hours playing cards and socialising with his old friends, who, like him, were retired taxi drivers. When I asked him why he travelled here to the central square he told me that this was a common place where taxi drivers would take a break or wait for busier periods, and that it was a habit that he and his former colleagues, who lived in different neighbourhoods across the city, had picked up when they worked, and continued now in their retirement. For men to socialise together in the street, whether at the Praça XV de Novembro, elsewhere in the centre, or in the other neighbourhoods of the city, was, he told me, a timeless practice. He had seen it when he was a boy, it had continued to be a space of male socialisation when he was a man and began to frequent the square himself, and it remained so now. He simply took it for granted that this was a space where men could socialise together and said that it was not a question to which he had devoted much thought.

He went on to muse that he and his friends could of course gather in their homes, but that after a lifetime of working outside the home he felt uncomfortable being there during the day, as it reminded him that he had retired and was growing old. Now that he thought about it, it did occur to him that maybe he had also subconsciously never proposed doing so because he believed that a group of men in the apartment would disturb his wife. When I asked him why this would necessarily be a disturbance, he paused and admitted that it was actually that it was their habitual use of palavrões (curse words) and casual blasphemy that he thought would offend her. A place like

Figure 9.2 Men playing dominoes at the north end of the Praça XV de Novembro. Image author's own

146   *Theorising Cultures of Equality*

this, he explained, was one where they could be themselves in a way that he thought would do no harm to anyone else. This confirmation of a gendered division of space is remarkably similar to that described by Setha Low (2000: 42) in her ethnographic research into the gendered dynamics of public spaces in Costa Rica. Indeed, the words of her 70-year-old male interviewee that '[t]he plaza is now my place of employment now that no longer work. I am underfoot at home. The house is my wife's domain, and I feel better being out of the house during the day' could have been uttered by Felipão and his friends.

The association of domestic space with women was clear, although as feminists have long theorised, and I have discussed elsewhere (Turner, 2014), this is absolutely not to argue that women necessarily, or even usually, wield more gendered power in the home, and nor should it be overlooked that an intersectional analysis is necessary to understand power relations between women in the household (Pinho and Silva, 2010). More pertinent for our purposes here is DaMatta's (1991: 55; my translation) theorisation of the dynamic and mutually constructive dynamic between the home and the street, wherein:

> there are spaces in the street that can be closed or appropriated by a group, social category or people, becoming their 'house', or their hang out [...] the street can have places which are occupied permanently by social categories who 'live' there 'as if they were at home.

The street serves as an extension of the home for these men, or perhaps even as a replacement for the home in terms of homosociality. This again mirrors anthropological analyses elsewhere, for example in Newcomb's (2006: 298) research into the gendering of urban space in Morocco and men's usage of the street outside the home for socialising with male friends.

The Spatial Practice of Urban Gender Inequality

While the gendered segregation of space is by no means as rigid in Brazil as Newcomb (2006: 298) describes it to be in Morocco, there are uncanny similarities in her characterisation of women's movement in the public sphere:

> For women, streets, unlike cafés, do not encourage lingering. The street is a pathway between destinations: market, school, work, or home. While women are always in motion, men lounge on corners or outside cafés.

A high proportion of my interactions with my female research participants also took place in cafés, which women described to me as affording a degree of respite from the street. Whilst it is certainly not rare for women to socialise in the street in Florianópolis, there was often no way to do so without experiencing patriarchal oppression. Often this takes a very overt form, for example in the male practice known as buzinando, wherein men in cars passing women would honk their horns, shout sexist comments through the window, and generally sexually harass passing

The City Animated by the Spirit of Patriarchy   147

women. The volume of the horns and the shouts above the sounds of the streets made this one of the most noticeable forms of harassment for the non-harassed (namely men such as myself), but time and again I was told by women of the subtler forms of harassment—the glances, the whispers, and the brushing of hands over the body. More covert still, and couched by men as a positive and complimentary practice, were the kinds of pseudo-compliments and unwanted attention included by Gardner (1995) within her theorisation of 'public harassment', and since discussed in a wide range of locations (see, for example, Adur and Jha 2018; Guano, 2007; and Meza-de-Luna and García-Falconi, 2015), and recently defined as part of an intersectional suite of 'Street-based Micro-interactional Assaults' by McCurn (2017). Of the different forms of harassment that I was told about, none aroused greater frustration among the women whom I knew than this, being regarded as the most insidious and frequent patriarchal display.

Considering this overwhelming and multi-fronted assertion of male dominance over the street, it is perhaps not a surprise that never once did I see a woman sitting with the men and socialising or playing cards or dominoes. On a number of occasions I asked women with whom I was walking through the centre of Florianópolis whether they ever had or would do so. All of them said no, and when I asked why, the answers were invariably oriented around the expectation that they would not feel comfortable or welcome there. The key issue was that it was completely self-evident to them, as it had been to Felipão, that this concrete furniture was a space for men. It had not needed stating, and no signs were necessary to formalise the arrangement. There was also no suggestion on the part of these women that they might want to challenge this status quo, as Fernanda told me, in the exasperated tone that she often resorted to when confronted by my questions about such obvious things, 'Why would I want to sit there? I can't imagine ever wanting to sit there. It is a place for old men'. It was put even more starkly to me when one day I walked through the centre with Maria and Paulo, a couple in their mid-twenties, and I asked them what they thought would happen if I sat down with the men and asked to join their game of dominos? Paulo replied that it might be awkward, but that they might find it interesting that a gringo wanted to play. I then asked Maria what would happen if she asked to play, and she responded 'I wouldn't even think about it, it is like they are at home playing, but away from their wives, they'd never let a woman interrupt'.

The spatial is therefore a key element that must be factored into our understandings of how gender is experienced and lived in the city, including the ethnographic interactions between me, my research participants and the material city that I present here. In order to be able to 'see', or otherwise discern, this gendering of space Tonkiss (2005: 111) points to a dynamic through which gender becomes 'visible in the city in the symbolic coding of spaces, through modes of spatial practice and interaction, in terms of material divisions and exclusions in space'. To this point I have focused on practice, using the examples of men's occupation of space for socialisation and modes of interacting with women through what these women often experience as McCurn's (2017) 'street-based micro-interactional assaults'. Whether or not such assaults occur around

148 *Theorising Cultures of Equality*

these tables and chairs – and given that I never observed a woman attempting to sit with the men, and no woman I spoke to had even considered doing so, I have no ethnographic evidence of this – what is absolutely clear is that in practice they are occupied almost exclusively by men and are gendered accordingly.

Materiality and Gender Inequality

This is not, however, the complete picture, and in order to more fully correspond with my experience of these ethnographic encounters, I need also to account for the materiality of the city, for the concrete tables and chairs themselves. Tonkiss (2005: 94) argues that gender and sexuality 'are not defined by the limits of the individual body: they involve social relations that extend across and are shaped by space'. If we are to begin to understand the role of space – and how social relations are 'shaped by' it, not just in it – we cannot stop at considering gendered things done by gendered people, and allow ourselves to assume that the material venue for this 'doing' is an apolitical, asocial and acultural stage, which takes meaning only through practice. Indeed, as Tonkiss (2005: 94) goes on to argue:

> the problem of gender or sexuality in the city is not merely a question of what kind of body is walking down the street, but of the social and physical environments which they inhabit and reproduce. The street, that is, can be seen as 'sexed' and 'gendered', not just the person who uses it.

If we think back to the earlier quote from Tonkiss (2005: 111) an obvious point at which to begin is what she calls the 'symbolic coding of spaces'. Within the symbolic realm we might consider that many of the tables are embossed with chess boards, and that chess is historically, symbolically and through practice coded as highly masculinised (Galitis 2002: 73–7). Although I never saw chess being played on these tables, with the masculine pursuit of homosocial games instead being represented through cards and dominos, it is important to consider that the mere presence of this familiar eight-by-eight battlefield symbolically could render the territory as male.

To understand how this links to practice, we might follow Pierre Bourdieu (1992) and his argument that in the houses and settlements of the Kabyle people of Algeria, masculine domination is 'objectified' in architecture and material construction. What this means is that a culture (understood in Bourdieu's terms as a symbolic field in which practice unfolds) will be reflected in the built environment through the objectification of that culture. Christopher Tilley (2013: 60) neatly captures this idea when he explains that '[o]bjectification in such a perspective is the concrete embodiment of an idea' – in our case the idea being that the street is a space of masculine leisure and freedom, and its embodiment being the establishment of a space of male sociality in the literal concrete chessboard. This way of thinking in terms of the relationship between practice and the symbolism of urban space is very necessary and is perhaps sufficient to build an accurate and persuasive enough understanding of the gendering of urban space to

The City Animated by the Spirit of Patriarchy 149

be able to act upon these gender inequalities through legislation, design or activism. However, I believe that it is not all that is happening, as from my perspective as a participant in these ethnographic encounters, there remains something incomplete about such a symbolic account to me.

'Something' More, be it Spectres or Spirits

There were in my ethnographic encounters traces of a 'something other' – a 'something' that, while it was only ever present in an affective register, was fundamental. For this reason, I will now proceed to perform what, in my reading of their work, Holbraad and Pedersen (2017) describe as the fundamental and important task of the anthropologist, namely the description of the ethnography that we experienced with the various others involved, in the terms of the ethnography itself, not those that our pre-existing concepts and theories set out for us. It is not therefore that this 'something' is simply interesting to me, or a mere curiosity, but much more fundamentally I would argue that it is a something that must be accounted for if these ethnographic encounters are to be understood in their own terms (at least as far as I, as one of the participants, understands them).

The difficulty here is that this 'something' offers up few traces of itself, and ethnographically these traces revealed themselves not principally through discourse, but more subtly through the practices of people and particularly through their dispositions as they entered into relationships with the non-human others that populated the space of the street. This human disposition was sharply gendered and revealed itself, for example, through the different bodily practices of men and women in relation to the tables. Large groups of men would gather and orientate themselves to press inwards on the table, whether participating in or observing the games they would be drawn towards the concrete (see Figure 3). This disposition contrasted sharply with that of women, whom I very rarely observed sitting at these tables, and only then when men were not present. On such rare occasions the women were always alone or in pairs, not in large social groups, and were seated facing outwards, orientated away from the furniture. I did not notice initially quite how marked this was until one day I asked Juliana and Alessandra, with whom I walking through the centre on a particularly hot day, if they wanted to sit at these tables, then unoccupied, to rest for a while. They responded both verbally and corporeally, saying no and performing a slight yet meaningful shying away from the tables, as though they were repelled by the same force that seemed to draw men towards them. This physical reaction, when only the tables and chairs and we three humans would have been present, was so noticeable – and to me unusual – that it led me to realise that in order to approach an understanding of, and be able to correspond to, the ethnography, I had to include all the participants, both human and Other.

An attention to the material has become so popular as to constitute a 'turn' spread across many disciplines, with objects coming to be understood as 'actants' (Latour, 2005), 'things' now needing to be 'engaged with on their own terms' (Henare et al., 2007: 1), and ontologies becoming object-orientated (Bryant,

Figure 9.3 Men gather around a card table on Rua Felipe Schmidt in central Florianópolis.
Image author's own.

2011), to list but three influential examples. Such perspectives have created an opening to new conceptualisations of 'actors/subjects', within which:

> Material forms, as objectifications of social relations and gendered identities, often 'talk' silently about these relationships in ways impossible in speech or formal discourses. The things themselves mediate between persons at a silent and unconscious level of discourse.
>
> (Tilley 2013: 60)

This idea of the silent talk of objects is highly compelling, but I am left with a sense that in order to really take the tables and chairs seriously I could not approach them as speaking agents, for to do so would be to deny them their alterity, refuse their table-ness. What I suggest is necessary is a mode of communication with 'things' which is decoupled from discourse, and here I find helpful Hartigan's (2017: 255) suggestion that if we are to interview plants we might abandon any idea of '"listening", as in language-based analytics, the aim here shifts sensorially'. To communicate with these tables and chairs, it would do little good to attempt to listen to them, but I could perhaps attempt to use other senses, both mine and those of my fellow human research participants', to enter into non-linguistic relationships with them and feel them.

The City Animated by the Spirit of Patriarchy   151

This leads me then to affect, at least as it has been conceived of by some within anthropology. The way that the tables and chairs seemed to impose some kind of repulsive force on the women certainly speaks to a kind of affect that follows Yael Navaro-Yashin's (2009: 13) definition of a 'the non-discursive sensation which space or environment generates'. From this it makes sense to me to think of these objects as generating in women the sensation of being unwelcome, just as it seems to draw many men in. Particularly important here is the recognition of the relational nature of this affect – that people and objects alike must be present in relationship with each other for such sensations to be ethnographically discernible. As Navaro-Yashin (Ibid.; emphasis in original) says of the Cypriot ruins that she encountered:

> neither the ruin in my ethnography, nor the people who live around it are affective on their own or in their own right, but both produce and transmit affect relationally.

Also important to remember is that such '"assemblages" of subjects and objects must be read as specific in their politics and history' (Ibid.: 9), because it is clear that the politics and history of the city, as an assemblage of material environment and human sociality, is a history and politics of gender, and even more precisely of a patriarchal endeavour of city-making.

There is a substantial literature exploring the historical and archaeological development of the city, including the always gendered nature of this history (Foxhall and Neher, 2013). What I find most pertinent for what I would like to propose is, however, a somewhat throwaway passage from Tim Ingold's (2007: 102) rurally focused book *Lines: A Brief History*, where he says that:

> Perhaps what truly distinguishes the predicament of people in modern metropolitan societies is the extent to which they are compelled to inhabit an environment that has been planned and built expressly for the purposes of occupation. The architecture and public spaces of the built environment enclose and contain.

The urban in this perspective represents the colonisation of nature and the occupation and violent structuring and containment of the world. The very act of human colonisation and occupation of territory is gendered and associated most with masculinity, and when we combine this with Wilson's (1991) argument that while the city is often symbolically linked to 'freedom', 'license' and 'excess', it is usually designed according to rationalist principles of government, regulation, order, progress, design and planning – principles that feminists recognise as not being the neutral and inevitable principles of a teleological vision of modernity, but rather a patriarchal mode of being in the world. This, then, leads me to argue that the city is a construction of patriarchy, and from this that the affect of the city is first and foremost patriarchal.

152 *Theorising Cultures of Equality*

Spectres

The clearest way to explain the impact of this patriarchal affect is through the sole occasion that one of my interlocuters, Clarice, was able to discursively express, albeit obliquely, her sense of being repelled by the street furniture, and only then through reference to a half-remembered samba lyric:

> I don't know why I don't want to sit over there, there's no-one there, I mean, and nothing will happen, but I feel like the seats don't want me to use them. I know it sounds crazy, but I can only think of some old samba, like by Clementina [de Jesus] or someone, where she sings something about shivering when she walked past a particular street because it is haunted by the souls of the pains of abused women [é assombrada pelas almas das dores das mulheres abusadas].

This sense of being haunted, of space carrying history to the present through affect, is beautifully elaborated by Bobby Benedicto (2013: 29) in his discussion of the affect of the largely derelict ruins of Imelda Marcos's drive to construct modernity in the Filipino capital, Manila. He argues that embedded in the materiality of the ruins are:

> the invisible and ineffable resonances accumulated in these spaces: the echoes, affinities, imaginations, and frequencies of memory and history that are, at times, elicited as feelings by ruined buildings and the objects that occupy them.

Describing these affects as ghostly hauntings of the dictatorship which spark feelings and emotions in us and force us to react, he builds a sense of an affective cityscape which approaches a register through which I feel that I can almost describe my ethnographic experiences in an effective way. This recent work, together with that of anthropologists of affect, gender and sexuality, such as McGlotten (2014) and Dave (2011), is opening up new ways to understand the role of affect in producing urban (in)equalities. In all such examples, context is central to the analyses elaborated, meaning that any mobilisations of their theories and approaches must necessarily be contingent and partial.

To continue with Benedicto's (2013) use of affect, there are two key points at which my ethnography must diverge. The first divergence comes when he stops short of assigning to the ghosts any sense of agency, saying instead that 'It is [...] the beholder who defines the ruin' (Ibid.: 32). Such a focus on the beholder would in my attempts to account for my ethnography result in a writing away of the tables and chairs, reducing them to the props used by humans and little more. I think, however, that perhaps what more importantly separates the context that Benedicto explores from my ethnographic encounters is the notion of haunting, and what I believe this notion implies in terms of temporality and presence. I understand the concept of 'haunting' used in this sense to imply the

The City Animated by the Spirit of Patriarchy   153

presence of something which, while 'real' no longer (the Marcos dictatorship being over), has an afterlife that has a contemporary affect, and therefore that it is as present as anything material, whether people or the material city. In stating a divergence here, I am aware that I risk appearing to argue here against a central thesis of this chapter, namely that affect is every bit as 'real' as discourse, practice or symbols. Argyrou (2017: 53) confirms what a mistake this would be in his discussion of Derridean 'hauntology' when he describes:

> Derrida's playful use of the theme of the spectre or ghost that exists and does not exist, is present and not present [...] What it considers to be real is a ghost, present as a disembodied, insubstantial, immaterial being; but precisely because of this, it is not present, since a body without substance, materiality, flesh and blood is not a real being, but rather a vision, a phantom, an apparition.

I find this concept of haunting deeply compelling, and in Benedicto's (2013) usage it is thrilling, but there remains for me, I think inevitably, the sense of a somewhat passive ongoing effect of memory and history rather than an active force. To put it more bluntly, I think that most feminists would agree that conceptualising patriarchy as a spectre that haunts the city risks implying that patriarchy is dead, and that we experience only its aftereffects. This is the reason that I need a way to understand and relate these affective ethnographic encounters with patriarchy that explicitly recognises its active and ongoing presence.

Spirits

The need for a means to conceptually understand and communicate the ethnographic encounters which I have described above leads me finally to the idea of animism, which I will now suggest is a helpful means to explore the ethnographic sense of relationships being entered into by different participants, human and other. Ingold (2006: 10) explains that animism in its traditional anthropological conceptualisation is 'a system of beliefs that imputes life or spirit to things that are truly inert' – the belief, for example, that spirits reside in rivers or trees. This traditional understanding is therefore not one that I would seek to promote here, for neither I nor my research participants believed that spirits, in any religious or spiritual sense, inhabited the tables and chairs in the centre of Florianópolis. Instead, we come closer when we understand animacy as:

> not a property of persons imaginatively projected onto the things with which they perceive themselves to be surrounded. Rather [...] it is the dynamic, transformative potential of the entire field of relations within which beings of all kinds, more or less person-like or thing-like, continually and reciprocally bring one another into existence. The animacy of the lifeworld, in short, is not the result of an infusion of spirit into substance, or of agency into materiality.
>
> (Ibid.)

154　*Theorising Cultures of Equality*

What we have here is a recognition that all participants in a lifeworld play roles in continually bringing each other to life, with 'life' as we know it constructed through these relationships. I would like therefore to suggest that in order to take seriously my ethnographic encounters, there are considerable benefits to conceptualising the city in something of an animist mode, wherein what I would describe as the patriarchal spirit that animates cities enters into relationships with different gendered human subjects and brings into existence different modes of being alive in the city.

This, I would argue, is a particularly anthropological mode of conceptualising the city, but it is not necessarily aligned with other anthropological contexts. The mountains discussed by de la Cadena (2010), for example, might be thought to have spirits in indigenous beliefs, but rather than using the language of animism to discuss them she refers to them as 'Earth-Beings', in part to deliberately emphasise that rather than being apolitical spirits, they are political actors in the Andean context that she describes (Ibid.: 365). I seek to make no such claims regarding the city, which does not meet the definition of an 'earth being' for the simple reason that unlike in de la Cadena's context it was not thought of as such by my research participants. This is because neither they nor I expressed any form of belief that the tables and chairs might in any sense be 'alive'. I am far more interested here in thinking not in terms of the dichotomy of living/non-living that Ingold (2006) deconstructs, but instead in more Strathernian (1988) terms about all participants in this ethnographic encounter – I, other people and the material world – as individuals through whose relationships the encounter was substantiated. I find that an opening up of what we might consider animacy to be, to the extent that we can imagine that tables and chairs might be animated by a spirit of patriarchy with which we might engage when entering into a relationship with such things, affords us a conceptual framework to be able to understand why, for example, women might be repelled by this concrete furniture while men are drawn to it. Understanding that this spirit has a history, a present and a future, and that it has been and will continue to be both shaped by and itself shape the practice and discourse of people, the affect of the city might hopefully be understood and engaged with in a way that corresponds with our experiences of it. This is just what I hope to do by conceptualising the city as being animated by the 'Spirit of Patriarchy' – opening up a way to describe the ethnographic presence of affects that operate through relationships formed between differently gendered humans and the materials of the city that they encounter.

These relationships must always be rooted in a historicised understandings of the city – this patriarchal spirit has a history which has developed over time through masculine domination. It is also co-constructed with and through patriarchal practices, discourses and symbolism, and rather than seeking to supplant or claim primacy over these factors, I hope that it might instead complement them, by providing a creative means of making sense of affective phenomena. Although space here prevents me from exploring such co-present factors, this spirit is not, I would emphasise, alone. It intersects with racial, class and sexual dominance(s) and inequalities, and in the Brazilian instance it

The City Animated by the Spirit of Patriarchy 155

is certainly a spirit of patriarchy that is simultaneously and equally white supremacist, heteronormative and bourgeois.

Conclusion

I will conclude here with a reiteration that the point I am arguing is not that there 'are' spirits in the city or that ghosts live in chairs, nor that humans believe there to be. Rather, I am arguing that when I take seriously the material city as a participant in my ethnographic encounters, I am forced to reconceptualise that city as being a producer of affect as it enters into relationships with humans. This is a tool for me as an anthropologist to understand that which I experienced, and a means to compellingly communicate this experience to others. It is not, as I emphasised in the introduction, an attempt to represent the city or its inhabitants, but rather an attempt to represent my experiences and the partial and located understandings that I have developed of them. It is through the concept of animism that I feel most able to correspond with the affects of the ethnography and those people and things with which I inhabited the spaces of the city. That affect should be a key consideration in our theorising is by now well established, and this is certainly true when it comes to gender and its intersecting categories.

The recognition that the city itself genders practice, discourse and symbols – and has a role in the construction and maintenance of the inequalities encountered therein – must remain central to any theorisation of the ongoing attacks by the patriarchy on the construction of anything resembling a culture of equality in urban spaces. The question of how we account for and theorise the affects of cultures of (in)equality in different contexts remains open, however, and very productively so, and there is no doubt for me that any answers to this question must be multiple, grounded in their contexts and attuned to the affective. Here I have accounted for just one of the ways in which it is not just human practice, discourse and symbolism that impose gender inequalities on cities, but also the material and immaterial elements that render the city itself not just a stage in which human lives unfold, but as an active and affective element in the relationships that construct these lives.

Bibliography

Adur, Shweta M. and Jha, Shreyasi. (2018). '(Re)centering street harassment – an appraisal of safe cities global initiative in Delhi, India', *Journal of Gender Studies*, 27(1): 114–124.

Argyrou, Vassos. (2017). 'Ontology, 'hauntology' and the 'turn' that keeps anthropology turning', *History of the Human Sciences*, 30(1): 50–65.

Benedicto, Bobby. (2013). 'Queer Space in the Ruins of Dictatorship Architecture', *Social Text*, 31(4): 25–47.

Bondi, Liz andRose, Damaris. (2003). 'Constructing gender, constructing the urban: A review of Anglo-American feminist urban geography', *Gender, Place & Culture: A Journal of Feminist Geography*, 10(3): 229–245.

156 *Theorising Cultures of Equality*

Bourdieu, Pierre. (1992). 'Appendix: The Kabyle House or the World Reversed'. In: *The Logic of Practice.* Cambridge: Polity: 271–283.

Bryant, Levi R. (2011). *The Democracy of Objects.* Ann Arbor, MI: Open Humanities Press.

DaMatta, Roberto. (1991). *A casa e a rua: Espaço, cidadania, mulher e morte no Brasil.* Rio de Janeiro: Editora Guanabara.

Dave, Naisargi N. (2011). 'Indian and Lesbian and What Came Next: Affect, Commensuration, and Queer Emergences', *American Ethnologist*, 38(4): 650–665.

de la Cadena, Marisol. (2010). 'Indigenous cosmopolitics in the Andes: conceptual reflections beyond "politics"', *Cultural Anthropology*, 25(2): 334–370.

De Meis, Carla. (2002). 'House and Street: Narratives of Identity in a Liminal Space among Prostitutes in Brazil', *Ethos*, 30(1/2): 3–24.

Foxhall, Lin and Neher, Gabriele (Eds.). (2013). *Gender and the City before Modernity.* Chichester: Wiley-Blackwell.

Galitis, Ingrid. (2002). 'Stalemate: Girls and a mixed-gender chess club', *Gender and Education*, 14(1): 71–83.

Gardner, Carol Brooks. (1995). *Passing By: Gender and Public Harassment.* Berkeley, CA: University of California Press.

Guano, Emanuela. (2007). 'Respectable ladies and uncouth men: The performative politics of class and gender in the public realm of an Italian city', *Journal of American Folklore*, 120(475): 48–72.

Hartigan, Jr, John. (2017). *Care of the Species: Races of Corn and the Science of Plant Biodiversity.* Minneapolis, MN: University of Minnesota Press.

Henare, Amiria, Holbraad, Martin, and Wastell, Sari. (2007). *Thinking Through Things: Theorising Artefacts Ethnographically.* London: Routledge.

Holbraad, Martin and Pedersen, Morten Axel. (2017). *The Ontological Turn: An Anthropological Exposition.* Cambridge: Cambridge University Press.

Ingold, Tim. (2006). 'Rethinking the animate, re-animating thought', *Ethnos: Journal of Anthropology*, 71(1): 9–20.

Ingold, Tim. (2007). *Lines: A Brief History.* London: Routledge.

Ingold, Tim. (2013). *Making: Anthropology, Archaeology, Art and Architecture.* London: Routledge.

Latour, Bruno. (2005). *Reassembling the Social: An Introduction to Actor-Network-Theory.* Oxford: Oxford University Press.

Lefebvre, Henri. (1991). *The Production of Space.* Oxford: Blackwell.

Low, Setha M. (2000). 'Cultura in the Modern City: The Micro Geographies of Gender, Class and Generation in the Costa Rican Plaza', *Horizontes Antropológicos*, 6(13): 31–64.

Lugones, Maria. (2007). 'Heterosexualism and the Colonial / Modern Gender System', *Hypatia*, 22(1): 186–209.

McClintock, Anne. (1995). *Imperial Leather: Race, Gender and Sexuality in the Colonial Contest.* New York and London: Routledge.

McCurn, Alexis S. (2017). '"I Am Not a Prostitute": How Young Black Women Challenge Street-based Micro-interactional Assaults', *Sociological Focus*, 50(1): 52–65.

McGlotten, Shaka (2014). 'A brief and improper geography of queerspaces and sex-publics in Austin, Texas' *Gender, Place & Culture: A Journal of Feminist Geography*, 21(4): 471–488.

Meza-de-Luna, Maria-Elena andGarcía-Falconi, Sulima. (2015). 'Adolescent Street Harassment in Querétaro, Mexico', *Journal of Women and Social Work*, 30(2): 158–169.

The City Animated by the Spirit of Patriarchy   157

Mohanty, Chandra Talpade. (1988). 'Under Western Eyes: Feminist Scholarship and Colonial Discourses', *Feminist Review*, 30: 61–88.

Navaro-Yashin, Yael. (2009). 'Affective spaces, melancholic objects: Ruination and the production of anthropological Knowledge', *Journal of the Royal Anthropological Institute*, 15: 1–18.

Newcomb, Rachel. (2006). 'Gendering the City, Gendering the Nation: Contesting Urban Space in Fes, Morocco', *City & Society*, 18(2): 288–311.

Oswin, Natalie. (2008). 'Critical geographies and the uses of sexuality: Deconstructing queer space', *Progress in Human Geography*, 32(1): 89–103.

Perry, Keisha-Khan, Y. (2004). 'The roots of black resistance: race, gender and the struggle for urban land rights in Salvador, Bahia, Brazil', *Social Identities: Journal for the Study of Race, Nation and Culture*, 10(6): 811–831.

Perry, Keisha-Khan, Y. (2013). *Black Women against the Land Grab: The Fight for Racial Justice in Brazil*. Minneapolis, MN: University of Minnesota Press.

Pinho, Patricia de Santana and Silva, Elizabeth B. (2010). 'Domestic relations in Brazil: Legacies and Horizons', *Latin American Research Review*, 45(2): 90–113.

Quintas, Fátima. (2007). *Sexo à moda patriarchal: O feminino e o masculino na obra de Gilberto Freyre*. São Paulo: Global Editora.

Rosaldo, M.Z. (1980). 'The Use and Abuse of Anthropology: Reflections on Feminism and Cross-Cultural Understanding', *Signs*, 5(3): 389–417

Spain, Daphne. (1992). *Gendered Spaces*. Chapel Hill, NC: University of North Carolina Press.

Spain, Daphne. (2014). 'Gender and Urban Space', *Annual Review of Sociology*, 40: 581–598.

Strathern, Marilyn. (1988). *The Gender of the Gift*. Berkeley, CA: University of California Press.

Tilley, Christopher. (2013). 'Objectification'. In *Handbook of Material Culture*. London: Sage Publications Ltd: 60–73.

Tonkiss, Fran. (2005). *Space, the City and Social Theory: Social Relations and Urban Forms*. Cambridge: Polity.

Turner, Jimmy. (2014). 'Uma cultura atrasada: The Luso-Baroque Manezinha, Hyper-Whiteness, and the Modern Middle Classes in Florianópolis, Brazil', *Journal of Latin American and Caribbean Anthropology*, 19(1): 84–102.

Wilson, Elizabeth. (1991). *The Sphinx in the City: Urban life, the Control of Disorder, and Women*. Berkeley, CA and Los Angeles, CA: University of California Press.

10 Power from the Peripheries

Art, culture and masculinities in Rio de Janeiro

Tatiana Moura, Marta Fernández and Victoria Page

Introduction

This chapter reflects on the potential that artistic and cultural practices produced by subjects from the periphery have to create alternative subjectivities that disrupt and challenge the hegemonic masculine, white and economically privileged order in Brazil. Specifically, we consider the multiplicity of peripheral and black masculinities that contest criminalised stereotypes in Rio de Janeiro. We argue that artistic and cultural movements such as *passinho* and *slam* disturb territorial divisions of the city, together with structural inequalities of white supremacy, patriarchy and heteronormativity, albeit in distinct ways. We see peripheral areas as areas of potential instead of areas of absence and need, and we argue that the artistic and cultural movements from these areas demonstrate the innovative, resistant and creative capabilities of the peripheries and their residents. Arguing in favour of a 'paradigm of potential' (Silva et al., 2016), this chapter is divided into three parts; the first outlines the dominant understandings of the peripheries and their embedded coloniality, together with an overview of *passinho* and *slam* in Rio de Janeiro. The second part reflects on masculinities in these movements. The last part discusses the criminalisation of culture from the peripheries at length from a decolonial perspective.

Art, Culture and the Urban Peripheries of Rio de Janeiro

The Peripheries

Urban peripheries across the Global South and North are stereotyped as sites of violence and criminality. Such stereotyping negates not only the root causes and factors that (re)produce violence and conflict in the peripheries, but also the multiplicity of positive examples that exist within each context. Favelas across the city of Rio de Janeiro are imagined as territories apart from the city, as the non-city, vis-à-vis the formal city (Pinheiro, 2011). The city is divided, with 'good citizens' – taxpayers with access to rights and services – envisioned on one side and, in the hegemonic imagination of the former, those who are constructed as threats to the good citizens' safety and privileges, on the other

Power from the peripheries 159

side. Rio de Janeiro is structured around profound sociospatial inequality, producing what Santos (2007) terms, an *abyss and abyssal lines*. Santos (2007: 71) argues that the universe 'on this side of the line' only prevails to the degree that it exhausts the field of relevant reality: beyond the line, there can only be invisibility and inexistence – or, at least, the inexistence of relevant or understandable forms of being. On one side of the line, the privileged classes live on the 'asphalt' and on the other side, the poorer residents live on the hillsides, separated physically in peripheral territories. However, invisibility gives way to a hyper-visibility when favela residents – understood as loud and dangerous – cross radical lines of separation in any way that disrupts hegemonic power relations and the subordinate position of the favela its residents.

Stereotyped representations of the peripheries where a city's most impoverished social groups reside are influenced by and drawn from public policies and private social investments. In addition to not meeting the reality of residents' demands, these policies and investments contribute to reinforcing processes of material and symbolic expropriation, weakening collective strategies built by groups from the peripheries to exercise their right to the city. Stigmatisation occurs in both dominant (hegemonic) and in subaltern (non-hegemonic) countries within the current global socioeconomic and political order. Assumptions are often sociocentric, and the examination of peripheries is typically based on cultural/aesthetic and urban models determined by hegemonic social groups and dominant classes. These groups establish what is healthy, pleasant and appropriate for the functioning of the city. They also define a particular concept of order and what forms of social behaviour and action are deemed appropriate. This denial of the subjectivities and rights of those on the peripheries is frequently fused with stigmatisation of groups that cross with intersectional inequalities and colonial ideas of the 'Other'. For Santos (2007), this is about being placed on the other side of the abyssal line, across which there is only nonexistence and invisibility.

Such a colonial view of the peripheries as spaces of absence and lack negates the plurality of experiences and practices in the peripheries, particularly the potentiality of these spaces as places of creativity and knowledge creation. *Passinho* and *slam* are only two examples of a multitude of cultural manifestations from the periphery that demonstrate the creative potential of groups to produce innovative artistic and cultural movements. As noted previously, they are also examples of the creative means through which groups from the periphery promote and demand equality and rights. Peripheries must be recognised for their everyday practices that create the social fabric of the city, including their potential for invention, differentiated forms of occupation of space and counter-hegemonic communication arrangements specific to each periphery.

Art and Culture from the Peripheries: Passinho *and* Slam

Passinho and *slam* have emerged over the last ten years as popular cultural movements from and in Rio de Janeiro's urban periphery. Both art forms directly and indirectly challenge oppressive structural inequalities, evolving

160 *Theorising Cultures of Equality*

into spaces of resistance, albeit in distinct ways. They demonstrate the urban periphery as a space of creativity, potential, and resistance. They are territories leading calls for equality and social change in a context of growing political polarisation with the growth and political advances of the far-right and overt racist, sexist, and homophobic narratives and actions. The production of culture from the peripheries in Brazil is at the same time a creative act *and* an act of resistance over one's right to create—a way of 'inventing citizenship' (Facina, 2016: 110). It is important to situate art and culture from the peripheries within a complex and historical struggle over definition and meaning of culture from the periphery. At times such expressions are criminalised and prohibited, at other times ignored, and in other moments appropriated for political and consumer gains.

Passinho is a sub-genre of *funk carioca*, a musical genre derived from Miami bass and rap music. It emerged out of *baile funk* favela parties and spread across favelas in Rio de Janeiro through the uploading and sharing of YouTube videos. One of the first of such videos, 'Passinho Foda', was posted on 2008 by dancers in the Jacarezinho favela and is considered the birth of *passinho*. A dance with quick footsteps built on a range of styles including *frevo*, samba, and hip hop, *passinho* is frequently expressed through dance battles between male and female dancers. The dancers' creativity and originality are key. Since 2008 *passinho* battles have occupied numerous favelas, city metro stations and the wealthier neighbourhoods in the *zona sul* (south) of Rio. *Passinho* gained global fame after being featured in the 2012 Olympic Games closing ceremony in London and the 2016 Olympic opening ceremony in Rio de Janeiro. Notable groups and organisations on the *passinho* scene include Os Imperadores da Dança, Dream Team do Passinho, Rio Parada Funk, Passinho Carioca, Eu Amo Baile Funk, Os Clássicos do Passinho and Passinho da Favela. In 2017 *passinho* was declared cultural heritage under law 390/2017 (A Câmara Municipal do Rio de Janeiro 2017).

Slam similarly centres on battles between participants. Poetry battles are made up of multiple rounds with a three-minute time limit on each participant's poem. In contrast to *passinho, slam* was born in the United States in the 1980s (D'Alva, 2011: 121), gained global popularity and started to gain greater popularity in Brazil, both in and outside of peripheries, beginning in 2008. Notable groups and movements in Brazil include, Slam Laje, Nós da Rua, Slam das Minas and Slam Resistência. The objective of Slam Laje, formed in 2017 in the favela of Complexo do Alemão, is to incentivise marginal literature and poetry and to strengthen the favela's cultural movements. The collective's mission is to be shrewd and resilient in the occupation of their favela using battles (Slam Laje 2017). Slam Resistência operates with a particular protest perspective seeking to actively defend against state-led threats to culture and to the social environment (Slam Resistência, date unknown). Nós da Rua, created in 2017 in the Jacarepaguá favela, has a mission to 'unleash minds and represent culture' (Nós da Rua, 2017). Slam das Minas, in contrast with the other groups, is composed solely of women. This collective was first formed in 2015 in Brasilia and has grown quickly, expanding to other cities, notably Sao Paulo, Rio de Janeiro and Porto Alegre. According to Slam das Minas-Rio de Janeiro, 'Slam das Minas is a playful poetic game to develop the artistic power of women (whether hetero, bi, pans, lesbian, or trans) and queer, agender, non-binary, and trans people' (Slam das Minas-RJ, date unknown). *Slam* movements in Rio de Janeiro actively speak out against machismo, sexism, racism, homophobia, discrimination, violence and other topics affecting the city's residents. These movements articulate feminist agendas and anti-racism agendas defined by black women and people from the periphery, both through individual poets' contributions and organisations' communications.

Events organised in favela communities demonstrate these peripherical areas as spaces for artistic production and potentiality. The occupation of various city spaces is a common feature in *passinho* and *slam* movements. These events reorient movements across the city from periphery to centre, to centre to periphery and across peripheries, destabilising the centre of the city as the site for artistic consumption.

At the same time, insertion into public spaces in Rio's downtown and wealthy southern neighbourhoods of the city challenges the orientation and meanings of bodies in space. The focus of this insertion is specifically on those bodies whose legitimacy to occupy space is questioned, such as black youth, youth from the periphery, women and LGBTQI groups. As an example, Nós da Rua held its 2018 Slam final next to a bus station, BRT Taquara (Nós da Rua, 2018). Slam das Minas held an event in October 2018 in Praça Cinelândia, together with other movements to 'combat institutional racism and intolerance'. The site was chosen, as it is a public square and focal point for protests surrounding the presidential elections and polarisation around far-right presidential candidate, Jair Bolsonaro (Ubunto Rio, 2018). *Passinho* flash mobs have been held in a range of spaces, from train and metro stations (Batalha do Passinho, 2013; CUFA Filmes, 2013; Botinha O Pika Do YTB, 2015), to museums (Passinho Carioca, 2017) and public spaces (Hepnova 2012). *Passinho* has even been performed on stage at Rio's Municipal Theatre (Passinho Carioca, 2018), at Rio's Olympic stadium and at a famous samba venue, the Sambódromo (Queiroz, 2017).

The art movements of *passinho* and *slam* contain numerous examples of how art creation and processes of production promote equality. Occupying spaces throughout the periphery and beyond, these movements are building networks that renegotiate the city's divisions. Although *slam* can be seen to actively and overtly advocate for equality, challenging inequitable hegemonic structures, *passinho* strategically inserts its participants into market forces and mainstream cultural movements and showcases the value of individual dancers' and groups' talents. In both instances, essentialised images of the periphery and the criminalisation of bodies and culture from these areas are challenged.

Art, Culture and Masculinities in the Peripheries

Cultural and artistic movements from the urban periphery in Rio de Janeiro can be seen within a perspective of equality. Many cultural movements promote 'cultures of equality' by articulating demands at multiple levels: through verbal, physical, rhythmic and/or aesthetic mediums; by creating equitable

162 *Theorising Cultures of Equality*

practices within their organisations; and by occupying and redefining spaces throughout the city. In other words, these acts of artistic and cultural expression have the potential to challenge structures of inequality founded on patriarchy, white supremacy, heteronormativity and coloniality. These movements promote spaces of inclusion for plural alternatives, non-hegemonic ways of bringing forward discourses of equality, occupying spaces and shifting boundaries and meanings across spaces and bodies. Such bodies, notably those seen as young, black and male, suffer from essentialising and othering stereotypes associated with danger and criminality based on an assumed hyper-masculinity. If we take masculinity as referring to 'ways of being a man', or the 'set of norms, values and behavioural standards that express explicitly or implicitly expectations on how men should act and present themselves before others' (Miescher and Lindsay, 2003: 4), then a black masculinity is stereotypically associated with machismo, violence, dangerous sexuality and primitivism.

While various art and cultural movements from the peripheries are evident within *passinho* and *slam*, a constant theme is the significant role of young men in these movements. While women and girls participate in, and are well respected in, *passinho*, men dominate the scene. In an interview for a film on *passinho*, Leandra Perfects, a prominent figure within the scene, describes how the current goal for male residents of favelas is either to be a dancer or a drug-trafficker (Osmose Filmes, 2014). While a paradigm of dance-or-crime is a narrow one that does not account for the various desires that men and boys have for their careers, it demonstrates the symbolic power and status accorded to men who dance *passinho*. Although the male identities and models of masculinity in drug-trafficking and dance movements share public displays of physical prowess, the identities are markedly distinct.

In contrast to the reproduction of models of masculinities based on the control and use of violence, *passinho* and *slam* resist the use of violence. These movements specifically call out state-backed violence and challenge the criminalisation of black male bodies. They refuse the stereotyping models of peripheral and black masculinities and highlight the complex struggle to exist in the imaginary of the police and society outside of oppressive structural inequalities. *Slam* poets are creating spaces, occupying city spaces, challenging intersecting inequalities and promoting new understandings of the multiplicity of male identities – specifically peripheral and black masculinities.

While feminist literature increasingly focuses more on men's multiple experiences and expressions of gender, there remains a tendency to focus mostly on men's involvement in violence rather than understanding their non-involvement (Barker, 1998; 2005; Roque, 2012b). Given the connection of dominant versions of masculinity to the use of violence, it is crucial to understand how to negotiate models of masculinity away from violence and how to produce alternative models of masculinity that resist violence and promote equality. Considering artistic and cultural movements from the peripheries, the potential for a redefinition of 'masculinity' to a non-violent, inclusive model is clear.

Criminalisation of Culture from the Peripheries

Residents from Rio's peripheries cross city spaces every day to work as house-keepers, nannies, janitors, drivers and construction workers for the middle and upper classes. However, their bodies are criminalised, violated, contained or sent back to 'their territories' every time that their movement transgresses the limits of the subaltern integration to the city not prescribed to them. There are numerous examples of favela residents whose movements are not authorised by those who produce and radicalise the lines of the broken city. Every summer, military police officers stop buses and violently frisk young men with a specific profile – black and poor – who go from Rio's northern neighbourhoods to the space considered the most democratic part of the city: the beaches in the *zona sul*. Thus, the black man is represented as docile and subservient when useful for the interests of the hegemonic classes and as brutal when it destabilises the geographical and symbolic borders of the city (see Vigoya, 2018).

Pinheiro (2011) argues that the lives of young people who live in poor communities is generally centred on the 'here and now', without further integration into the cultural life of the city. This is because they cannot afford to circulate and do not feel comfortable in cultural environments associated with middle- and upper-class lifestyles. That is why, in 2014, *rolezinhos* or 'little excursions' or 'outings', arguably represented a form of resistance movement. *Rolezinhos* were gatherings organised on social networks by young men from the peripheries, who would go to Rio de Janeiro's shopping malls listening to funk music. *Rolezinhos* were considered transgressive enough to motivate the closing of malls (Watts, 2014) and to get managers to call the police, resulting in the expulsion of the youth without them having violated any law. The managers' attitudes, in turn, shed light on the racist and discriminatory character of the society that frequents Rio's malls to fulfil their consumer expectations (Lima and Baumgärtel, 2016). The examples above display the racism of Brazilian society, which will tolerate only black bodies entering the formal city's space in an atomistic manner – not collectively, as in the case of *rolezinhos* – and in order to serve. In fact, young black men are seen as especially frightening when they are in a group (Souza, 2013).

Rio de Janeiro is (re)imagined by the residents of privileged areas as a city that either domesticates those bodies into menial jobs or removes, confines and incarcerates them. The Brazilian prison system confines young men who are mostly poor, black and with low levels of education, revealing a society that desperately seeks to isolate, contain and purge its margins. To ensure the security, mobility and consumption of urban residents, favela residents should have their mobility as restricted as possible, and if necessary, through incarceration. When slavery was originally abolished in Brazil, the popular imagination feared that the liberation of slaves would send a horde of semi-barbaric men into society (Azevedo, 1987 in Souza, 2013). These former slaves continued to be subjected to all kinds of physical and symbolic violence to keep them in a subordinate position, contain or eliminate them (see Souza, 2013). The stereotypes attributed to black masculinity, based on physical strength but

164   *Theorising Cultures of Equality*

not strength of character, in turn, contribute to the idea that these men must have their mobility and strength repressed and controlled.

In a specific context of containing and disciplining periphery residents' bodies, numerous cultural and artistic activities become the targets of state control, surveillance and repression. This was the case with the large *baile funk* favela parties, which the authorities and media came to represent as associated with drug-trafficking, violence and criminality. During a search conducted by the armed forces in 2017 in the context of a larger operation targeting drug-dealers, a resident of the Manguinhos favela describes his interaction with soldiers. The resident describes how soldiers asked him whether he worked and what he did for work:

> I said I worked with culture. They laughed and looked at me with an air of mockery, asking which culture it was. I answered it was funk culture. I am a passinho dancer. Another soldier dismissed it, laughing, saying that was easy, asking if it pays. I wanted to respond on equal terms, but the fear of getting beaten was larger, so I just stood silent.
>
> (Moura, 2017; our translation)

We argue that the art produced in and by the periphery, while frequently not recognised as 'art', has the potential to destabilise the discourse constructed by actors who are economically, socially and racially privileged. These movements operate nationally and therefore have a large opportunity to contribute to cultures of equality. Art, in this sense, can greatly contribute to dismantling the construction, which is widely disseminated by the media, of the peripheral subject as a disempowered victim or a potential criminal. Traditionally, the favela and other peripheral spaces have been conceived either in terms of a state of nature marked by a cultural and artistic void, or as the producers of a lower culture, or as spaces marked by deviant and depraved culture. Historically, popular spaces and their residents have been understood in relation to a 'paradigm of absence', that is, through a focus on what they lack (Silva et al., 2016). Funk music, for instance, is understood as the product of a series of deficiencies: in education, in political awareness, in taste and in moral values (Lopes and Facina, 2012).

All these representations, in turn, converge around the construction of the formal city that produces legitimate cultural and artistic expressions, which should be taken to the peripheries to fill their cultural void, or even in order to correct/save/rescue favela residents from their violent and deviant lives. Proposals of cultural actions in those territories often claim to attempt to save favela residents by ensuring that they stay away from crime and, as highlighted by Jailson de Souza Silva et al. (2016), be integrated into formal labour markets – usually lower-skilled and lower-paid jobs. Silva et al. (2016) propose a new 'paradigm of potential' to interpret social practices found in the favela, one that values the inventiveness and plural aesthetic expressions affirmed by residents in relation to their own experience of urban life. Going against the logic that reduces the periphery to a homogeneous space, marked

Power from the peripheries 165

by poverty and lack, this paradigm draws attention to the possibility of creation. This vision sees the potential to invent other ways of existing, new references and powerful networks of life assertion that challenge dominant ways of life from a peripheral condition (Lacaz et al., 2015). Even in spaces where the state does not provide basic education, health, transportation, sanitation, leisure and cultural services, a territory can harbour new forms of everyday life, producing subjective displacements in relation to the hegemonic way of existence. Hence, 'misery gives rise, not only to an experience of lack and need, but also to a method of production that finds other material and immaterial forms of sustaining and reinventing itself' (Ibid.: 63; our translation). Attempts are made through the unique joining of music and the body, to challenge the alienation that black male bodies have been subjected to (Vigoya 2018: 116). Through art, black men become subjects capable of challenging the white gaze that seeks to set them in stereotypes (Ibid.: 117–8).

The art produced by peripheral subjects has the potential to produce and give visibility to another periphery which, unlike in media representations, affirms itself through its agency, inventiveness and non-violet pathways. Through art, the residents of favelas and other peripheries may alter the regimes of visibility and invisibility that make up the collective imagination. In doing so, they lend a political meaning to aesthetics, as they disturb dominant borders between the invisible/irrelevant and the visible/praiseworthy (see Rancière, 2005). Art can thus contribute to ensuring that peripheral subjects treated as inexistent can assert themselves and interfere in dominant representations of gender, race and class.

From a decolonial perspective, we understand that the internal borders drawn across the city of Rio de Janeiro coincide with those of the modernity/coloniality binomial (see Quijano, 2005) Modern thought constitutes itself as a privileged locus of enunciation which, from the assumption of the Other's colonial inferiority, continues to justify oppression, exploitation and assimilation (Mignolo and Tlotanova, 2006: 206). Therefore, a decolonial aesthetic articulates practices that subvert the hegemony of the modern/colonial project which has historically regulated not only the economy, but also knowledge, senses, perceptions and gender (Vazquez and Mignolo, 2013; Lugones, 2015). In Vazquez and Mignolo's words (2013: vii):

[Decolonial aesthetics] is a heterogenous historic-embodied movement, it perceives the wound of coloniality hidden under the rhetoric of modernity, the rhetoric of salvation. Decolonialisation is at once the unveiling of the wound and the possibility of healing. It makes the wound visible; tangible; it voices the scream.

Brazilian Decolonial Aesthetics

In Brazil, this decolonial aesthetical gesture has been present, for instance, in the creation of 'Teatro Experimental do Negro' (TEN, or Black Experimental

166 *Theorising Cultures of Equality*

Theater). TEN was created in 1944 as a reaction to the colonialism/racism of Brazilian theatrical representations that mirrored society's widespread racism. Inspired by the 'Negritude' movement and idealised by Abdias Nascimento, TEN sought to promote the liberation of black people, through theatre, from the situation of spiritual, cultural and political servitude in which they were inserted. This servitude continued long after the formal end of slavery (Nascimento, 2004), when, owing to their race and poverty, Black people were segregated in favelas and other public housing arrangements (Nascimento, 2002). The purpose of TEN was thus to rescue an Afro-Brazilian culture long silenced by a society which, from colonial times, has been informed by a European imaginary, loaded with pseudoscientific conceptions of black inferiority (Nascimento, 2004).

The underappreciation of black culture, which is the object of Abdias's concern, remains present in relation to numerous artistic expressions taking place in Rio de Janeiro's peripheries, such as funk music and *passinho*. According to Simone Sá (2014), the relative cultural invisibility of funk in discussions of Rio's creative industries and its demonisation by a segment of the media that connect it to violence leave aside other central aspects of funk, such as its aesthetical and social dimensions. Many of funk's critics, described by Adriana Facina (2008), argue that the poverty of the lyrics and their grammatical 'errors' represents the failure of Brazilian public education. Although Brazil's public education system is indeed under-resourced and inadequate, one must, according to Facina (2008), contextualise the different ways that social groups appropriate language. These modifications entail complex cultural creation processes which should not be simply understood as mistakes. For Adriana Lopes (2009), funk music transforms the language of favelas into an artistic form, filling it with slangs and significance that escape formal, standard language.

According to Lopes (2009), the identity of Rio's funk music is highly heterogeneous and disputed, acquiring multiple meanings, which may range from fun and sensuality to a vehicle for social critique. Through funk music, young people from Rio's favelas show their lifestyles and the ways that they experience their 'microworlds' (Lopes, 2009), challenging the places of exclusion, poverty and precarity routinely assumed for them (Lacaz et al., 2015: 66). While the favela is constructed as a homogeneous place of violence in the hegemonic discourse, funk music describes favelas from the standpoint of plural everyday practices using hyper-localised language. This localised language of funk music provides an alternative cartography for the city of Rio de Janeiro (Lopes 2009), lending the favela a new meaning and drawing alternative maps and paths over the city. Through funk's counter-narrative, each favela and its parts (streets, corners and places of recreation) are enunciated and receive proper names, visibility and legitimacy. Thus, while challenging the homogenisation of favelas and their residents, funk lyrics also avoid the opposite risk of romanticising them. Favelas are presented in their heterogeneity and complexity, with positive aspects, but also as spaces of oppression, difficulties and suffering (Ibid.).

Power from the peripheries   167

Drawing from the analyses of the authors described above, we argue for understanding funk culture as a set of practices that produce new subjectivities and cartographies. Such practices are performed by those participants who, while living and (re)inventing local experiences, are also submitted to all sorts of violence (of race, class, place and gender) which constitute the hegemonic order – both in the space of favelas and when they cross the borders imposed by the privileged side of the city. Through such aesthetic practices, peripheral subjects (re)signify the hegemonic discourse of gender and race that incarcerates their bodies, humiliating and robbing them of their dignity. For Lacaz et al. (2015: 63; our translation),

> Art, when meeting our body, becomes singular to the extent that it can produce in us things not previously experienced. It holds the power to make differ our ways of being in the world, through creation and rupture of the prescriptions which today frame our lives according to models with such well demarcated borders.

Therefore, when thinking from their bodies, their locations, their diasporic lives, their border thinking (see Andalzua, 1999; Mignolo and Tlotanova, 2006; Saldívar, 2006; Grosfoguel, 2009), their mutilated beings (Fanon, 1968), their still open colonial wounds, those subjects defy the abyssal borders and regimes of visibility/invisibility produced by the dominant culture.

Conclusion

Through art forms such as funk, *passinho* and *slam*, individuals and groups from the periphery of Rio de Janeiro can reinvent themselves and produce new forms of existence, challenging hegemonic narratives that place them in a space marked by widespread poverty, crime and disorder. Such narratives not only neglect the potential and creativity of the peripheries, they essentialise problems of violence and poverty and see them as endogenous causes. Against the dominant idea of a forked order that separates and interiorises the peripheries vis-à-vis the formal city, this chapter seeks to show the relational and connected nature of these spaces. The asphalt, in the case of Rio de Janeiro for example, affirms its superiority by visualising favelas as spaces of radical alterity and cheap labour.

In this manner, this chapter politicises and questions the naturalisation of violence and multiple forms of oppression (gender, race, class and geography) that affect the favelas and favela residents. These forms of oppression cannot be explained without contemplating both past and present systematic inequalities in Brazilian society. The peripheries in both the Global South and North, and in particular those of Rio de Janeiro, are presented here from the paradigm of potential, as spaces of creative agency. These spaces create movements that, on a daily basis, subvert power relations. This chapter has sought to understand artistic and cultural expressions form the periphery beyond the idea of resistance

168 *Theorising Cultures of Equality*

and reaction to hegemonic values, but as innovative practices, producer of alternative sensitivities, references and modes of existence. Traditionally such practices were understood as instrumental forms, directed towards solving problems in the peripheries, saving them from themselves and from criminality and deviance without calling into question the existing unequal order.

We seek to instead show that artistic and cultural practices produced by residents of the periphery are not limited to solely finding solutions to problems within the current order; for example, reducing incidents of violence and therefore increasing feelings of security for the privileged strata of society. Artistic and cultural movements that arise naturally out of peripheries are creating spaces, occupying cities, challenging intersecting inequalities, and promoting new understandings of the multiplicity of male identities – specifically peripheral and black masculinities. Given the connection of dominant versions of masculinity to the use of violence, it is shown that art performed in peripheral spaces can contribute especially to the production of non-violent masculinities.

Bibliography

Anzaldúa, G. (1999). *Borderlands/La Frontera: The New Mestiza*, 2nd edition. San Francisco: Aunt Lute Books.

Barker, G. (1998). 'Non-violent males in violent settings: an exploratory qualitative study of prosocial low-income adolescent males in two Chicago Neighbourhoods', *Childhood*, November, Vol. 5.

Barker, G. (2005). *Dying to be Men*. New York: Routledge.

Câmara Municipal do Rio de Janeiro. (2017). Projeto de Lei 390/2017. Accessed at: http://mail.camara.rj.gov.br/APL/Legislativos/scpro1720.nsf/f6d54a9bf09ac233032579de006b-fef6/6895f9ddd8688d5a8325818a005a6323?OpenDocument&fbclid=IwAR0F2bu1y-Blz4uCSOJFLinmfCq137ARzUA0g7ryNMqZM19fjsIZ2W_4BhY

CUFA Filmes. (2013). Duelo do Passinho, YouTube. Available at: www.youtube.com/watch?v=Aq0Bixcd94I. Accessed on 23 October 2018.

D'Alva, R.E. (2011). 'Um microfone na mão e uma ideia na cabeça – O poetry slam entra em cena' *Synergies Brésil*, 9: 119–126

De Sousa Santos, B. (2012). *Epistemologies of the South: Justice against Epistemicide*. London and New York: Routledge.

Facina, A. (2008). '"Vou te dar um papo reto": linguagem e questões metodológicas para uma etnografia do funk carioca', Encontro de Linguagem e Identidade. Anais, Campinas: Instituto de Estudos de Linguagem, Unicamp.

Facina, A. (2016). 'Cultura como crime, cultura como direito: a luta contra a resolução 013 no Rio de Janeiro', in (ed.) EDUFMA. *Discussões epistemológicas: as Ciências Humanas sob uma ótica interdisciplinar*. Sao Luis: Universidade Federal do Maranhão.

Fanon, F. (1968). *Os Condenados da Terra*. Rio de Janeiro: Civilização Brasileira.

Grosfoguel, R. (2009). 'A Decolonial Approach to Political-Economy: Transmodernity, Border Thinking, and Global Coloniality', *Kult 6* (Special Issue): 10–38.

Lacaz, A.S., Lima, S.M.; Heckert, A.L.C. (2015). 'Juventudes Periféricas: Arte e Resistências no Contemporâneo', *Psicologia e Sociedade*, 27(1): 58–67.

Lima, F.C. andBaumgärtel, S.A. (2016). 'O flashmob e o rolezinho: considerações sobre a construção estética de um corpo político coletivo num espaço de ostentação capitalista', *Urdimentos*, vol. 1(26): 128–143.

Lopes, A.C. (2009). 'A favela tem nome próprio: a (re)significação do local na linguagem do funk carioca', RBLA, Belo Horizonte, 9(2): 369–390.

Lopes, A.C. andFacina, A. (2012). 'Cidade do funk: expressões da diáspora negra nas favelas cariocas', *Revista do Arquivo Geral da Cidade do Rio de Janeiro*, no. 6: 193–206.

Lugones, M. (2015). 'Toward a Decolonial Feminism', *Hypatia* 25(4): 724–759.

Miescher, S. andLindsay, L.A. (2003). 'Introduction: Men and Masculinities in Modern African History'. In S. Miescher and L.A. Lindsay, *Men and Masculinities in Modern Africa*. Portsmouth, NH: Heinemann.

Mignolo, W.D. andTlotanova, M.V. (2006). 'Theorizing from the Borders. Shifting to Geo- and Body-Politics of Knowledge', *European Journal of Social Theory*, 9(2): 205–221.

Moura, T. (2007). *Rostos Invisíveis da violência armada. Um estudo de caso sobre o Rio de Janeiro*. Rio de Janeiro: 7 Letras.

Nascimento, A. (2004). 'Teatro Experimental do negro: trajetória e reflexões', *Estudos Avançados*, vol. 18(50).

Nascimento, A. (2002). *O Quilombolismo: Documento de uma Militância Pan-Africanista*. Brasilia/Rio de Janeiro: Fundação Cultural Palamares.

Nós da Rua. (2017). Facebook page. Available at: www.facebook.com/pg/nosdaruapoesia/about/?ref=page_internal. Accessed on 23 October 2018.

Nós da Rua. (2018). Facebook page. Available at: www.facebook.com/nosdaruapoesia/photos/a.290871738004018/535119453579244/?type=3&theater. Accessed on 23 October 2018.

O Globo. (2016). 'Placa em banheiro do Country Club informa que babás não podem entrar', 26 June. Available at: https://oglobo.globo.com/rio/placa-em-banheiro-do-country-club-informa-que-babas-nao-podem-entrar-19372359 (por Natália Boere/Ludmilla de Lima)

Osmose Filmes. (2014). Trailer A batalha do Passinho: O filme, YouTube. Available at: www.youtube.com/watch?v=n1ITxvCJKFY. Accessed 20 July 2016.

Passinho Carioca. (2017). Passinho Carioca Flash Mob, YouTube. Available at: www.youtube.com/watch?v=jqdgoWiOu8A. Accessed on 23 October 2018.

Passinho Carioca. (2018). Passinho Carioca no Teatro Municipal, YouTube. June 2018. Available at: www.youtube.com/watch?v=SMUWZDMlH90. Accessed on 23 October 2018.

Pinheiro, D. (2011). 'A Cidade-Espetáculo e as Favelas Visibilidade e Invisibilidade Social da Juventude no Rio de Janeiro', *Contexto & Educação*, vol. 26(85).

Queiroz, M. (2017). 'Rio Parada Funk reúne milhares de pessoas em 8 horas de bailes no Sambódromo', *O Globo*,. Available at: https://g1.globo.com/rio-de-janeiro/noticia/rio-parada-funk-reune-milhares-de-pessoas-em-8-horas-de-bailes-no-sambodromo.ghtml. Accessed on 23 October 2018.

Quijano, A. (2005). 'Colonialidade do Poder, Eurocentrismo e América Latina'. In *Colonialidade do Saber: eurocentrismo e ciências sociais. Perspectivas latino-americanas*. Edgardo Lander. ColecíonSurSur, CLACSO, Ciudad autônoma de Buenos Aires.

Rancière, J. (2005). *A partilha do sensível: Estética e Política*.

Roque, S. (2012). 'For what reasons do male youth avoid "mobilizing"? Managing minimal possibilities in Bissau', In *Jovens e trajetórias de violências. Os casos de Bissau e da Praia*. Coimbra: CES/Almedina.

170 *Theorising Cultures of Equality*

Saldívar, J.D. (2006). 'Border Thinking, Minoritized Studies, and Realist Interpellations: The Coloniality of Power from Gloria Anzaldúa to Arundhati Roy'. In: L. Martín Alcoff, M. Hames-García, S.P. Mohanty and P.M.L. Moya (eds), *Identity Politics Reconsidered*. New York: Palgrave Macmillan.

Santos, B. de S. (2007). 'Beyond Abyssal Thinking: From Global Lines to Ecologies of Knowledges', *Review*, XXX, 1: 45–89.

Santos, B. de S. (2007). 'Para além do pensamento abissal: das linhas globais a uma ecologia de saberes', *Novos Estudos CEBRAP*, 79, November: 71–94.

Silva, J. de S. and Barbosa, J.L. (2005). *Favela: alegria e dor na cidade*. Rio de Janeiro: X-Brasil, Senac-Rio.

Silva, J. de S., Siva, E.S., Balbim, R. and Krause, C. (2016) 'Um olhar possível sobre o conceito de mobilidade e os casos da favela da Maré e do Complexo do Alemão'. In (eds) R. Balbim, C. Krause *and* C. Cunha Linke , *Cidade e Movimento: Mobilidades e Interações no Desenvolvimento Urbano*. Brasília: IPEA.

Sjoberg, L. andVia, S. (2010). 'Conclusion: The Interrelationship between Gender, War and Militarism'. In Sjoberg, L. and Via, S. (eds). *Gender, War and Militarism: Feminist Perspectives*. Westport, CT: Praeger.

Slam das Minas-RJ. (Date unknown). Facebook page. Available at: www.facebook.com/pg/slamdasminasrj/about/?ref=page_internal. Accessed on 23 October 2018.

Slam Laje. (2017a). Facebook page. Available at: www.facebook.com/pg/batalhadepoesia/about/?ref=page_internal. Accessed on 23 October 2018.

Slam Laje. (2018). Facebook page. Available at: www.facebook.com/batalhadepoesia/. Accessed on 23 October 2018.

Slam Resistência. (Date unknown). Facebook page. Available at: www.facebook.com/pg/slamresistencia/about/?ref=page_internal. Accessed on 23 October 2018.

Souza, R.R. de. F. (2013). 'Homens negros e brancos e a luta pelo prestígio da masculinidade em uma sociedade do Ocidente', *Revista Antropolítica*, no. 34: 35–52.

Ubunto Rio. (2018). Facebook event. Available at: www.facebook.com/events/252968445404976. Accessed on 23 October 2018.

Vazquez, R. andMignolo, W. (2013). 'Decolonial AestheSis: Colonial Wounds/Decolonial Healings', Social Texts Online. Available at https://socialtextjournal.org/periscope_article/decolonial-aesthesis-colonial-woundsdecolonial-healings/.

Vigoya, M.V. (2018). 'As Cores da Masculinidade. Experiências Interseccionais e práticas de poder na Nossa América'. Papéis Selvagens.

Watts, J. (2014) 'Brazilian flashmob forces shopping mall to close', *The Guardian*, 20 January. Retrieved from: www.theguardian.com/world/2014/jan/20/brazilian-flashmob-shopping-mall-closes-rolezinho.

YouTube. (2012). Hepnova, Passinho do Paz – Flash Mob do Gamba no Arpoador. Available at: www.youtube.com/watch?v=N9Ep-7H12oY. Accessed on 23 October 2018.

YouTube. (2013). Batalha do Passinho, Todo Mundo no Passinho. Available at: www.youtube.com/watch?v=O0EqgLk_wc8. Accessed on 23 October 2018.

YouTube. (2015). Botinha O Pika Do YTB, Passinho Foda – No Metro. Available at: www.youtube.com/watch?v=0tCW1EQDlnw. Accessed on 23 October 2018.

11 Decolonial Joy

Theorising from the Art of *Valor y Cambio*

Frances Negrón-Muntaner

> It is only with hindsight that I can see
> what a brave thing it was to do,
> to just print our own money
>
> (Hopkins, 2019)
>
> Let me at least return to joy.
>
> (LaValle, 2009)

On 9 February 2019 I co-launched Valor y Cambio (Value and Change) in Puerto Rico, a Caribbean archipelago that has been subject to US colonial-capitalist rule for more than a century and increased neoliberalisation since 2006.[1] A pun on the Marxist concept of *valor de cambio* or exchange value, Valor y Cambio is a storytelling, community-building and solidarity economy project that contains an interactive art installation and six bills of a community currency, Personas de Peso Puerto Rico (People of Weight Puerto Rico), or *pesos* for short. A community currency or 'moneda social' is a type of non-market money that is created and adopted by groups to value skills, knowledge and talents and facilitate their exchange. In general, they do not replace the main currency, but offer ways to identify collective needs, strengthen local activity, and build economies that are not based on profit, extraction or accumulation. There are over 5,000 community currencies in circulation around the world, Spain alone has close to 300.

From the start, Valor y Cambio had three goals: one, to offer a widely accessible platform for participants to consider what they value; two, to introduce the notion of community currencies; and three, to provide a practice of an exchange economy capable of fostering different social relationships. Valor y Cambio also proposed that complimentary currencies constituted a potential tactic for countries such as Puerto Rico, which have high unemployment and poverty rates, but also high levels of education and collective knowledge. Moreover, the project envisioned community currencies as a means to promote critical conversations about what is generally termed 'the economy' and some of its core assumptions, including the necessity for capitalist 'development' and 'employment'.

On the ground, Valor y Cambio is a participatory and public experience: To take part, people approach a refurbished ATM machine called the VyC

172 *Theorising Cultures of Equality*

(the acronym for Valor y Cambio) and speak into a camera and recorder for up to 3 minutes. The VyC asks participants to tell stories about what they value, how their communities can support what they value, and which people or groups are already sustaining these values. Participants can then exchange the bill for items at the partner businesses and organisations that agree to accept the currency for a period of time. Through these exchanges, Valor y Cambio materialises an economy where the main unit of value is storytelling: in exchange for the story that participants tell the VyC, they receive a bill with a QR code that they could use to access the currency's stories through their mobile phones. Furthermore, in exchange for the establishments' accepting the pesos, the project shares their stories on social media. These general principles are written on the bills themselves, which detail that Valor y Cambio's aims and means are 'to tell stories of value' and to create a 'collective bank' of stories in a manner that is 'voluntary and free'.

The need for a project such as Valor y Cambio arose from a desire to combat Puerto Rican suffering resulting from what is generally called 'the debt crisis'. A complex process rooted in over a century of colonial-capitalism − a logic of expropriation, extraction, and subordination that serves the interest of global capital through colonial practices and epistemologies − its immediate trigger was the ten-year phase-out (1996–2006) of Section 936 of the US Internal Revenue Code. Originally approved in 1976, the measure was designed to guarantee high profit margins to American corporations by extending tax breaks to companies that operated in Puerto Rico. In 1996, however, Congress abolished the tax exemptions to fund an increase of the minimum wage stateside inducing a wave of plant closings, the loss of over 100,000 jobs, and a deeper recession in Puerto Rico than the one experienced in the United States.[2]

The crisis deepened when, in 2015, Governor Alejandro García Padilla announced that as a result of extensive borrowing to offset shortfalls, the island's government had amassed such an enormous public debt − US $72 billion, in addition to US $50 billion in pension obligations − that it was 'unpayable' (Corkery and Williams Walsh, 2015). A year later, the US Congress responded by passing the Oversight, Management, and Economic Stability Act (Duffy, 2016), which returned Puerto Rico to a direct form of colonial-capitalist rule. This 2016 federal law created a fiscal control board composed of people with deep ties to the banking industry, including entities directly involved in producing the debt, and granted them broad powers to extract payment by privatisation and cuts to all of life's fundamentals, including, healthcare, education, infrastructure, and pensions. As a result of these policies, close to 500,000 people have migrated; there are now over 5 million Puerto Ricans living in the United States (Guadalupe, 2016).

The suffering reached a breaking point after 16 September 2017, when Hurricane Maria, a category 5 storm, made landfall in Puerto Rico. Maria demolished the archipelago's decrepit electricity network and other infrastructure, leaving half a million residents with damaged or destroyed homes, and an energy blackout that lasted almost a year. The political aftermath was no less devastating; it ushered in disaster capitalism and a necropolitical response by the state that resulted in hunger, homelessness, the deaths of at least 4,645 people and the migration of another 100,000 residents – about 4 percent of the population. Poverty rates soared to near 50 percent.

Following the hurricane, it similarly became evident that *la crisis* is not a temporary predicament. Instead, it is the symptom of a new mode of colonial-capitalism. Since the United States invaded Puerto Rico, different sectors of US capital have subjected the island to three forms of colonial-capitalist extraction: agricultural (1898–1945), manufacturing (1945–2006) and now neoliberal debt (since 2006). Each has been injurious in its own way. Agricultural extraction ruined Puerto Rican landowners, expelled peasants from the land and created single-crop monopolies. Manufacturing modernised the economy and expanded the middle class, but it was predicated on extensive structural unemployment and mass migration of the so-called 'surplus' population. In some ways, the newest modality may be the most extreme: its goal is not only to extract profit or push out labour, but also to found an 'empty island' – a process that requires an even greater takeover of land and population expulsion than the prior periods (Negrón-Muntaner, 2018b).

To the extent that Valor y Cambio remains an ongoing project that includes a final tour in Puerto Rico, a report of the recorded stories, and a documentary film, it is impossible to presently draw firm conclusions on its effects or impact. However, at this point, I have found it urgent to reflect on two unexpected outcomes of the project: the joy that greeted it, and the community-currency initiatives that it immediately inspired. In retrospect, this reception anticipated the 'hot summer' mass protests and subsequent people's assemblies that erupted a few months later across Puerto Rico and its diaspora, and raised a range of questions regarding the centrality of emotion to politics and art (Negrón-Muntaner, 2019). Valor y Cambio likewise generated a concept that I will formally introduce here and which may be increasingly relevant as anti-neoliberal protests spread throughout the world: decolonial joy.

Art of Change: On Designing Valor y Cambio

If the austerity crisis and post-Maria abandonment represent the larger contexts for Valor y Cambio, as an artistic intervention, the project's design largely stemmed from Unpayable Debt: Capital, Violence and the New Global Economy, a working group that I co-led with anthropologist Sarah Muir at Columbia University's Center for the Study of Social Difference (2016 to 2019). Unpayable Debt's goal was to pursue comparative work and collective action against the imposition of debt as an extractive regime and form of governance. The working group included members and affiliates who were scholars, journalists, artists, activists and students, none of whom was formally trained in economics. This last characteristic proved critical to the development of Valor y Cambio, as it prompted us to draw from multiple methods and perspectives, and to conclude that debt structures all aspects of our lives beyond those considered to be economic, including subjectivity and political organisation.[3]

174 *Theorising Cultures of Equality*

Figure 11.1 Journalist at Latte que Latte, 11 February 2019

After two years of research and discussions, I began to consider how we could more directly contribute to challenging neoliberalisation and share what we had learned, particularly with others affected by debt and austerity. To this end, in May 2018 several members conducted a listening tour with activists who were working on food security, participatory governance and

Figure 11.2 Bill 25 with QR code

related issues. Initially, we wanted to explore the possibility of organising an assembly that would facilitate knowledge exchange and link existing grassroots efforts to create a greater political force. Unexpectedly, many activists in Puerto Rico strongly discouraged us from attempting this, citing that they were exhausted, did not have the energy or resources to collaborate or build broad coalitions, distrusted mainstream political parties and media, and even

Figure 11.3 Participants in line at the Miramar Food Truck location, 16 February 2019

176   *Theorising Cultures of Equality*

others doing similar work. While dispiriting at a certain level, these conversations proved to be fundamental. The widespread rejection of traditional forms of dialogue and organising implied the need to design and imagine an entirely different kind of intervention.

Initially at a loss, Valor y Cambio's concept started to cohere as a result of at least three clarifying moments. The first took place when Vanessa Pérez-Rosario, scholar and managing editor of the journal *Small Axe*, interviewed me about Unpayable Debt's work and asked me to think of a concept that I had not devoted much time to before: money. What it is? How does it acquire value? How can money be disruptive (Pérez-Rosario, 2018)? In the process, I realised that while money itself was 'nothing', it told stories, signified values and facilitated a range of human relationships. Even further, I came to view that the creation of money can serve, 'as a means of [...] fostering political resistance' and invite trust in alternative political projects (Notar, 2002: 124), in the words of anthropologist Beth A. Notar.

The second moment was the knowledge that a few years after the 2008 financial crisis, the government of Ireland facilitated a conversation about what people valued as a way to rethink aspects of the nation's educational curricula and produce new social relations and subjectivities. This led to another set of key questions that recontextualised the prior ones on money. If in a debt crisis, there is not only the challenge of less resources but also of how to use existing resources, how do polities and communities determine what they will support? In other words, what do they value? How do these values orient power and policy? (Blease, 2017).

The last moment involved art. In May 2018 I also curated a show called *Puerto Rico Under Water: Five Art Perspectives on the Debt Crisis* at the Center for the Study of Ethnicity and Race's at Columbia University. Early on, our working group had identified the arts as an important practice in contexts of neoliberal crisis globally, including in Argentina, Brazil, Greece, Mexico and Spain. In fact, one of our initial questions was: 'What are the roles of information, education, and the arts in disrupting debt regimes?' (Negrón-Muntaner, 2018). The curatorial process confirmed how in Puerto Rico, art was investigating fundamental aspects of the debt not addressed by the majority of scholarship, including the affect and surrealness of debt and money itself. The process likewise made me more aware of the work of Sarabel Santos Negrón, one of the artists included in the exhibit, who had produced a series of photographs of objects left behind in increasingly abandoned landscapes or what I termed the 'debris' of the austerity crisis. After the show, I reached out and asked if she would be interested in collaborating what I began to call the 'Puerto Rican money' idea. She agreed.

One of the most complex and time-consuming parts of Valor y Cambio's design was the imagining of a new currency. To conceive it, Santos Negrón and I worked for almost a year to develop the initial series of six 'banknotes', which featured 1, 2, 5, 10, 21 and 25 denominations. During this period, we studied art, national and community currencies from all over the world, particularly those of islands, which tend to employ a broad colour palette, visualise a rich

Decolonial Joy 177

sense of place and include a greater diversity of people than the US dollar. To select what stories the bills would circulate, Santos Negrón and I conducted an informal survey of people living in Puerto Rico and the diaspora. We asked them what persons, communities or places both embodied the four core values that we had adopted for the project – equity, solidarity, justice and creativity – and allowed us to discuss critical challenges of the present such as access to healthcare, education, and land; racism, sexism, and migration.

After considering the responses, we selected an iconic community and nine non-living figures who practiced a wide range of politics. To avoid creating a hierarchy among them, we assigned a chronological order to the denominations, beginning with those born in the 18th century through to the twentieth. Ultimately, the currency highlighted the siblings Gregoria, Celestina and Rafael Cordero, black and Christian pioneers of public education in the early 19th century; Ramón Emeterio Betances (1827–98), an early promoter of public health, abolitionist, and anti-colonial organiser; anarchist, feminist and labour organiser Luisa Capetillo (1879–1922); social justice activist and poet Julia de Burgos (1914–53); humanitarian and baseball star Roberto Clemente (1934–72); and Marangelys Torres Morales, Jerald Constanzo and Krystal Géigel Ramírez, three young leaders selected by the eight Caño Martín Peña communities – the only in Puerto Rico to collectively own their land–to represent their story.

To bring awareness to the politics of storytelling and the importance of imagination to politics, we also introduced story elements that were not widely known or missing from the official archives. For instance, the 1 peso bill included composite drawings of Rafael Cordero's sisters, who despite their many contributions to the public education of girls have been largely ignored by scholars and hegemonic national narratives (Méndez Panedas, 2019), and for whom no contemporaneous portraits exist. We likewise used unorthodox numbers such as 21 in the Clemente denomination. This gesture was meant to not only note Clemente's exceptional career as a baseball player (his number as a Pittsburgh

Figure 11.4 The '21' peso bill portraying Roberto Clemente

178 *Theorising Cultures of Equality*

Figure 11.5 The '1' peso bill of the Cordero siblings

Pirate was 21), but to signify that stories are complex, do not have to come in multiples of five and that monetary policy could effectively be in 'our hands'.

The creation of the Caño Martín Peña bill, number 25, also allowed the project to engage with a largely unremarked paradox: the bills were designed to foster localised solidarity economies, yet most of the figures, while diverse in multiple senses, were already incorporated into national and nationalist narratives. This tension between local and national seemed unavoidable if the goal was to have a broad dialogue across the Puerto Rican archipelago. So, to address this inconsistency, the 25 bill underscored the importance of local economies, participatory forms of governance and collective land tenure. Following our own rule, we narrated the Caño's 'birth' in the 1930s, making it the last bill in the series. Tellingly, the fact that this bill had the highest denomination and featured living young people was generally understood to

Figure 11.6 The '25' bill featuring three youth leaders to represent the eight communities of El Caño Martín Peña

most clearly exemplify the project's critique to neoliberal capitalism and desire for a different present and future.

Despite living in the era of BitCoin and other digital currencies, we chose to create a paper currency that can be passed from hand to hand as we thought that this would enable conversations and facilitate the circulation of narratives. To test this idea, in January 2019, we took some early currency prototypes to farmers markets in Hato Rey and Humacao. We quickly discovered three things: one, that the bills indeed served to tell stories and that the stories were meaningful; two, that very few people had ever heard of the term 'moneda social' before our meeting but readily grasped the concept of an exchange economy; and three, that it often took less than a minute for most to agree to participate. This early level of support was remarkable, as we were basically suggesting to small business owners that they may potentially 'lose money' and 'waste time' for more than a week.

Significantly, many of those who agreed without hesitation were women, who offered two key reasons for their support. For one, exchange economies were familiar. In the succinct words of a farmer from Humacao, 'exchange is how women take care of their families'. The building of exchange economies and other forms of *autogestión* (self-governance) involving food, housing, and transportation is also how countless Puerto Ricans survived after Hurricane Maria, an experience that was still fresh in people's minds (Santos Negrón,

Figure 11.7 'Se aceptan pesos' poster at Latte que Latte Cafe, 11 February 2019

180 *Theorising Cultures of Equality*

2019). As Virma Brull, the owner of Deaverdura in Old San Juan, the project's first site, recalls, 'Here in my restaurant, we started operating right away. Everyone brought what they had and we cooked' (Brull, 2019). This is consistent with how, during an austerity crisis, women are particularly pressured as they are tasked with social reproduction and care of family and community in precisely the areas undermined by austerity policies such as education and health (Federici, 2012). At the end, that Valor y Cambio was conceived and largely executed by women became perceived as part of the design, inviting greater trust and rapid incorporation into existing networks of exchange and *autogestión*.

Eight Days That Shook Some Worlds

A month later, however, not all business owners or organisational directors agreed to participate. Several declined out of fear that community currencies were illegal or a scam. Others, including some of our team members, had concerns that the state would retaliate against participating organisations or even arrest us. Regardless, the decision was made to take the risk. After nearly a year of planning and with the ultimate support of 42 businesses and organisations, Valor y Cambio hit the road.

Over the course of eight non-consecutive days – from 9 February to 17 February – the VyC visited five locations, two public schools and a youth leadership programme. From the first day, the public reaction surprised everyone: hundreds of participants stood in line for hours until evening, rain or shine, to obtain a bill. A number of people came every day and others every time that they could. On the last day of the project in the city of Bayamón, the VyC was open for 14 hours, until midnight, to honour the petition of people who worked as cooks, waiters and bartenders in the area to participate after their shifts ended.

Immediately, the outcome begged the question: as the line to obtain the bills was not to access fuel, a job or even a concert ticket: why was this happening? What made the wait worth it? One thing became clear: it was not 'for the money' – at least it was not for the exchange value of the bills. In a country suffering from a profound austerity crisis, the vast majority of people who participated, more than 1,000, did not utilise the currency. Of the dispensed 1,600 bills, which amounted to thousands of dollars, less than 100 bills, totalling 150 pesos, were used. Instead of circulating the bills for the exchange of products or services, participants exchanged ideas, broke down into tears or smiles when they obtained the bills and asked how we could 'keep this movement going'.

As I engaged with participants each day, I heard a host of reasons why people retained the bills. Not a few said that they did so because the project and the bills were 'works of art' and that they were 'beautiful'. Others held on to them because the bills affirmed their identities, not only as Puerto Ricans, but as women, blacks, young people and residents of El Caño. Yet for another group, the bills represented the end of colonial capitalism and the possibility of a new beginning. The return of numerous people to the VyC, again and

Decolonial Joy   181

again, to repeat the experience and obtain a new bill, recalls theologist Ruben Alves's verse: 'for in each repetition, the beauty is reborn new fresh' (Alves, 2010).

That hundreds of participants opted to keep the bills could appear as a form of individual appropriation or hoarding. Notably, the keeping of community money is not unique to our project. Activist Rob Hopskins, for instance, has written that many viewed the Totnes Pound, a complimentary currency in the United Kingdom, as 'souvenirs' and symbols of community pride. However, the politics of the Puerto Rican response are arguably of even greater complexity. On the one hand, that participants understood the bills as 'art' was in itself politically meaningful as artists are often more valued than political figures for their role in maintaining cultural memory and reproducing collective identity under colonialism (Negrón-Muntaner, 2019). On the other, unlike most residents of Totnes, who are citizens of a nation-state with its own money, Puerto Rico has never had a national currency and has been subject to US colonial-capitalism and its symbolically loaded currency – the dollar – for over a century.

Equally significant, the US dollar is not only that of another country and a colonial power with complete control of Puerto Rico's monetary policy and federal money allocations. It similarly enshrines the coloniality of power, that is, 'the long-standing patterns of power that emerged as a result of colonialism, but that define culture, labour, intersubjective relations, and knowledge production well beyond the strict limits of colonial administrations', in the words of philosopher Nelson Maldonado Torres's (Maldonado-Torres, 2007). This is evident in that the dollar contains only figures of men who identify themselves as white, are representatives of the state, and/or agents of racist, genocidal and heterosexist policies.

In this context, the idea of a local currency created for communal well-being, which operates by exchange, and circulates images and stories of women, blacks, migrants and children of immigrants, writers, doctors, educators, athletes, thinkers, feminists, union organisers, individuals but also families and communities, disrupted the manner in which Puerto Ricans are discounted daily by the US currency, politically, economically and culturally. It likewise affirmed a range of stories, perspectives and political praxis as valuable and underscored that there are other ways of counting and telling. And it did this using the most powerful discursive and economic symbol of US colonialism in Puerto Rico: money.

To rejoice at the currency was then to challenge multiple layers of dispossession. Therefore, to the extent that this stage of the project lasted only eight days and there was doubt that it could be extended or repeated, the majority of participants opted to keep the bills as a symbol: of communities, of struggles, of memory, of beauty, of hope. If money is a 'promise' of payment and the body that imposes austerity in Puerto Rico was created by a law called PROMESA, the peso is a very different kind of promise. Which is why for many, the value of the bill exceeded what could be exchanged with it. The peso was, in addition to beautiful or valuable, a piece of each participant's desires and history with which they refused to part or transact.

182 *Theorising Cultures of Equality*

Figure 11.8 Participant holding the Julia de Burgos bill at University High School in Rio Piedras, 13 February 2019

But even before I asked participants why they were not using the bills and I heard their reasons, I witnessed an emotion that was not entirely new to the project: joy. Countless times, several months before the machine first touched the ground, I too felt joy working on Valor y Cambio. This emotion was one that I seemed to communicate to people who visited the tour locations. Day after day, I spoke to participants who thanked me for the project. Significantly, they did not thank me for my 'work', as people normally do, but 'por tu alegría', for 'your joy'.

At times I distrusted this joy. All joy is not 'good', or intends to do good: 'Joy', writes theologician Miroslav Volf, 'can be self-absorbed (I rejoice only in my own good); joy can be indifferent to others (I rejoice with gusto over my distant friend's fortune but am unmoved by the pain at my doorstep); joy can be perverse (I rejoice in the misfortune of others)' (Volf, 2016). Moreover, as philosopher Slavoj Žižek's has argued, if 'enjoyment' coheres national identity through the notion that others want to 'steal' a group's enjoyment and corrupt them with theirs, joy can lead to violence against the 'foreign other' and fix subjects into 'the existing framework of domination', in critic Jodi Dean's terms (2016: 25). This was evident in on site and on line discourse, where some participants underscored that what decolonial joy referred to was 'OUR (Puerto Rican) joy' (Facebook, 2019).

Yet, without ignoring the above complexity, the explosion of joy that greeted the project often went beyond ethnic affirmation and its pitfalls. Joy appeared at the precise moment when many, myself included, 'felt' the possibility of a different now, one where neither colonialism nor coloniality ruled over our lives. While this reaction is not free of fantasy in Žižek's sense – the imaginary relation to the other – not all (political) fantasies are the same or are equally generative (Žižek, 2008). This realisation immediately raised two additional questions: could this widely shared response that so pervaded Valor y Cambio's inquiry into value in the so-called 'oldest colony in the world' be described as not only joy but a specific kind, 'decolonial joy'? And, if so, what does the concept make politically possible and how to define it?

The Terms of Joy

Although joy is one of the most fundamental human emotions, theorising the politics of joy in general and decolonial joy in particular is not without difficulties. First, 'decolonial' is often defined as the antithesis to 'coloniality', which, in scholar Joseph Drexler-Dreis's words, 'refers to the cultural and epistemological frameworks – including the ontological (for example, gender and racial), theological, and social imaginaries – generated during the political process of colonialism, which have yet to disappear after political decolonization' (Drexler-Dreis, 2015). In the case of the Puerto Rican archipelago, a formal colony, the reception to Valor y Cambio raises the question of whether what I am referring to as decolonial joy would not be better described as 'anti-colonial' or even 'national' joy, that is, a joy fundamentally springing from a desire to replace the colonial nation-state, found a new nation-state, or affirm national sovereignty rather than disrupt the matrix of coloniality.

There is no doubt that some participants' joy could also be described in this way. Not a few cried at seeing the currency because holding it in their hands made them feel as 'if Puerto Rico was already an independent country' (Manning, 2018). However, to the extent that the inhabitants of Puerto Rico have been subject to colonialism *and* coloniality for over 500 years; and many Puerto Ricans today are ambivalent toward nation-state building, due in part to the fear this process may bring not less but greater coloniality in the hands of a white and male elite, the decolonial imaginary appeared to be more widely shared. In this regard, for decolonial joy to prevail in a formal colonial context is, among other things, to insist on the necessity for a decolonial politics under any configuration of power, including a formal colony, nation-state or other alignment (Negrón-Muntaner, 2017).

Second, while it is arguably impossible to talk about love without joy, decolonial theorists have to date almost exclusively focused on love. This is evident in the works of a wide range of decolonial thinkers, such as Chela Sandoval, Drexler-Dreis and Maldonado-Torres. For Sandoval, who coined the term, decolonial love is simultaneously a 'technology of social transformation' and a 'category of analysis' that can be defined as an 'attraction [...]

184 *Theorising Cultures of Equality*

and relation carved out of and in spite of difference' (Sandoval, 2000). Maldonado-Torres in turn stresses the ethico-political dimensions of love from the point of view of philosopher Frantz Fanon's *damné*, who '"cries out in horror"... and aspires – through the decolonial praxis of love,... to create a transmodern world "in which many worlds fit" and where the global dictatorship of capital, property, and coloniality no longer reign' (Maldonado-Torres, 2008). Similarly, engaging with both Fanon and the writer James Baldwin, Drexler-Dreis views decolonial love as a tool, method, and hermeneutic to 'shatter the structures of colonial modernity' and foster 'the reconstruction of a world that allows for a new way of being human, eclipsing current hierarchies within a modern/colonial world' (Drexel-Dreis, 2015).

The notion of joy, however, is not altogether absent from decolonial theory. In his work on beauty and art, philosopher Enrique Dussel has argued that the joy of being alive is 'the substance of all possible aesthetics and art' (La Razón, 2009; Dussel, 2018). Although not fully theorised, the term itself is briefly mentioned in scholar Dean Itsuji Saranillio's book *Unsustainable Empires: Alternative Histories of Hawaii's Statehood* (2018). The concept appears in a passage discussing theorist Candace Fujikane's notion of 'settler ally' in relation to 'ea', which in this context refers to both life and sovereignty: 'The term "settler" roots us in the settler colonialism that we seek to rearticulate so that we never lose sight of those conditions or our positionality or the privileges we derive from it. At the same time, the term encompasses the imaginative possibilities for our collaborative work on ea and land-based decolonial nation-building. For there is joy, too, in these practices of growing ea…we rejoice in the practice, we move ourselves to the *decolonial joy of practicing ea*' (my emphasis, quoted in Saranillio, 2018; and Fujikane, forthcoming.).

Overall, influential feminist scholarship in the Americas and Europe has devoted limited attention to joy, generally favouring pleasure or anger as key categories. Tellingly, scholar Sara Ahmed is one of the most prominent feminists invoking joy, albeit as a negative-positive: killjoy. In her words, 'There is solidarity in recognizing our alienation from happiness, even if we do not inhabit the same place (and we do not). There can be joy in killing joy. And kill joy we must, and we do' (Ahmed, 2010). Whereas one could argue that decolonial joy is a killjoy of coloniality, Ahmed's main target is actually 'happiness' which she at times conflates with joy, thus assuming that killjoy is the reverse of (or its imperative) happiness. Yet, I would argue, that joy is not the same as happiness, can be perfectly compatible with not being happy, and can be experienced with greater intensity in relation to pain. I will return to that.

A more akin genealogy stems from the work of black feminists who invoke joy as a politics. In her influential text *Uses of the Erotic*, writer Audre Lorde linked joy to the life source of the erotic and the possibility of connection across difference, a relation that has also been explored by decolonial feminists. As Lorde writes: 'For once we begin to feel deeply all the aspects of our lives, we begin to demand from ourselves and from our life-pursuits that they feel in accordance with that joy which we know ourselves to be capable of' …

Decolonial Joy 185

'The sharing of joy, whether physical, emotional, psychic, or intellectual, forms a bridge between the sharers which can be the basis for understanding much of what is not shared between them, and lessens the threat of their difference' (Lorde, 2000). Contemporary black feminist activist adrienne maree brown has likewise argued for joy as a form of resistance and community: 'Finding ourselves, finding each other – finding our fight and our joy – that's what this moment is about' (brown, 2019).

In various ways, black feminist joy, decolonial love and Fujikane's conceptualisation of joy as a decolonial practice of life and communal (rather than state) politics provide valuable entry points into the possibilities of decolonial joy. At the same time, to the extent that in all these contexts, joy is not at the center of reflection, leaves a range of critical questions unexplored. To address some of these gaps, in the next section, I will expand the dialogue between Valor y Cambio and several theorists of joy, including Friedrich Nietzsche, Baruch Spinoza, Miroslav Volf and Ann Mische. Through this counterpoint, I will focus on the temporality, pain and tensions of decolonial joy and broaden the scope of questions one may ask about this concept and praxis.

Decolonial Joy, or What's Joy Got To Do With It?

To the extent that Valor y Cambio was a temporal experience, it is useful to begin with describing *when* joy was felt by participants: it was not waiting in line, although people reported that they enjoyed speaking to others. It was generally not during the recording nor exchange with the VyC, although some people had an emotional response in telling their story, including crying and laughter. It was generally at the exact moment when participants received the bills from the VyC dispenser, particularly when they obtained the figure they hoped for. This temporal dimension of joy recalls philosopher and theologist Thomas Aquinas's observation that joy 'is a response to having been "united" with what we love' (cited in Volf, 2016).

One of the most compelling examples of what one may call 'the moment of joy' was that of a young artist and teacher, Eduardo Paz, who stood in line for hours for several days because he wanted to receive one particular bill: the 1, featuring the Cordero siblings. When he finally did, on 18 February, I asked Paz why this bill brought him so much joy: 'Let's say that if I talk, I will cry. He was an educator. Basically, it represents what I am: an Afro-descendant man, fighting, educating and showing his roots through the different situations that life can present. [The bill] is worth a lot'.[4]

As suggested by Paz's experience and commentary, this rejoicing was not a passive act. In order to obtain the bills, participants had to engage in a series of interactions that required time, effort and mental investment. But even without this particular design, to experience joy requires what Volf described as 'the *construal* of the object of joy as good; it is tied to how I perceive things rather than to what things are in themselves [...] (Ibid). In other words, to feel

186 *Theorising Cultures of Equality*

Figure 11.9 Eduardo Paz showing the '1' bill in Bayamón, 17 February 2019.

joy, a subject will need to actively imagine relationships to him or herself, as well as to other objects and subjects, and determine their value.

Consistently, Paz's reaction underscored that there was joy in the story that the bill told and the possibilities this story opened. In his case, the joy was in contrast to W.E.B. DuBois' concept of double consciousness, it was the joy of (at least) a dual valorisation: his valorisation of Rafael Cordero, a black

Decolonial Joy   187

educator in the 19th century, and the projects' public valorisation of Cordero, and all who like him are black teachers. The convergence gave a particular content to Paz's joy: that for a moment, the world valued what he valued, and the world valued him. This recalls Volf's observation that joy can be defined as an *'emotional attunement between the self and the world – usually a small portion of it – experienced as blessing'* (Volf, 2016, italics in original).

At another level, Paz's joy in the story of black educators is about asserting people's individual and collective capacities under conditions of colonialism and coloniality that continuously attempt against their thriving. This dimension is consistent with philosopher Baruch Spinoza's notion of joy as a 'concept of resistance' that arises when a subject is able to actualize his or her capacities and 'persevere in its own being' (Spinoza, 2003: 82). Or as philosopher Gilles Deleuze put it, 'you experience joy when you satisfy, when you effectuate one of your capacities [...] (Blake, 2013). In circulating stories of past capacity, Valor y Cambio sought to also expand present capacities by challenging the enduring colonial myths of Puerto Ricans as fundamentally lazy, inferior and lacking in value (Negrón-Muntaner, 2018).

Joy then not only implicates the world but also assumes a politics, that is, a field of power. As Nietzsche has observed, there is a temporal desire in joy: 'All joy wants eternity – wants deep, wants deep eternity' (Nietzsche, 1883). In other words, if joy is, 'what is missing', it wills itself as a permanent state of justice (Mische, 2014). Furthermore, as Volf elaborates, 'In this willing joy sets itself tacitly against features of the world over which one cannot or should not rejoice, and does so without resentment and judgment'. In this regard, to retain the bills, so that they would not be exhausted or 'lost', allowed for decolonial joy to be continuously rekindled.

The ways that the bills prompted joy, however, does not exhaust the question of temporality and history. Participants frequently commented that the project had been successful because it came 'at the right time', and this assessment returns us to the historical juncture of the project and one of the paradoxes of joy, or how joy is felt alongside or in counterpoint to pain, suffering or mourning. Whereas the 'moment of joy' was the embodied experience of receiving the bills, the 'time of joy' related to the larger context that renders such an object and occasion a gift. In the case of Valor y Cambio, joy emerged as the most common emotion to greet the project due to the collective suffering that Puerto Ricans had been experiencing for over a decade. It was the triple pain of the austerity crisis, hurricane Maria and its aftermath, and the migration of so many Puerto Ricans that made our project's assertion of capacity and love feel like a blessing. This may similarly explain why numerous people who visited the project said goodbye to me using an expression rooted in Christian practice: 'Que Dios te bendiga' (May God Bless You).

In other words, the exuberance of joy was not despite suffering but because of it. Joy, as literary scholar Matthew Mutter has observed in his work on W.B. Yeats, is not only inseparable from loss and suffering, the most intense joy may emerge from 'challenges to joy, even catastrophe' (Wright, 2016). The term

188 *Theorising Cultures of Equality*

catastrophe is critical. As I have argued elsewhere on the trope of the 'emptying island', what Puerto Rico has been experiencing is catastrophic (Negrón-Muntaner, 2018). But I use the term catastrophe not as simply a synonym of disaster. Instead, I propose to build on literary scholar Alexandra Perisic's (2017) observation that catastrophes – a term derived from the 'Greek katastrephein, meaning to "overturn"' – can be understood as a moment of 'overturning' in which collective reflection and action are still viable (Perisic, 2017: 118). In other words, facing the disaster of colonial-capitalist modernity, Puerto Ricans have brought about catastrophe, or overturning. Similar to other public art projects such as the 2018 'memorial of shoes' tribute and demand for those who died as a result of Maria (Zaitchik, 2018), Valor y Cambio, provided a space for the creative resignification of suffering, an 'alter-signification' in Drexler-Dreis's terms (Drexel-Dreis, 2015).

The joy produced by participating in Valor y Cambio thus envisioned the collective potential of both decolonial joy in the present and a joyful decolonial future. This is consistent with Volf's remark that, 'Joy is best experienced in community. Joy seeks company ('come and rejoice with me') (Volf, 2016). It is likewise present in Nietzsche's question about how humanity will assume strength in the face of the tragic nature of life' (McIntyre, 1997) through revenge or communal joy – and his answer, 'to share not suffering but joy' (Ibid). It is similarly consistent with sociologist Ann Mische's observation that 'joy comes from the immersion in and enjoyment of simultaneous motion *forward* in time and *across* social space' (Mische, 2014).

In this sense, while some participants appeared to enjoy the fetishisation of the bills or the affirmation of 'our Puerto Rican (national) thing', others related their joy as part of a process of founding an expansive decolonial politics. If for neuroscientists such as Antonio Damasio, joy is an embodied emotion and feeling is *'the perception of a certain state of the body along with the perception of a certain mode of thinking and of thoughts with certain themes'* that weaves in emotion with memories and meaning (Damasio, 2003: 86; italics in original), decolonial joy signifies more than a particular emotion. The cognitive process to envision decoloniality also assigns meaning to joy and materialises a 'feeling' for justice. In other words, what I call decolonial joy is the (active) manner by which people become aware of, reason with, and connect the emotion of joy to a desire for decolonial justice. Akin to what Damasio (1999: 35) calls the 'satisfaction of seeing justice served', decolonial joy encompasses and connects both emotion and feeling, to redress pain, suffering, and anger.

Coda: Multiplying Joys

Joy, however, was not the only concept used to describe how people felt at receiving the bills. In interviews and conversations with participants, many expressed that they would be keeping their bills because they bore hope. As farmer and activist Yanna Muriel put it, 'We have been undergoing a long economic crisis. Hurricane María proved that the island and federal government are untrustworthy. VALOR Y CAMBIO brought hope, in a time when most was

Decolonial Joy   189

lost. I believe that farmers and elaborators can organize to create a local currency, which can meet the specific needs within the market. As it is, most of us exchange goods, harvests and sometimes services' (Fitzpatrick, 2019).

In theory, joy and hope are often at odds. Mische has observed that hope is a 'future-oriented discourse, which, unlike joy 'is based on the 'not yet', on the sense of potentiality' (Mische, 2014). In addition she has argued that, 'hope in this sense involves discipline, patience, self-denial, postponement of gratification until an as yet undefined future moment [...]' (Ibid). Tellingly, Spinoza views hope as an ambiguous and problematic notion: 'Hope is nothing else but an inconstant pleasure, arising from the image of something future or past, whereof we do not yet know the issue' (Spinoza, 2003: 79). Even further, for Ahmed hope is reactionary: to the extent that hope is a promise of future happiness, it can express a melancholy for a lost object and constitute a form of control that keep subjects to stay 'in place' (2019). One political risk is that, as Ahmed observes, objects that bring joy and happiness - as the peso - may never realise them while their pursuit may make us oblivious to the suffering of the present.

Still, in Valor y Cambio, the joy of the present, the connection to a past, and the possibility of a more just future were at times intertwined, recalling Alves' conception of hope not as deferment but as a knowledge that actions in the present may only completely flourish in the future. In his words, 'Let us plant dates/ even though those who plant them will never eat them./We must live by the love of what we will never see' (Alves, 2004). This is evident in how some participants found hope and joy in how the project facilitated their own initiatives. In this sense, decolonial joy inspired 'a greater ease in the capacity to act' (Damasio, 2003: 137) rather than postponement. Which is perhaps why decolonial joy has been sustained over time, giving rise to another unexpected outcome: the rapid emergence and consolidation of community currencies and solidarity projects.

The first example is the Caño Martín Peña communities, which began to design their own community currency, the first in Puerto Rico, after our project ended the initial tour. In late 2018 I visited El Caño to ask permission to tell their story in our 25-peso bill. After a 20-minute conversation with Alejandro Cotté Morales, then director of citizen participation and social development at Proyecto Enlace, he agreed to discuss my request with the community leadership and stated that El Caño had an immediate use for an alternative currency. To learn more, El Caño asked to be included in Valor y Cambio's tour, and the project visited the community's farmers' market, Mercado Agro-Artesanal Barrio Obrero Pa'ti, on the third day. Finally, on 1 October 2019, El Caño launched its own currency, the *Pasos* (steps) del Caño Martín Peña. The Pasos are so named as they will be issued to residents whose actions allow the community to 'step closer' to their goals.

A second project is that of JustXChanges in New York – a collaboration with activists Libertad Guerra and Angel López, supported by the Loisaida Center and the Ford Foundation. The project consolidated after Valor y Cambio visited the center and the Nathan Cummings Foundation to be part of the Pasado y Presente: Art After the Young Lords exhibition in May 2019,

190 *Theorising Cultures of Equality*

curated by Guerra and Yasmín Ramírez. JustXChanges aims to create a city-wide community currency and solidarity economy networks among three communities in the city, starting in 2020. Its initial network will include the Lower East Side and the Bronx.

Of course, not all was joyful. While joy was widely shared and experienced, what made people joyful was often different, at times leading to conflicts. For instance, a small number of people who participated in the project apparently did so with the main objective of cashing in on decolonial joy. For them, the currency was, if not 'real' money, an object which could (and should) be converted into a quick profit. Unsurprisingly, in less than 48 hours, at least two people were selling the pesos on the eBay platform for as much as US $125, leading to intense arguments on line between sellers and other participants. Comments in relation to the two most visible press and broadcast items on the project similarly showed that conservatives and likely paid internet trolls did not experience decolonial joy but colonial-capitalist disgust. Of the over 400 comments left on *El Nuevo Dia* and Telemundo's website on their Valor y Cambio coverage, the overwhelming majority were insults to the artists and mockery of the idea that Puerto Ricans could ever have a valuable currency or have a thriving economy without the United States (Fullana Acosta, 2019). For many in this group, the bills represented a reviled authoritarianism or 'communism' and the sure destabilisation of the status quo, US hegemony and their way of life.

Equally important, although the expressions of joy appeared alike, their political locations were diverse, underscoring the complexities of joy as politics, decolonial or otherwise. For example, children and young people tended to express joy when they received the bills. They were, however, significantly less attached to the currency or its stories, and used the bills more frequently than adults to meet specific needs. This was particularly pronounced during the Puerto Rico tour when Valor y Cambio visited a public school in Punta Santiago, Humacao, where nearly all students expressed their fear of hunger, and immediately exchanged the bills for food.

In addition, most participants' joy critically addresses at least one of the matrixes of power that characterised colonial-capitalist modernity. Yet, gauging from the many conversations that spontaneously occurred throughout the tour, their visions of what a decolonial future is or may look like, and the conceptual and political frameworks guiding them were not only different but sometimes at odds. Easily recognisable political referents included nationalist, feminist, anti-racist, anarchist, populist, labor, queer, and Marxist. Given this, there is no guarantee that what the majority enjoys correlates with an autonomous, non-hierarchical politics; or that decolonial joy will turn into a 'feeling' for justice encompassing everyone.

This raises the question of the durability of decolonial joy on an actual political terrain. If decolonial joy, as all joy as Nietzsche would have it, seeks eternity, what to do with the various temporalities and locations of decolonial joy? That is, if there is no decolonial joy but, rather, multiple forms of radical joys, how does one sustain the other? Part of the answer may lie in the ability of the joyful subject to *share* his or her specific form of joy, which recalls Sandoval's notion of decolonial love and Lorde's black feminist joy. In both cases, joy and love could be capable of bridging difference, although not all difference at all times. Another part lies in the ability for collectivities and polities to generate conditions for multiple joyful occasions to take place. In this regard, if the process of producing common narratives to enable collective action remains a political necessity, the achievement of consensus or the presumption of total cohesion is neither possible nor desirable.

Still, while questions remain in conceptualising decolonial joy, as these words attest, for those of us who felt this joy, all we have wanted to do since then is to pass it on. And on. The author wishes to thank Suzanne Clisby, Nelson Maldonado-Torres, and Katerina Gonzalez Seligmann for their support, generosity and rigorous comments on this essay.

Notes

1 Over time, Valor y Cambio became a team that included visual artist Sarabel Santos Negrón, designers Walter Santaliz and Julio Torres, computer engineer Victor Maldonado, just economy communicator Dayani Centeno, solidarity economy activist Joel Franqui, co-ordinator Francesca Carroll Lausell and social media expert Adriana Berríos, as well as volunteers and filmmakers in Puerto Rico and New York.
2 Dylan Matthews, "What the Hurricane Maria migration will do to Puerto Rico – and the US," *Vox.com*, 5 October 2017, www.vox.com/policy-and-politics/2017/10/5/16403952/hurricane-maria-puerto-rico-migration.
3 During the three years that the group was active, it produced various items of public scholarship, including *No More Debt: Caribbean Syllabus* (https://caribbeansyllabus.wordpress.com/caribbean-syllabus/) and *Global Syllabus* (forthcoming).
4 In Spanish: 'digamos que si hablo voy a llorar. Fue un educador. Básicamente representa lo que yo soy: un afrodescendiente, luchando, educando y mostrando sus raíces a través de las distintas situaciones que puede presentar la vida, y [la figura del billete] vale mucho.

Bibliography

Alves, R. (2010). 'Our Father... Our Mother'. *Transparencies of Eternity*. [*Transparências da eternidade,*2002] Translation: Jovelino and Joan Ramos. Miami, FL: Convivium Press, 2010: 11.
Alves, R. and Cervantes-Ortiz, L. (2016). 'A Theology of Human Joy: The Liberating-Poetic-Ludic Theology of Rubem Alves', *Perspectivas Online*. Accessed 19 September 2019. Retrieved from http://perspectivasonline.com/downloads/a-theology-of-human-joy-the-liberating-poetic-ludic-theology-of-rubem-alves-3/.
Ahmed, S. (2010). 'Killing Joy: Feminism and the History of Happiness', *Signs: Journal of Women in Culture and Society*, 35(3): 571–594.
Arbasetti, J.C. et al. (2017). '100 Years of Colonialism: How Puerto Rico Became Easy Prey for Profiteers', *In These Times*. Accessed 19 September 2019. Retrieved from https://inthesetimes.com/features/puerto_rico_colonialism_hurricane_vulture_funds.html.

192 Theorising Cultures of Equality

Anon, Territories and Insular Possessions. *[USC02] 48 USC Ch. 20: PUERTO RICO OVERSIGHT, MANAGEMENT, AND ECONOMIC STABILITY.* Accessed 19 September 2019. Retrieved fromhttp://uscode.house.gov/view.xhtml?path=/prelim@ title48/chapter20&edition=prelim.

Blake, Terence. (2013). '*English Transcription of Deleuze on JOY*', 17 August. Retrieved from https://terenceblake.wordpress.com/2013/08/17/english-transcript-of-deleuze-on-joy/

Blease, C. (2017). 'Philosophy can teach children what Google can't', *The Guardian*, 9 January. Retrieved from www.theguardian.com/commentisfree/2017/jan/09/philosophy-teach-children-schools-ireland.

Brown, A. (2019). 'Motor City Pride: A Speech Unspoken', *adrienne maree brown*. Accessed 19 September 2019. Retrieved fromhttp://adriennemareebrown.net/2019/06/10/motor-city-pride-a-speech-unspoken/.

Corkery, M. and M. William Walsh. (2015). 'Puerto Rico's Governor Says the Debts are "Not Payable"', *The New York Times*. 28 June. Retrieved from www.nytimes.com/2015/06/29/business/dealbook/puerto-ricos-governor-says-islands-debts-are-not-payable.html.

Damasio, A. (2003). *Looking for Spinoza: Joy, Sorrow and the Feeling Brain*. New York, Harvest.

Dean, J. (2016). 'Why Žižek for Political Theory?', *International Journal of Zizek Studies. Vol. 1, No.* 1:18–32.

Drexler-Dreis, J. (2015). 'James Baldwin's Decolonial Love as Religious Orientation', *Journal of Africana Religions Penn State University Press*, Vol. 3: 251–278.Accessed 19 September 2019. Retrieved from https://www.jstor.org/stable/10.5325/jafrireli.3.3.0251

Drexler-Dreis, J. (2019). *Decolonial Love Salvation in Colonial Modernity*. New York, NY: Fordham University Press.

Duffy, S.P. (2016). H.R.5278–114th Congress (2015–2016): PROMESA. US Congress. Accessed 19 September 2019. Retrieved fromwww.congress.gov/bill/114th-congress/house-bill/5278.

Dussel, E. (2018). 'Siete hipótesis para una estética de la liberación', *Praxis: Revista de Filosofia*, No. 77, January–June: 1-37.

Federici, S. (2012). *Revolution at Point Zero: Housework, Reproduction, and Feminist Struggle*. Brooklyn, NY and Oakland, CA: Common Notions (PM Press).

Fitzpatrick, M. 2019). 'VALOR Y CAMBIO: Uplifting Puerto Rico With Value and Change', *Latino Rebels*. Accessed 19 September 2019. Retrieved from https://www.latinorebels.com/2019/03/14/valueandchangepr/.

Fujikane, C. (Forthcoming). *Mapping Abundance for a Planetary Future: Kanaka Maoli and Critical Settler Cartographies in Hawai'i*. Durham, NC: Duke University Press.

Fullana Acosta, M. (2019). 'Crean pesos de Puerto Rico inspirados en figuras importantes del país', *El Nuevo Dia*, 8 February. Retrieved from www.elnuevodia.com/entretenimiento/cultura/nota/creanpesosdepuertoricoinspiradosenfigurasimportantes delpais-2475550/

Guadalupe, P. (2016). 'Who are the Members of the Puerto Rico Fiscal Control Board?', *NBCNews.com*. Accessed 19 September 2019. Retrieved from www.nbcnews.com/news/latino/who-are-members-puerto-rico-fiscal-control-board-n640811.

Hopkins, R. (2019). '*My talk at the celebration of the life and times of the Totnes Pound*', Rob Hopkins. Accessed19 September 2019. Retrieved from https://www.rob-hopkins.net/2019/04/05/my-talk-at-the-celebration-of-the-life-and-times-of-the-totnes-pound/.

Interview with Virma Brull. (2019). San Juan, Puerto Rico.

Interview with Yarelly Manning. (2018). *Miramar*, Puerto Rico.

Decolonial Joy 193

La Razón. (2009). 'La alegría de estar vivo es el contenido del arte: Dussel', 2 October. Retrieved from: www.google.com/search?q=La+alegri%CC%81a+de+estar+vivo+es+el+contenido+del+arte%3A+Dussel&oq=La+alegri%CC%81a+de+estar+vivo+es+el+contenido+del+arte%3A+Dussel&aqs=chrome..69i57.19j0j7&sourceid=chrome&ie=UTF-8.

LaValle, V. (2009). *Big Machine.* New York: Spiegel and Grau Trade Paperbacks.

Lorde, A. (2000). *Uses of the Erotic: the Erotic as Power.* Tucson, AZ: Kore Press.

Maldonado-Torres, N. (2007). 'On the Coloniality of being: Contributions to the development of a concept', *Cultural Studies*, Vol. 21, No. 2–3: 243. Accessed 19 September 2019. Retrieved from www.tandfonline.com/doi/abs/10.1080/09502380601162548?journalCode=rcus20.

Maldonado-Torres, N. (2008). *Against War: Views from the Underside of Modernity.* Durham, NC: Duke University Press: 244.

McIntyre, A. (1997). The Sovereignty of Joy. Toronto: University of Toronto Press.

Méndez Panedas, R. (2019). 'Celestina Cordero: una maestra negra puertorriqueña en la época de la esclavitud', *Afroféminas*. Accessed on 19 September 2019. Retrievd from https://afrofeminas.com/2019/01/28/celestina-cordero-una-maestra-negra-puertorriquena-en-la-epoca-de-la-esclavitud/.

Mische, A. (2014). 'Joy in Movement', Yale Center for Faith & Culture. Accessed from 19 September 2019. Retrieved from https://faith.yale.edu/sites/default/files/mische_joy_in_movement_.pdf.

Negrón-Muntaner, F. (2017). *Sovereign Acts: Contesting Colonialism Across Indigenous Nations and Latinx America.* Tucson, AZ: University of Arizona Press.

Negrón-Muntaner, F. (2018). 'Blackout: What the Darkness Illuminated', *Politics/ Letters*, 2 March. Retrived from http://politicsslashletters.org/blackout-darkness-illuminated-puerto-rico/.

Negrón-Muntaner, F. (2018). 'The Emptying Island: Puerto Rican Expulsion in Post-Maria Time', *E-misferica*. Accessed19 September 2019. Retrieved from https://hemisphericinstitute.org/en/emisferica-14-1-expulsion/14-1-essays/the-emptying-island-puerto-rican-expulsion-in-post-maria-time.html.

Negrón-Muntaner, F. (2019). 'Puerto Rico Remade', *Dissent Magazine*. Accessed 19 September 2019. Retrieved from www.dissentmagazine.org/online_articles/puerto-rico-remade.

Nietzsche, F. (1883). 'A quote from *Thus Spoke Zarathustra*', Goodreads. Accessed 19 September 2019. Retrieved from https://www.goodreads.com/quotes/8195170-o-man-attend-what-does-deep-midnight-s-voice-contend-i.

Notar, B. (2002). 'Viewing Currency Chaos: Paper Money for Advertising, Ideology, and Resistance in Republican China'. In Terry Bodenhorn, ed. *Defining Modernity: Guomindang Rhetorics of a New China, 1920–1970.* Ann Arbor, MI: The University of Michigan Press.

Pérez-Rosario, V. (2018). 'Unpayable Debt: Capital, Violence, and the New Global Economy An interview with Frances Negrón-Muntaner' *Small Axe.* Accessed 19 September 2019. Retrieved from http://smallaxe.net/sxlive/unpayable-debt-capital-violence-and-new-global-economy-interview-frances-negron-muntaner.

Sandoval, C. (2000). *Methodology of the Oppressed*, Minneapolis, MN: University of Minnesota Press: 187.

Santos Negrón, S. (Forthcoming). *Nature of Exchange.*

Saranillio, D.I. (2018). *Unsustainable Empire. Alternative Histories of Hawai'i Statehood.* Durham, NC: North Carolina, Duke University Press.

194 *Theorising Cultures of Equality*

Volf, M. (2015). 'Joy and the Good Life', ABC Religion and Ethics. Retrieved from www.abc.net.au/religion/joy-and-the-good-life/10096486.

Wright, S. (2016). 'What Is Joy?', *BYU English*. Accessed 19 September 2019. Retrived from http://english.byu.edu/what-is-joy/.

Zaitchik, A. (2018). 'Thousands of Shoes Honor Hurricane Maria's Victims in San Juan', CityLab. Accessed 4 June 2018. Retrieved from: www.citylab.com/equity/2018/06/thousands-of-shoes-honor-hurricane-marias-victims-in-san-juan/561944/.

Žižek, S. (2008). *For They Not Know What They Do: Enjoyment as a Political Factor.* New York: Verso.

Index

Page numbers in **bold** refer to figures.

able-bodiedness, compulsory 67, 68
abortion 95, 102–103, 106–107
absence, paradigm of 164
absolute equality 5–6
active view 12–13
affect 149–155, 155
Ahmed, Sara 18, 42, 184, 189
al-Qaeda 119
Alsop, R. 8, 18
alternative futures 16, 112–121
Alves, Ruben 181, 189
Americans with Disabilities Act 70, 72–73
Anderson, Benedict 98
Anderson, Elizabeth 7
Andresen, S. 46
androgyny 117
animism 153–155, 155
anthropological approach 10–11
anthropological description 10–11
anti-gender movements 44, 52; backlash against 94, 102–108, 108; Catholic Church 95, 98, 100–101, 104; and economic disadvantage 96; and national identity 97–99; and nationalism 94, 97–99, 108; Poland 3, 94–109; sociopolitical context 94–97; Stop Gender Ideology! Parliamentary Committee 101–102; and women's rights 99–100, 106, 108
anti-Muslim stereotypes 35
Appadurai, A. 4
Arfini, Elisa A.G. 6, 15
Argentina 89
Argyrou, Vassos 153
arts, the 16, 112–121; contribution 112; importance 120–121; power of 112–113; recycling 114–115, 115–116; re-mixing 117–120
Associazone Orlando 20n2
attitudes, changing 2
autogestión (self-governance) 179–180

Barad, Karen 64
Baril, Alexandre 64, 69–72
Beijing Platform for Action 52
Benedicto, Bobby 152
Benhabib, S. 4
Beveridge, F. 39
biological essentialism 100
Black Protest 94, 102–108, 108
body politics 63
Bondi, Liz 143–144
Borderias, Cristina 87
Bourdieu, Pierre 11, 148
Brace, Laura 13–14
Bradbury, Ray 119
Brazil: criminalisation of culture 163–165; decolonial aesthetic 165, 165–167; Florianópolis 17, 142–155, **150**; gendered division 144–146, **145**; male dominance 147; masculinities 17, 158–168; *passinho* 158, 159–160, 162, 167; patriarchy 17, 142–155; Rio de Janeiro 17, 158–168; *slam* 158, 159–160, 162, 167; urban gender inequality 146–148
Brull, Virma 180
Busi, Beatrice 6, 15
Bustelo, M. 41
Butler, Judith 68

care work 83; gender gap 83–86
Carmichael, Stokely 118, 119

196 *Index*

CASCO Art Institute, Utrecht 19
Catholic Church 51–52, 76, 84, 95, 98, 100–101, 104
Cavaghan, R. 45
Cicogna, Patricia 79
cities: affect 149–155, 155; gendered division 144–146, **145**; gendered inequalities 142; male dominance 147; materiality of 148–149; patriarchy 142–155; relational nature 149–151, 152–155; spectres 152–153; spirits 153–155, 155; urban gender inequality 146–148
citizenship 9, 160; and democracy 50; and masculinity 34
civic engagement 50
civilisational supremacy 38
civil society 50–51
Clare, Eli 63, 67
Clisby, Suzanne 1
colonialism 181, 184, 188
coloniality 188
Columbia University, Center for the Study of Social Difference 173
communal well-being 181
community currency 171, **175**, 176–180, **177**, **178**, **179**, 180–183, **182**
comparative policy research 40
co-optation of feminisms 42
Corso, Carla 83
cosmopolitanism 125–126, 130
Council of Europe 77–78, 90
Covre, Pia 83
Cowan, J.K. 9–11
creativity 112, 160
Crenshaw, Kimberlé 7
criminalised stereotypes 158
critical perspective 2
cross-cultural dialogue 138
cultural agents 27
cultural critics 4
cultural frameworks 3
cultural impunity 135
culturalism 4
cultural practices 2
cultural production: criminalisation 163–165; equality 9–13; urban peripheries 159–160
cultural sites 2
culture: definition 3–4; and inequality 11; and rights 9–10; understanding 2

Dalla Costa, Mariarosa 81
Damasio, Antonio 188

DaMatta, Roberto 144, 146
Dave, Naisargi N. 152
Dean, Jodi 182
Debate Feminista 18
debility 71
decolonial aesthetic 165, 165–167
decolonial joy 18, 183, 183–184, 185–188, 190–191
decolonial love 183–184
de la Barre, François Poulain 9
de la Cadena, Marisol 154
Deleuze, Gilles 187
DEMAU 79
de Meis, Carla 144
democracy, and citizenship 50
Diagnostic and Statistical Manual of Mental Disorders (American Psychiatric Association) 66
difference, discourse of 119
disability: accessing 72–74; formations of 69–72; and globalisation 65; intra-actions of transgender 67–69; as queer 67–68; as stigma 63; and transgender 14–15, 63–74; transgender as 69–72; vocabulary 71
disability bathrooms 64–65
disability politics 64
diversity 14–15
Dölling, I. 46
Drexler-Dreis, Joseph 184, 188
DuBois, W.E.B 186
Dussel, Enrique 184

Earth-Beings 154
Edelman, Lee 117
emancipatory politics 84
embodied discomfort 19
empowerment, triangles of 40
Enderstein, A.M. 14
Engdahl, Ulrica 67
Englund, Harri 11–12
Enlightenment, the 25–36; feminism 28, 28–36; and gender 13–14; and human nature 25–26; natural history discourses 25–28; subordination of women 28; women's claim to humanity 28–36
entanglement 64
equalities architecture 3, 4
equality: absolute 5–6; achieving 2; active view 12–13; criteria 5; as cultural artefact 4; cultural production 9–13; definition 2, 5–9, 77–78; importance 4–5; and inequality 6–7; passive view

12–13; as provocation 18; radical critique 6; relational 6–7; vernacular forms 11–12
equality-building 39
equality policies 42
equality stories 38, 53
equality work, tensions and challenges 41–44
Espineira, Karine 65–66
ethnography 11–12
EU referendum 1
European Commission 88
European Institute for Gender Equality 40, 76
Europeanness, claims to 2
European Union 52, 96–97
evolution 27
exchange value 171

Facina, Adriana 166
Fanon, Frantz 184
fantasy 16, 112–121
Farris, Sara 14
Federici, Silvia 82
feedback loops 51
female sexuality, male regulation of 7
feminine mystique 82
feminism, Enlightenment 28, 28–36
feminisms: co-optation of 42; re-mixing 113–115
feminist activism 14
feminist knowledge transfer 41, 47–48
femonationalism 14
Fernández, Marta 17
Ferree, Max 48
Fligel, A. 99, 103
Florianópolis, Brazil 17, 142–155, **143**, **150**; gendered division 144–146, **145**; inequalities 142; male dominance 147; materiality of 148–149; spectres 152–153; spirits 153–155; urban gender inequality 146–148
Footnotes on Equality exhibition 18–19
Fouque, Antoinette 79
freedom 30
Friedman, Susan 11, 16
Fujikane, Candace 184
funk 166–167
futurity 117

Garcia, Neil 16
Gardner, Carol Brooks 147
Gdula, M. 105

gender: definition 3; and the Enlightenment 13–14; medical regulation 64–67; and national identity 97–99; social assignment 67; subject positions 3
gender-based violence 90, 102
gender difference 2
Gender Dysphoria 64
gendered inequalities: cities 142; theorisations of 143–144
gender equality 4, 77–78; Italy 76
gender equality architecture 50–51
Gender Equality Index 76, 95
gender equality policies 40
gender expertise 39–41, 41, 43, 44
Gender Identity Disorder 66, 73
gender ideology 52; Poland 95, 101–102
gender inequality 6–7, 39
gender knowledge 44, 45–46, 50
gender-neutral toilets 14–15, 63, 64–65
gender nonconformity, legal regulation 72–73
gender performativity 68
gender stereotypes 100
gender training 3, 14, 38–54; definition 40; domains 50–51; emancipatory ethos 43; and gender expertise 39–41, 41, 43, 44; gender knowledge 44, 45–46; interpretive frameworks 46; knowledge circulation 44, 46–48, 53; multi-level nature of 38, 41, 48; research 40–41; resistances 43–44; social complexity theory 48–52; tensions and challenges 41–44; theoretical architecture 38–39, 44–52, 53, 53–54
Global Financial Crisis, 2008 176
globalisation 125; and disability 65
Golańska, Dorota 97
Gosepath, S. 5–6
governance 43
GRACE (Gender and Cultures of Equality in Europe) project 1–2, 18–19, 19–20n2, 19n1
Graff, A.
Graff, Agnieszka 97–99, 103
Greenblatt, Stephen 112
Gregor, A. 94–95, 97
Grzebalska, W. 94–95, 96, 97, 99, 101, 108
Guardian, The 1
Guerra, Libertad 189–190

Halberstam, Jack 65
Hall, Kim Q. 68, 70

198 *Index*

Halsaa, B. 40
haunting 152–155
Hays, Mary 6–7, 13–14, 25, 29–30, 31, 32, 34, 34–35, 36
heteronormativity 68
Hettinga, Leike 14–15
Hoard, S. 41
Holbraad, Martin 149
Holli, A.M. 40
homo/hetero binary 138
homosexuality 16; depathologisation 69; masculine tradition 130; the Philippines 124–138; sexual exile structures 125
hope, and joy 188–189
Hopskins, Rob 181
housework, and paid work 80–83
Humanism 134–135
humanities: importance 120–121; value of 112
humanity; women's claim to 28–36; zoological frontiers of 25–28
human nature 25–26
human rights 94–95

identity 129, 181
identity politics 72
imagination 13, 112, 120–121, 177
imperialism 38
inclusion 14–15, 63
inequality 31; centrality of 49; and culture 11; and equality 6–7;; gender 6–7; and privilege 6–7; production 2; regimes of 49–50
Inglehart, R. 3
Ingold, T. 142, 151, 153
inspiration porn 65
interdependency 12
International Classification of Diseases, World Health Organization 66
International Feminist Collective 81
intersectionality 7–8
Ireland 176
Istanbul Convention 96, 102
Italy 6, 15, 51–52, 76–91; ageing index 84; austerity policies 84; Berlusconi premiership 84; Catholic Church 76, 84; emancipatory politics 84; family law decree 88–89; female employment 84; feminisation of work 86–90; feminism 76, 76–77, 77–80; gender care gap 83–86; Gender Equality Index 76; Law 75 80; legal reform 80; Manifesto di Rivolta Femminile 78;

Marxist feminism 80–81, 90; pension reform 88; Pillon Decree 88–89, 91; Second Republic 84; sex workers' movement 83; thought of sexual difference 76–77, 79–80; Wages for Housework campaign 77, 80–83, 90–91; work-life balance initiatives 88

Jagger, Alison 5, 6
Janion, Maria 98
joy 173, 182–183, **182**, **186**; decolonial 183, 183–184, 185–188, 190–191; durability 190–191; and hope 188–189; multiplying 188–191; sharing 185, 190, 191; temporal dimension 185–187; terms of 183–185
JustXChanges 189–190

Kafer, Alison 64–65, 69
Kantola, J. 43
Kauffman, S. 49
Kay, A. 51
Keim, W. 48
Kempa, Beata 101
knowledge circulation 44, 46–48, 53
knowledge dissemination 124
knowledge production 47; reflexive 14
Korolczuk, Elzbieta 103, 104, 105, 106–107, 107, 108
Krieg, Josephine 67
Kubisa, J. 103, 107
Kunz, R. 47

Lacaz, A.S. 167
language 26
Lauretis, Teresa de 79
Lennon, K. 8, 18
LGBT activism, the Philippines 124
liberty 30
Lipinski, Adam 96
literature 16, 112–121; contribution 112; importance 120–121; power of 112–113; recycling 114–115, 115–116, 117; re-mixing 117–120
Livingston, Julie 71
Lonzi, Carla 78
Lopes, Adriana 166
López, Angel 189–190
Lorde, Audre 184–185
Lotta Femminista 81
Low, Setha 146

Macaulay, Catharine 35
McCurn, Alexis S. 147

Index 199

McGlotten, Shaka 152
machismo 129
MacKinnon, Catherine 6–7
McRuer, Robert 65, 67–68, 68
Magsaysay, Ramon 127–128
Majewska, Ewa 103, 104, 105, 106, 108
Maldonado-Torres, Nelson 181, 184
Marazzi, Christian 87
Marden, Roland 31–32
market economy 34
marketisation 42–43
Marshall Plan 83
Marxism 101
Marxist feminism 80–81, 90
masculinity and masculinities 6–7, 17,
  158–168, 168; alternative subjectivities
  158; black stereotypes 163–164; and
  citizenship 34; criminalised stereotypes
  158; definition 162; and violence 162
Meretoja, Hanna 113
#metoo hashtag 89–90
Micro-interactional Assaults 147
Mignolo,W.D. 165
Mische, Ann 188, 189
Mitchell, D.T. 67
Mollow, Anna 67–68
money 176; community currency 171,
  175, 176–180, **177**, **178**, **179**,
  180–183, **182**
Montano, Severino, *The Lion and the
  Faun* 16, 124–138; anti-woman
  attitude 129, 130–131, 132, 137;
  biographical accounts 127;
  biographical interpretation 127, 133;
  characters sexual definitions 132;
  comparison with Nadres 132–133;
  conceptual clarifications 126;
  cosmpolitanism 130; cultural
  background 124–126; focalisation 135;
  homosexual encounters 129, 131;
  Humanism 134–135; influences 131;
  lack of formal merit 133–138;
  Montano's plays 130–131, 135;
  mythologising 130; narrative 127–129;
  narrative language 135–137; narrator
  132; personal background 126–127;
  politics 134; post-colonial signifier
  125; problems 129; representational
  content 129; sexual exile structures
  125; sexual politics 132; subplots 128;
  use of English 133
Morales, Alejandro Cotté 189
Morocco 146
Moura, T. 164

Moura, Tatiana 17
Movimento di Lotta Femminile 81
Muir, Sarah 173
Muraro, Luisa 80
Muriel, Yanna 188–189
music 116
Muslim women 14, 35
Muthu, Sankar 27
Mutter, Matthew 187–188

Nadres, Orlando, *Hanggang Dito na
  lamang at Maraming Salamat* 132–133
Nascimento, Abdias 166
national identity 97–99
nationalism 97–99, 108
natural history discourses 25–28
Navaro-Yashin, Yael 151
negative associations 63
Negrón-Muntaner, Frances 17–18
neoliberal crisis 176
neoliberalisation 42, 174
neoliberalism 97, 108
Newcomb, Rachel 146
Niekerk, C. 25, 27
Nietzsche, Friedrich 187, 188
non-linguistic relationships 150–151
Nordvall, H. 44
Norris, P. 3
Notar, Beth A. 176
Nousiainen, K. 43

Obama, Barack 112
obligation 12
O'Brien, Edward 133
O'Brien, Karen 33, 35, 36
Oleksy, E.H. 98
orang-utan, the 25–28

Page, Victoria 17
Pankowski, R. 96, 100
Pasado y Presente: Art After the Young
  Lords exhibition 189–190
passinho 158, 159–160, 162, 167
passive view 12–13
path dependency 51
patriarchy 6, 17, 31, 35, 77, 142–155;
  affect 149–155; gendered division of
  space 144–146, **145**; objectified
  148–149; relational nature 149–151,
  152–155; spectres 152–153; spirits
  153–155; urban gender inequality
  146–148
Paz, Eduardo 185–187
Pedersen, Morten Axel 149

200 *Index*

perceptions, changing 2
Peres, Tony 131
Pérez-Rosario, Vanessa 176
Perfects, Leandra 162
Perry, Keisha-Khan, Y. 144
Philippines, the: Americanisation 126; anglophone literature 136–138; conservatism 137; homosexuality 124–138; LGBT activism 124; male bisexuality 130; post-colonial signifier 125; sexual exile structures 125; sexualisation 126; sexual politics 139n5
Phillips, Anne 18, 33
Pietrzak, E. 99, 103
Pinheiro, D. 163
Poland 15–16; Act on Family Planning 95; All Women's Strike 102, 108; anti-abortion law proposal 102–103, 106–107; anti-'gender' backlash 3; anti-gender movements 94–109; Black Protest 94, 102–108, 108; Catholic Church 95, 98, 100–101, 104; Gender Equality Index 95; gender ideology 95, 101–102; gender stereotypes 100; human rights 94–95; messianism 98; national identity 97–99; nationalism 94, 97–99, 108; Ombudsman for Equality and Civil Society 96; political landscape 94; reproductive rights 96, 104–105; sociopolitical context 94–97; Stop Gender Ideology Parliamentary Committee 101–102; women in 98, 99–100; women's rights 95, 99–100, 106, 108
policy hinterlands 43
Politique et Psychanalyse 79
populism 15
potential, paradigm of 158
Potere Operaio 81
power: colonialities of 48, 181
power relations 14, 31, 41, 146
Prawo i Sprawiedliwość 99
private/domestic space, as feminine 143, 145–146
privilege, and inequality 6–7
Prügl, E. 41, 45
psychiatric manuals 66
Puar, Jasbir 63, 64, 71, 72
public space, as masculine 143, 144–145, **145**
Puerto Rico: *autogestión* (self-governance) 179–180; community currency 171, **175**, 176–180, **177**, **178**, **179**, 180–183; debt crisis 172–173; distrust 175–176; and joy

182–191, **182**, **186**; Valor y Cambio (Value and Change) project 171–191
Puerto Rico Under Water: Five Art Perspectives on the Debt Crisis exhibition 176

queer sexualities 68
queer space 144
Queer Theory 117
Quintas, Fátima 144
Quotidian app 19–20n2

racism 2, 119
Rae, Douglas 5
Rancière, J. 12
rape, responses to 7
rationality 31–32
reason 26, 31
recognition, politics of 4
recognition-versus-rights debate 2
recycling 114–115, 115–116, 117
redistribution 7
reflexivity 41
relational equality 6–7
re-mixing 116, 117–120
reparation 7
reproductive labour 15, 76–91; Catholic Church and 76, 84; definition 80; exploitation of 89; feminisation of work 86–90; gender care gap 83–86; outsourcing 85–86; Wages for Housework campaign 80–83, 90–91
reproductive rights, Poland 96, 104–105
re-vision 113, 116
revolution 115–116, 120
Rich, Adrienne 68, 113, 116
rights: and culture 9–10; and freedom 13
Rio de Janeiro, Brazil 17, 158–168; criminalisation of culture 163–165; criminalised stereotypes 163; decolonial aesthetic 165, 165–167; funk 166–167; *passinho* 158, 159–160, 162, 167; peripheries 158–159; *rolezinhos* 163; *slam* 158, 159–160, 162, 167; sociospatial inequality 159
Rizal, José 131
Rosaldo, M.Z. 143
Rose, Damaris 143–144
Rousseau, Jean-Jacques 26, 27, 30
Rowbotham, Sheila 113
Różalska, Aleksandra 3, 15–16
Rozbicki, M. 30
Ruston, R. 28
Ruston, Sharon 33

Saffioti, Heleith 8
same-sexual desire 137
Samuels, Ellen 68
Sandoval, Chela 183–184
Santos, Angelito 129
Santos, B. de S. 159
Santos Negrón, Sarabel 17–18, 176–177
Saranillio, Dean Itsuji 184
Sá, Simone 166
Scherrer, C. 45
Schueller, Malini Johar 72
Schwenken, H. 46
sexism 2
sexual difference theorists 5
sexual difference, thought of 76–77,
    79–80
sexual exile structures 124
sexual freedom 78
sexual harassment 146–147
sex workers' movement 82–83
Silva, Jailson de Souza 164
slam 158, 159–160, 162, 167
slavery and the slave trade 9, 33, 163–164
Smith, Linda 11
Snyder, S.L. 67
social change 49
social complexity theory 48–52
social divisions, production 2
social justice 7
social relations 49
social systems 49–50
space: gendering of 146–148; symbolic
    coding of 148
Spade, Dean 64, 72–73
Spain 171
Spain, Daphne 143
Spencer, Jane 26, 28
Spinoza, Baruch 187, 189
*Stanford Encyclopaedia of Philosophy,
    The* 5
stereotypes 4, 162, 163–164;
    anti-Muslim 35
stigmatisation 159
storytelling, politics of 177
strategic partnerships 40
Sturman, Rachel 25, 28, 30
Stuurman, Siep 4
Suess, Amets 65–66
Sylvia Rivera Law Project 72–73

Tan, Michael L. 130
Taylor, B. 33, 34
Teatro Experimental do Negro 165–166
temporality 117

Thompson, H. 41
Tilley, Christopher 148, 150
tipping points 51
Tonkiss, Fran 147, 148
transgender 14–15; accessing disability
    72–74; bathroom accessibility needs
    14–15, 63, 64–65; depathologisation
    64–67; and disability 14–15, 63–74; as
    disability 69–72; disability stigma 63;
    emancipation 63; inclusivity 63;
    intra-actions of disability 67–69; legal
    regulation 72–73; medicalisation 64,
    73; negative associations 63; rights 73;
    suffering 70
Turner, Jimmy 17, 19, 142–155
tyrants 32

United Nations, Women's Conferences 52
United Nations Women Training
    Centre 40
UnpayableDebt: Capital, Violence and
    the New Global Economy working
    group 173, 176
urban gender inequality 146–148;
    materiality of 148–149; relational
    nature 149–151, **150**
urban peripheries 158–159; art and
    culture from 159–160, 163–165, 166,
    167–168; creativity 160; criminalisa-
    tion of culture 163–165; masculinities
    161–162
utilitarian market model 42–43

Valor y Cambio (Value and Change)
    project 17–18, 171–191; clarifying
    moments 176; community currency
    171, **175**, 176–180, **177**, **178**, **179**,
    180–183, **182**; design and development
    173–180, **174**, **175**, **177**, **178**, **179**; and
    exchange value 171; goals 171; and
    hope 188–189; and joy 173, 182–191,
    182, **186**; need for 172–173;
    participation 171–172, **175**, 180–181;
    support 179–180, **179**; team 191n1
value 17–18, 171
Vargas, V. 40
Vazquez, R. 165
Vergès, Françoise 9
Verloo, M. 49, 50
vernacular forms, of equality 11–12
Villa, Jose Garcia 126–127, 130, 133,
    139n10
violence, use of 162
Volf, Miroslav 185, 187

202   *Index*

Wages Due Lesbians 82
Wages for Housework campaign 77,
  80–83, 90
Walby, S. 49, 50, 50–51, 90
Walker, Alice 117
Walters, Pau Crego 65–66
Wheeler, Roxann 27
Wieringa, S. 40
Wieslander, M. 44
Wilson, Elizabeth 151
Wilson, Kabe 16, 113, 113–115,
  117–120, 120
Winterson, Jeannette 1
Wokler, Robert 26, 26–27, 27, 30
Wollstonecraft, Mary 6–7, 9, 13–14,
  25, 27–28, 29, 30, 30–31, 33, 34,
  35, 36; *Vindication of the Rights of
  Man* 32
women 13–14; claimed moral inferiority
  28–30; claim to humanity 28–36;
  Muslim 14, 35; potential 35; rights 29,

30, 95, 99–100, 106, 108; subordina-
  tion 28, 31, 34–35
Women's, Gender and Feminist Studies
  47, 48
women's movement 14
Wong, F 41
Woodward 40
Woolf, Virginia, *Room of One's Own* 16
Workerist movement 81
work, feminisation of 86–90
work-life balance initiatives 88
World Health Organization, Interna-
  tional Classification of Diseases 66
Wynter, S. 9

Young, B. 45
Young, Iris Marion 7
Young, Stella 65

Žižek, Slavoj 182, 183
Zonana, J. 35